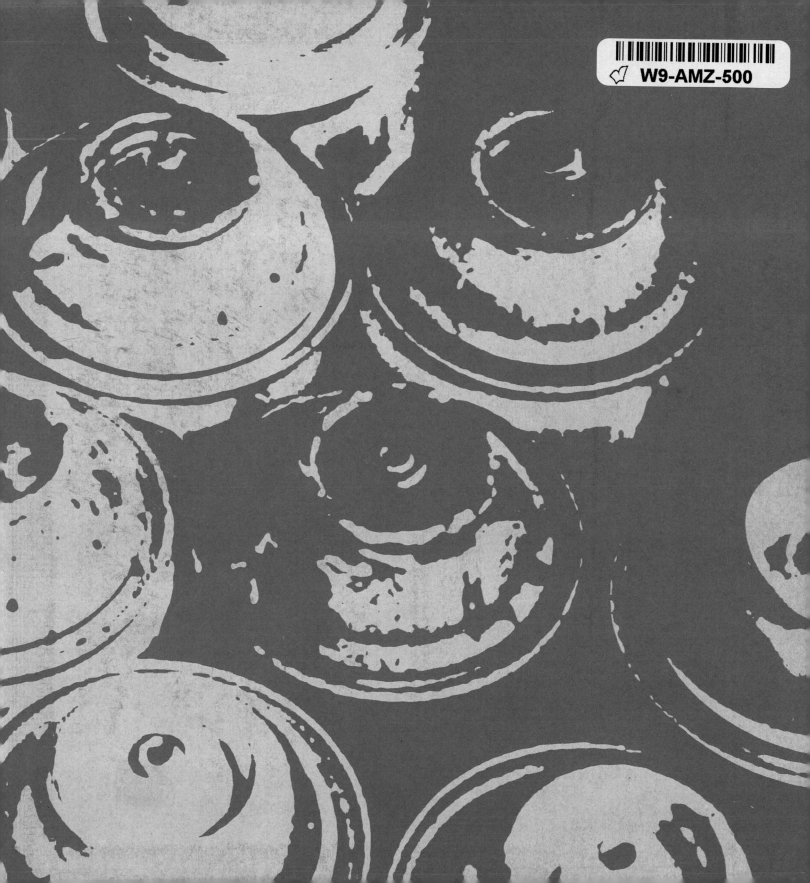

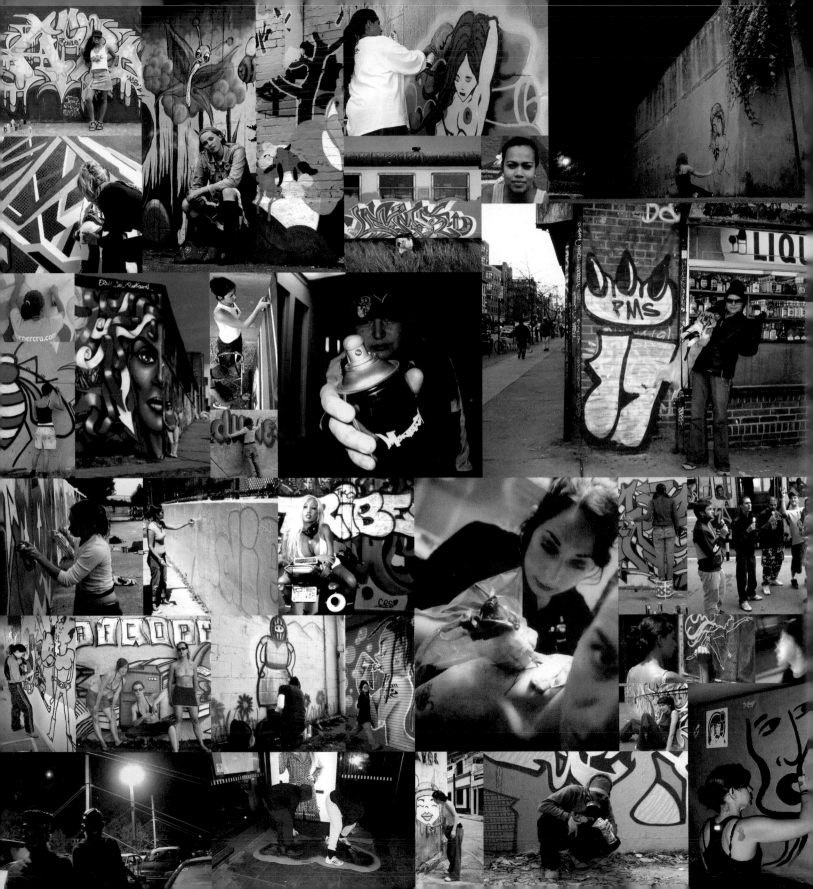

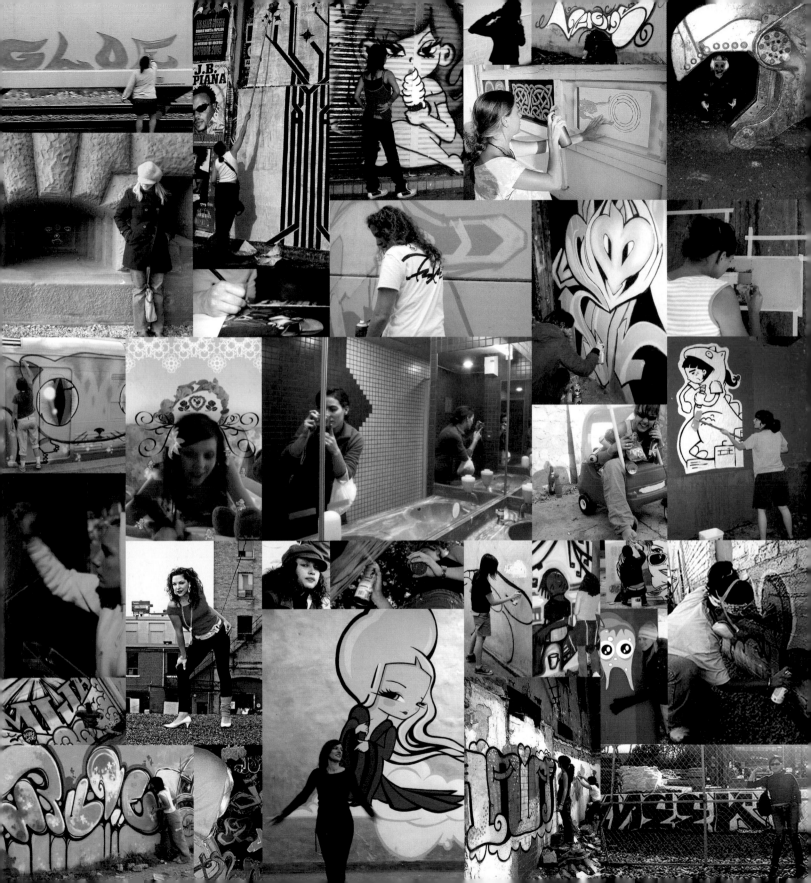

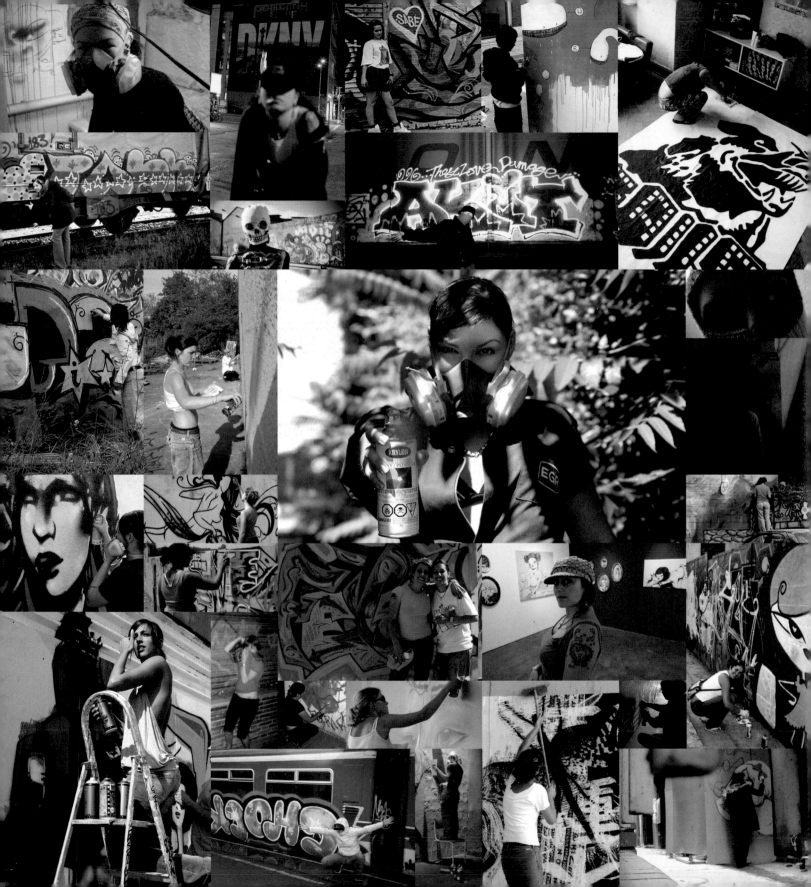

Graffiti Women

Street Art from Five Continents

by Nicholas Ganz

Foreword by Swoon

For Elena

contents

First published in the United Kingdom
in 2006 by Thames & Hudson Ltd, London
Editor: Rebecca Pearson
Designer: Samuel Clark
Production Manager: Virginia Liggitt

Library of Congress Cataloging-in-
Publication Data

Ganz, Nicholas.
  Graffiti women : street art from five
continents / by Nicholas Ganz.
    p. cm.
  ISBN 10: 0-8109-5747-7 (hardcover)
  ISBN 13: 978-0-8109-5747-3
  1. Street art. 2. Mural painting and
decoration––20th century. 3. Women
artists. I. Title.
  ND2590.G348 2006
  751.7'3––dc22
                        2006015287

Printed and bound in China
10 9 8 7 6 5 4 3 2 1

HNA ▪▪▪▪▪
harry n. abrams, inc.
a subsidiary of La Martinière Groupe
115 West 18th Street
New York, NY 10011
www.hnabooks.com

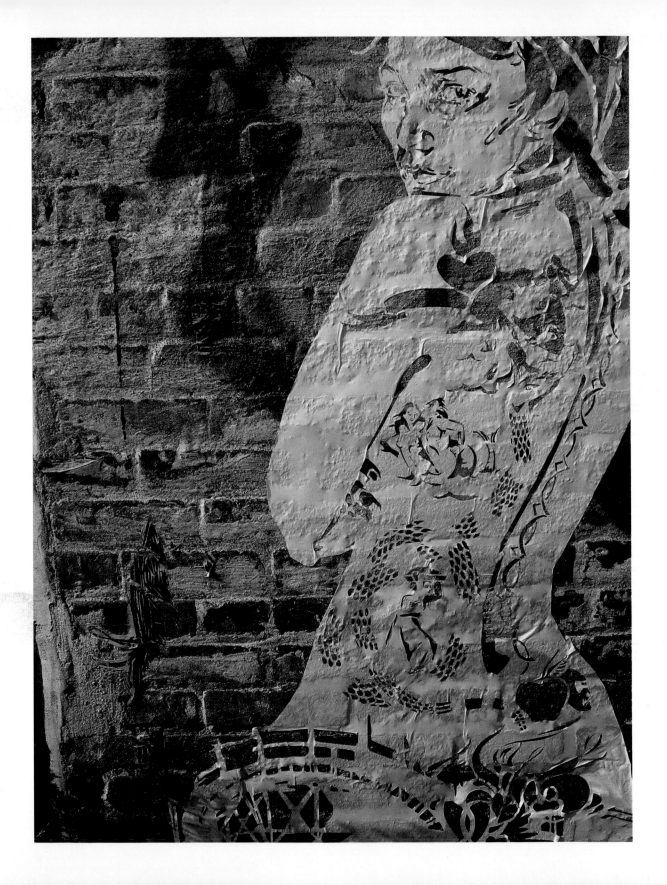

Foreword

At one point I didn't think it mattered that I was a 'female in a male-dominated field'. My chosen name wasn't 'Miss' anything, and my style, erupting of its own accord, didn't care to identify me as a skirt or trousers. Right? A non-issue, let's move on. Well, no, maybe it was more than just a non-issue – somewhere in there was a ripping undercurrent, determined to force it not to matter, an aggravated internal voice whispering sharply, 'Fucking hell. Get over it already! Let's level this shit. I know who I am. Always have. My mama and my mama's mama put in a lot of years of struggle that I might take my chosen path, unfettered by a stigma about my gender. I don't want your bad rap and I don't want your extra props, 'cause I don't need either. I'll wreck house one way or another so don't blink because I'm coming.' Yeah, I think this about describes her – lil' Swoon, aged twenty-two, something to prove.

I had been at it for a couple of years, making work on the street, when suddenly people started to want that Swoon guy to come to their town and do shows. I giggled and kept it to myself. Turns out it was kind of fun flipping people's expectations after all. I relished the looks of delight and the surprised descriptions – 'and she's only this big!' (holding up a hand to mark the midget line which, at five foot two, I barely clear). I decided to go ahead, travel and participate in those shows, and I found that so much of the time the only females represented there were girlfriends or sidekicks. Where were my lone wolf she mamas, tearing themselves a clear place to stand on? I knew they must be out there, but rarely was I meeting them. I was a touch lonely and a pinch angry.

In the meantime there was a lot of attention coming my way for being female, and it just made me feel alienated and objectified, not to mention patronized. 'Look at what the girls can do – aren't they cute?' To hell with that shit. I didn't want it. All except this one, very specific kind of attention that I couldn't have foreseen – the email from a sixteen-year-old girl in Georgia, an impromptu print-making seminar with three women in San Jose after an opening, or the girl in Berlin, at my very first show ever, who grabbed me by the hand in the middle of all of the madness and said, 'Listen, you changed my life'. I have never forgotten her face at that moment. I didn't know what to say – mostly I just wanted to cry – stared blankly, and then the river of chaos eddied around us and we returned to the party like it was nothing.

So, this is the thing: I'm from a small town in Florida. I was the 'art girl' and 'the freak who didn't shave her legs', and the one that the cheerleaders would pull aside to admit that sometimes they just wanted to curl up in bed and read a book. They'd flash a bit of wit and confide a hidden intelligence that they didn't dare to show in class. It's always an honour to be confided in, but mostly in these moments I just felt a slow burning rage. Why are you hiding this, and who are you hiding it from? I wondered. OK, sure, our mamas did a lot of work, but in the mid '90s, in the culture I grew up in, you had cheerleaders cheering on the game, and skate betties holding court at the halfpipe, but where was the culture of women doing things for themselves? This was my desperate question.

Sounds funny now, but when I heard little nineteen-year-old Ani DiFranco, with her shaved head, her acoustic guitar and her self-made label, it shook my small-town-girl world. Looking back, it could have been almost anything, as long as it was precisely this, a woman, someone I could identify with doing things in her own way at that exact moment. Riot Girl was a distant story that somehow never reached my town, and the '70s bra-burners an even more distant myth. Frida Kahlo? Beautiful in black and white, and dead as a doornail. I needed to see something that I could practically have made myself, and finding it was invaluable. It was a wind at my back.

The truth is, I never want to make anything that could be pigeonholed as 'women's work'. I'm way too interested in looking for something transcendent in the human experience. Further, I think that constantly trying to look at an artist's, or anyone's, work from the point of view of their race or gender is limiting and risks playing into stereotypes. So why on earth did I even agree to be a part of this book, much less write this foreword? Well, it's that thing I could not have foreseen, and which I cannot resist. You know? It's the mere idea that once or twice I might be a part of the process by which we show each other what we are made of, and where we lead each other by blazing example. That girl in Berlin, whose name I never got; I returned to Berlin six months later and found that she had turned one of the city's bus shelters into one of my favourite works of art ever. What's more, I see it often now, this look in the eyes of women who come out to say hello on opening night. It's a spark that says we are sharing a secret. We smile, and for a split second we are linking arms at the front line of a very subtle struggle. We smile because we are winning. I think if this were the only thing I had to keep me going, I would probably be just fine.

Swoon

Preface

'The cop who took my fingerprints and photographs said he would never have guessed girls' heads could be full of such crap!' Hera

People often view graffiti and street art as exclusively male domains, but this couldn't be further from the truth. Women have been just as active as their male counterparts since graffiti's very inception, be it in fewer numbers, venturing down dark side streets or dangerous stretches of rail track to catch tags or to piece. In the free gallery of the street, to which everyone has access, and where the artists can keep their identity secret or wipe out all traces of sex, anonymity has played a vital role. Many female spray artists take advantage of this aspect of the game; others prefer to make their pieces overtly feminine, such as Fafi and Miss Van.

The art form's transient nature hasn't helped to change this male perspective. Work is regularly buffed or destroyed, sometimes within hours of completion, with the result that artists' efforts often go unnoticed. Graffiti literature has also been a contributing factor, focusing almost exclusively on men. It would be impossible to offer a truly comprehensive representation of the female graffiti and street art scene from its beginnings to the present day, as there is little in the way of historical documentation. *Subway Art*, *The Faith of Graffiti*, *The Graffiti Subculture* and *Spray City* broke the mould by flagging up the work of female spray artists such as Eva62, Barbara62 and Lady Pink, but many artists have been overlooked.

In *Graffiti Woman* I have tried to rectify this oversight by including as many artists as possible from around the globe, both prominent figures and unknown artists. I have divided the featured artists into two sections according to their style and viewpoint: 'graffiti' or 'street art'. Graffiti is often associated with letters and the spraycan, but many new forms have emerged or developed in recent years that have enriched the scene, including stencils and stickers, often collectively grouped as street art. Graffiti and street art are separated not only by techniques but also by sociological elements. The former is largely governed by the desire to spread one's tag and achieve fame, and the old rules of 'getting up' still apply; it's about quality (your work must be better than everyone else's) *and* quantity (you have to piece like mad and catch as many tags as possible). Street art tends to have fewer rules and embraces a much broader range of styles and techniques.

For women, faced with the clear risks of attack or rape, the night-time escapades linked to graffiti are particularly dangerous. Many find that getting up is made doubly difficult by the fact that female spray artists are often taken less seriously or become the focus of gossip, with stories circulating about how they've slept their way to the top or how other spray artists have really done their pieces for them. The term that is so important for the graffiti and hip-hop movements – respect – sometimes seems to fall by the wayside.

As Lady Echo explains, 'A girl who is into painting graffiti has to work three times as hard as a guy to be considered as good, and even after that someone will try to use personal information to the detriment of your reputation. I have had many negative experiences, to the point that I considered quitting. In the end, those people who tried to bring me down have made me tougher and taught me not to put much emphasis on what people say about me.'

In some ways the street art movement seems more open to and tolerant of women. It attracts few or none of the 'male obstacles' you associate with the graffiti movement, and women tend to be seen in a positive light and supported. This could be something to do with the culture's 'young' history or the 'safer environment' of street art – stencilling or putting up a poster can take less time and therefore carries fewer risks – or the fact that street art seems to be an art form in which men don't feel the need to assert their masculinity to the same degree, an area where women aren't seen as 'the competition'.

'There are definitely more women who have got into [the scene] through the street art movement,' confirms German artist Mad C. 'Women feel more secure in this field. You don't have to prove yourself in front of an audience but can work in peace at home; you can paint over anything you cock up and just put the good stuff out there on the street. And you hardly have to worry about the legal implications. The main reason, though,

is the way it broadens the realms of possibility. There isn't the restriction of letters and added characters. In street art, for example, you can draw landscapes with filigree lines and bring them to the wall. There are simply so many more techniques and materials than in the graffiti field.'

During the research for *Graffiti Woman* it became clear that, for the women involved, the scene is a cluster of contradictory experiences – some good, others bad. Being a part of the movement hasn't been easy, and women often haven't enjoyed their fair share of the limelight, but it has become a much more level playing field. The past few years have seen more and more women coming up and a proliferation of exhibitions of their art. Female graffiti and street artists are increasingly being acknowledged for their key role and are finally getting the credit they so rightfully deserve. *Graffiti Woman* is a celebration of their work.

Nicholas Ganz

'My good friend Squid, bassist for the girl punk group The Lunachicks, grew tired of the question "What's it like to be a girl musician in a male-dominated field?" Her response: "The only difference between me and them is that I sit when I pee."' Dona

The Feminine Touch: The Highs and Lows of

Graffiti is one of the few areas in life where one's gender can be disguised. As a written word – and often a gender-neutral one – your identity can remain a mystery to those around you. And yet this distinctive subcultural benefit would seem to be less accessible if you are a woman. As I realized when I started speaking to female writers for my book, *The Graffiti Subculture,* a woman's gender can often be the most spot-lit aspect of her work.

I started researching this subject in the early 1990s, at a time when female writers were somewhat hard to find. There were a few well-known names, but nothing like the numbers of men writing. The reasons for this throw up a whole different set of issues about masculinity, which I won't go into now. What is of interest here are the 'experiences' that women appear to share as female members of this male-dominated culture. While their shape and form might differ, all would agree: life as a female graffiti writer can be extremely hard.

Women enter this subculture and appear to gain an automatic and tainted set of traditional feminine qualities – constructing her as a timid, delicate little thing with absolutely no fear threshold and a tendency to burst into tears at the slightest hint of danger. Lady Pink recalls the reactions that would usually meet her request to go with male writers to the train yards:

'They didn't take me seriously, some little girl like, "Take me to the train yard, take me to the train yard", and they wouldn't have anything to do with it…. I got the things, "Oh you'll scream, we'll have to protect you"…. I couldn't go off and cry and scream and carry on like a girl because that's what they expected. I had to prove myself too, that I wasn't a wimp.'

Male writers start graffiti and work to prove they are 'men', but female writers must work to prove they are not 'women' – i.e. demonstrate that they have the same 'balls', stamina and resilience as their male peers. Claw, a female writer in New York, is emphatic about shattering beliefs that women are out of their league in this subculture. To prove it, she pushes herself extra hard and paints in places that ensure this is fully understood:

'I want to do the riskiest, the most outrageous stuff because I'm a woman. So people would say, "How the fuck did she do that? A nice Jewish girl…nice Jewish girls don't write". I write and I write for women. I'm doing this to say, "You and your closed little mind, we can do this, anybody can do it, as long as they have the will and desire to do it."'

But balls alone are not enough. A female writer is always going to be 'just a girl' – until she shows that she is one hundred per cent 'down for' or dedicated to graffiti. And this demonstration is where life as a female graffiti writer probably gets its hardest. Through no fault of her own, a girl's route to fame is both quicker and easier than her male counterpart's, as Pink remarks:

'I was already famous as soon as I started, just because I was a girl.'

Although this short cut may look like a bonus, it is actually a severe hindrance. Writers are legitimized by the hard work and effort they put in, and the female writer's quick rise to fame strips her of her ability to demonstrate this. She gets fame without effort, which prevents her from ever really enjoying 'true authenticity' in other writers' eyes. In reality, she doesn't gain from her increased profile, she suffers.

Girls that persist, despite this hurdle, face further obstacles. Although women cannot be physically stopped from getting involved in graffiti, they can, through the exclusion of their competitive force, be denied a place within an all-male subcultural core. When I was conducting my research, it was evident that strategies operate to exclude women or secure their 'absent presence'. What was also clear was the way female writers recognize these strategies, and worked tactically in ways to undercut them.

The first centres around the issue of accountability. Boys, 'toys' or not, are generally expected to prove themselves by their own merits and learn to stand on their

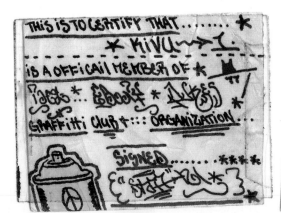

Kivu

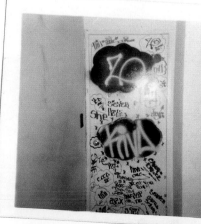

the Female Graffiti Experience

own two feet as 'men'. Girls, apparently, are not. The female writer is often helped or supported, which can be used to attribute her achievements to the men assisting her. By painting with a wide variety of writers, Lady Pink made it clear that she was responsible for her own work and deserving of her own credit:

'I went piecing deliberately with different groups so that everyone could see I could actually paint this stuff and I'm not having some guy do it for me.'

Claw makes similar claims by rejecting help:

'When people try to help me do my piece, I get really, "No, no, no, I have to do it, don't, I'm doing it", because I don't want anybody to, you know, say, "Oh, I saw Divo do her piece."'

The sexual rumours that often circulate about women within this subculture can work to deflect her achievements in a similar way. While male writers are recognized for what they do with their spraycan, greater interest is often shown in what the female writer does with her body, as Lady Pink recalls:

'Graffiti writers would just bad-mouth me and say I'm just some little slut, I'm probably just doing everybody when I go to the train yard. These rumours have stuck until now, people are still saying stuff, guys are still saying that they did so and so with me…you're either a dyke or a slut, that's it, so I had a lot of problems with that.'

Unlike a girl, a male writer's reputation or identity rests upon his graffiti, not his sexual activities, his demonstrations of masculinity, not his passive physicality. At the end of the day, he occupies a sphere that grants him a presence, a competitive force and an opportunity to be recognized. That sphere would seem to be a much harder place for a woman to occupy.

And yet, despite all this, there have been many women who have persisted – and, for the love of their craft, battled through and even changed such resistant attitudes. Twenty-five years on, and Lady Pink is still a forceful female presence within the American, and indeed global, scene. Many of her male contemporaries have since hung up their spraycans and retired, but Pink has

stuck around and played a key role in moulding this subculture into what it has become today. Her dedication alone has done much for the female cause.

Likewise, the graffiti scene itself is also changing. As the traditional subculture fragments and new offshoots develop, avenues are opening up to those who might have been alienated or excluded from its 'illegal core'. The more recent stencil boom appears to be nudging this gender bias back into greater balance. By diversifying graffiti's angles of involvement, and lessening some of its more extreme risks, women are showing more interest than ever before.

Women have been part of this subculture since its inception – albeit at the fringes. But only now does graffiti appear to be embracing their feminine touch. I, for one, look forward to seeing what new influences and meanings women will bring with them to the walls.

Nancy Macdonald
Author of *The Graffiti Subculture*

'Miss 17 and I are not out here as "female" writers. We are out to CRUSH and that has no gender specification. Man or woman, you have to be able to compete and rep your name on the streets.' Claw

A Global Snapshot

'Once, I was about to catch a spot and a cop stopped me. I had to pretend I was waiting for the bus. He tells me the bus has stopped running and it's not a safe area. He offers me a ride home. I'd have looked suspicious if I'd said no, so I got in the car, clinging on to my bag to stop the cans shaking. I was so nervous he was going to hear my paint and know automatically what I was up to. Boy did he kill my night! I was pissed!!!' Jel

The Americas

The **USA** was the birthplace of graffiti and is home to many of the most influential female graffiti and street artists, including the likes of Lady Pink, Swoon, Claw, Miss17, Siloette and Aiko (Faile). Back in the 1970s, when graffiti first took off in **New York**, Manhattan's Eva62 and Barbara62 teamed up to catch tags all over the city and became widely respected for their art. Although they are the best-known female graffiti artists of that era, Stoney and Cowboy (Brooklyn), Kivu181, Poonie, Z73 and Suki also played an important role. Lady Pink, New York's most renowned and respected female aerosol artist, came on the scene as the 1970s were drawing to a close, but most active female artists still cite her as a magical inspiration, a role model and a huge influence, and she remains an integral part of the scene today.

In the early 1980s Lady Heart and Abby (Queens) started to make an impact, and Brooklyn artists CC (Chick, RIP) and SS (Super Skates) bombed the New York subway, followed shortly after by Lower East Side's Lady Bug (mid-1980s). Lil Love, who would help her brother Lee Quinones with his pieces, also made a contribution to the American scene with her whole cars, along with Lizzie (who teamed up with Bronx-based Duster) and Tramp/Cyndah (who hit up trains with PJ).

Miss Maggs (Queens), one of the first bombers to achieve fame, was particularly active in the early 1990s and was instrumental in influencing a whole band of up-and-coming artists. Jakee, Diva, Dona, Utah/Ohio, D=Fla, Naisha, Queen Andrea, Muck, Erotica67, Lady Di, Jae9 and Doris all became prominent in the early to mid-1990s. More recently, a proliferation of extremely talented street artists like Swoon and Aiko have made their mark in New York, beautifying the cityscape with a broad variety of techniques.

On the opposite side of the country, the **West Coast** was fostering a scene of its own. San Francisco was a hotspot in the early 1990s, with the highly influential Ruby Neri (aka Reminisce or The Horse Lady), the late Margaret Kilgallen (who was married to well-known artist Twist) and Grace. Evon Sue and Never were key players in the LA scene

Lady Pink
Photo © Martha Cooper

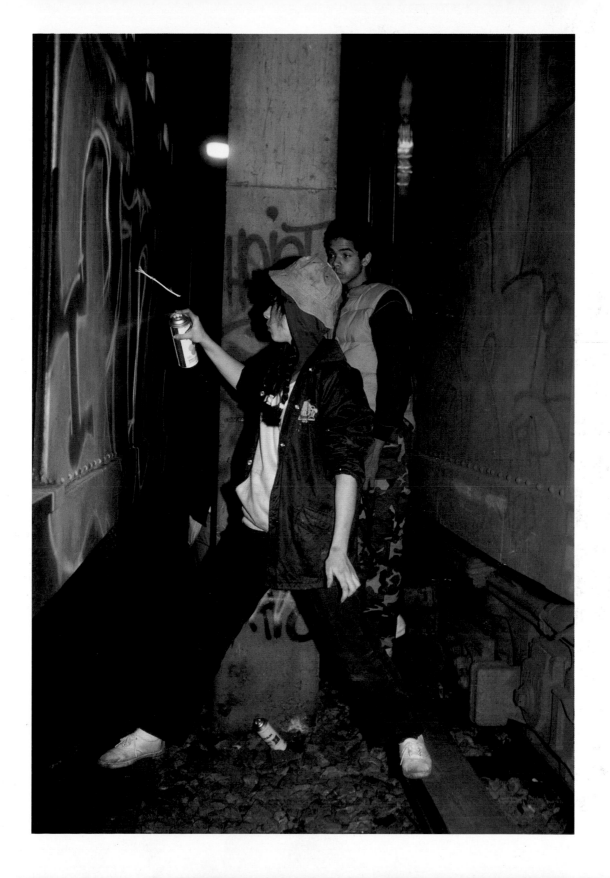

in around 1988, and Omega (known primarily for her complex pieces) was active from 1989, although she has since quit. From the late 1980s into the '90s, the number of female spray artists on the West Coast grew rapidly, and Tribe, Fem, 2tsie, Sherm, Kudles, Jerk, Perl, Jel and Erah became known. Freights, a medium through which artists could communicate with their counterparts all over the country, also provided an alternative outlet for many young female artists, including Femme9, Siloette, Are2, Gates (Denver), Spyder (Ohio) and Faset (NYC), as well as Pink.

In contrast to the USA, evidence of **Canadian** activity is thin on the ground. Toronto's Yoni, wife of Canada's first male spray artist (Ren), used to catch tags next to her husband's, although she has since quit. Cant4, another Toronto-based spray artist, got into graffiti in around 1995, followed shortly after by EGR with her accentuated figurative pieces. Bomba, Star, Air and Mes3 were around at the same time, and Montreal's Mao-Tze has sometimes pieced more aggressively than her male counterparts.

South America has produced several extremely creative female artists. Nina has been active since the mid-1980s and was **Brazil**'s first female aerosol artist, later followed by Jana Joana and Waleska. Rio de Janeiro had a rather late start by comparison – in 2000, when Om (Coletivo TPM) and Mieu started to paint, although only Om remains active today. Graffiti and street art have also made their mark in **Chile** and **Venezuela** through the work of ACB and Pian respectively, while in **Bolivia** the members of female-anarchical group Mujeres Creando use graffiti alongside their political actions to voice their resistance.

Europe

On the other side of the Atlantic, **the Netherlands** enjoyed a fair amount of early female activity. Amsterdam-based Mickey, who entered the scene in 1983, is widely celebrated as one of Europe's first female aerosol artists, and Vampirella (USA Crew) was active in the early 1980s. From the mid-1980s to the early 1990s tags by Jena (The Hague) would also crop up around the Netherlands.

Scandinavia also enjoys a significant female presence in graffiti and street art. Blue is one of the most prominent **Swedish** female spray artists and got into graffiti in 1985, following the likes of Shen, Abab and Shana, all of whom were active for a few years. From 1996 onwards, Tiger, Karma and Tur became known primarily for their work in underground stations and on walls, and Tiger was particularly prolific. Nowadays it is not uncommon to see pieces by Z Dad, who has been around since 2000.

Danish-born street artist Miss Riel now lives in **Germany**, where a large and lively female scene has developed through the likes of Casie, Mad C, Mace, Suez, Dani, Donna and FUCK YOUR CREW. Berlin has attracted numerous female artists over the years. Back in the late 1980s and early '90s a number of crews formed there, such as The Comic Luzies crew (founded in 1989, with Luri, Sherin, Kate, Joyle and Gina), The Monsters Crew (TMC) (f. 1993, with Same, Zeone, Nora and Skai), Real Home Girls (RHG), King Size Bombers (KSB) and Emancipated Jungle Sisters (EJS), and artists such as Danone, Luzie, Asem, Sher, Marianna, Same and Leys were also on the scene in the early 1990s. In Munich Gismo and the United Female Artists Crew were more or less contemporaries of their Berlin counterparts. DSA Girls (f. 2001, with Cayn, Amy, Wench, Xynon and Sonne) from Chemnitz and the German/Swiss crew AFC (with Soma, Lady Wave, Fany, Ream and others) are also prominent.

Switzerland's leading lady is long-standing artist Rosy. In around 2000 there was also a group of female writers who would stand out with stickers and large compositions of comic figures and signed their pieces *War Hier/Was Here*. Friendly Vandalism is a more recent addition.

Miss Tic and Nice Art Kollectiv's Ariane are among the many female *pochoir* artists that emerged in **France** in the 1980s, before the flood of tags and throw-ups that swept through the streets of Paris. In France another very particular form of graffiti also developed, initiated primarily by Toulouse's Miss Van and Mademoiselle Kat in the early 1990s. They were the first female artists to paint entirely female figures with a brush. Fafi, Lus, and Montpellier's Koralie are also associated with this form of graffiti. French pioneers include Fancie (who hit up trains), Lady V (one of the first to catch tags in the streets of Paris) and Klor, as well as Scottie, Clyde (RIP) from Bordeaux, Quest, Plume and Kensa from Toulouse.

Spain's graffiti and street art culture is also sizeable and vibrant, boasting such artists as Musa, Dune, Fly/Flai, Den, Makoh, Malicia, Yolie and Yubia. Musa set things moving in Barcelona in 1989, followed by Shy and Ir-n, who have both since quit. Between 1993 and 1996–97 there was also a female crew called IAO (with Soda, Woke and Otra), and Freaklub's Empty became widely known. The female duo La Mala Rodriguez and La Señora were active around Seville in the 1990s and also work as MCs.

Other key European players include Akit, who is famously credited as the **UK**'s first female graffiti artist and was active in the early to mid-1990s, and fellow Brit Chock. **Belgium**, **Italy**, **Portugal**, **Greece** and **Macedonia** also have an important female presence through the work of Keho, Omri, Louise, Supa B2, Fairy, Microbo, Lady Bug, Venus, Mofi and Psila.

Australasia, the Far East and South Africa

As in Europe, the **Australian** scene developed in the 1980s and was concentrated in the large cities. In Sydney the artists Rhythm and Rhyme teamed up to piece huge compositions on the rail lines, but they have since quit the scene altogether. In 1987 a purely female crew was founded – Girl Style Crew, although out of its members only Spice has remained active. Other Sydney-based artists include Chez, Shaz, Thorn, Mafia and Skoda. Tash, who got into graffiti in 1990, has achieved worldwide recognition and is also famed for her musical talent as Queen MC Tash.

On the other side of the country in Perth one early artist was Mayhem, who was active prior to 1988, before Poise shaped the cityscape. Further south in Victoria there is a large female crew of over twenty spray artists, DJs, breakers and MCs, which goes by the name of Ladiesluvhiphop. Other Australian aerosol artists include Melbourne's Krisy, Tiff, Aura, Lioness and Damsel, and Adelaide's Waste, Lace and Nish.

Across the water in **New Zealand**, Diva NZ has been active since 1998, and Mizery has been spray-painting characters since the late 1990s. Further afield, French-born Miss Lili, Redy and Shiro are all based in the Far East (in **China**, Hong Kong and **Japan** respectively).

South Africa also has just a small female presence. Ladybugs Crew used to be active in Cape Town, Supa is a stencil artist who now works on short films, and Meth has been piecing in Johannesburg. However, it is Faith47 who has achieved the most recognition, together with Swiss artist Smirk, who moved to Cape Town in 1998.

'Most girls have different handwriting from guys. Girls use rounder letters. You see this already in primary school. With this background a lot of girl writers use round letters when they first start out, although obviously not all of them. Girls also tend to use round characters like butterflies, hearts, big eyes – cute shit!' Mickey

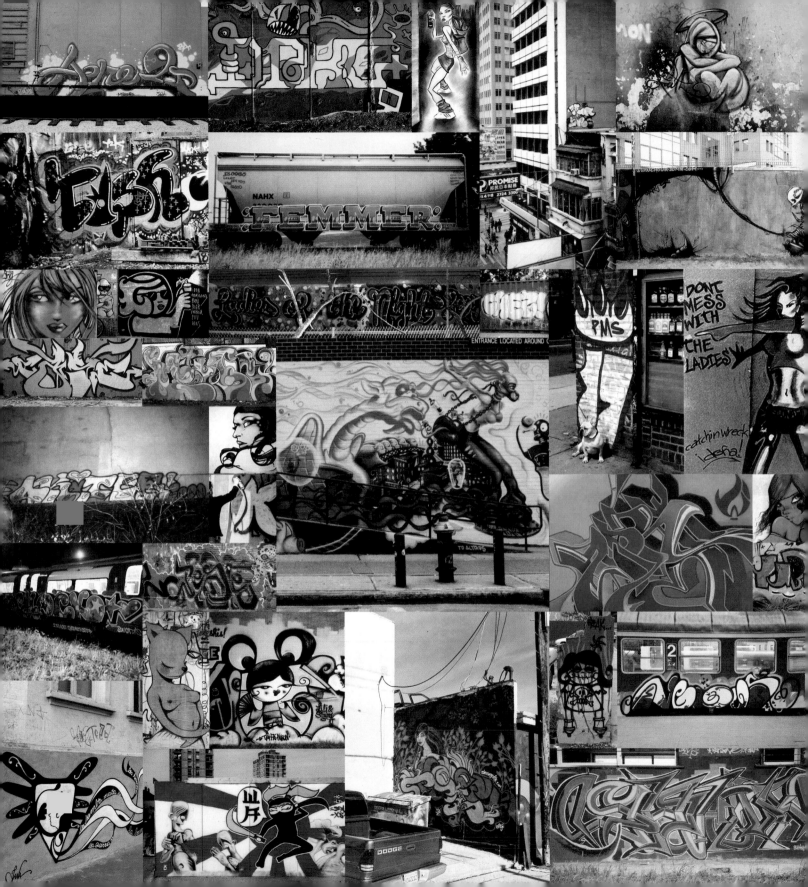

Graffiti

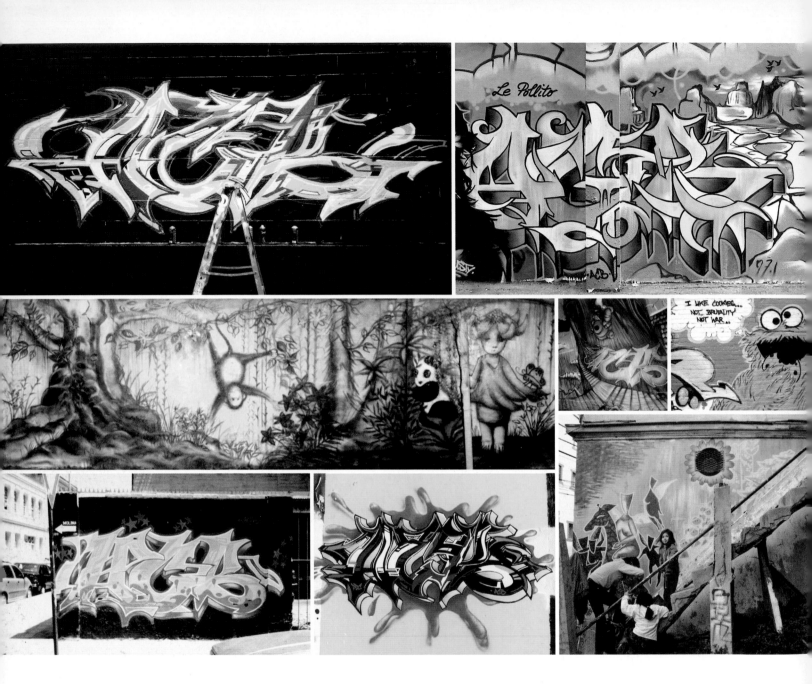

ACB

ACB's artistic talent shone through at an early age, and at thirteen friends introduced her to graffiti. The Chilean-born artist, who lived in New York for two years, has been active since 1996 and has been involved in numerous mural productions, youth workshops and lectures on hip-hop, graffiti and women at universities and cultural institutions.

She's now working on her *Mundo Feliz de ACB* ('ACB's Happy World') project: 'My art is for children, expressing happiness through vibrant murals with psychedelic colours and graffiti, and involving people from the community, friends and other artists. I want to convey joy and celebrate life, and I'd like my art to act as a substitute for nature in grey city areas.'

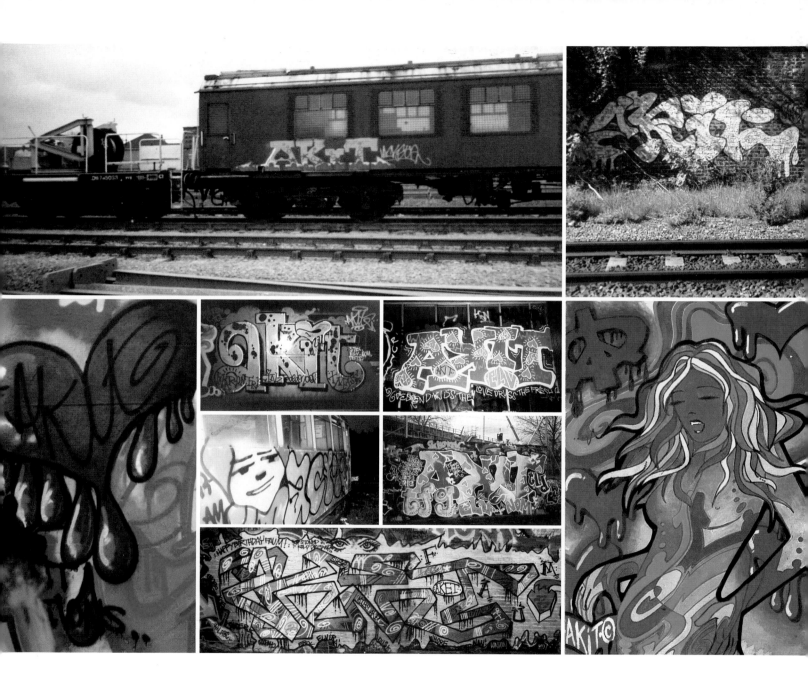

Akit

Londoner Akit pieced walls and trains in the early to mid-1990s. She says: 'I was fifteen. I knew a few writers, but I didn't think too much about graff to be honest. I liked it but I never thought about doing it until I was out with them one time and they were bombing. I thought, "That looks like a right laugh...I'll have some of that". I spent a long time practising and bombing before I actually executed a piece. By the time I was twenty-two, I had pretty much stopped. I haven't actually done any illegal pieces for eight years! I've dabbled with spraycans a couple of times since, but it's all or nothing really. I just want to bomb but I'm too old to get arrested for that! Many of my good friends are writers. I love graff and think about it every single day.'

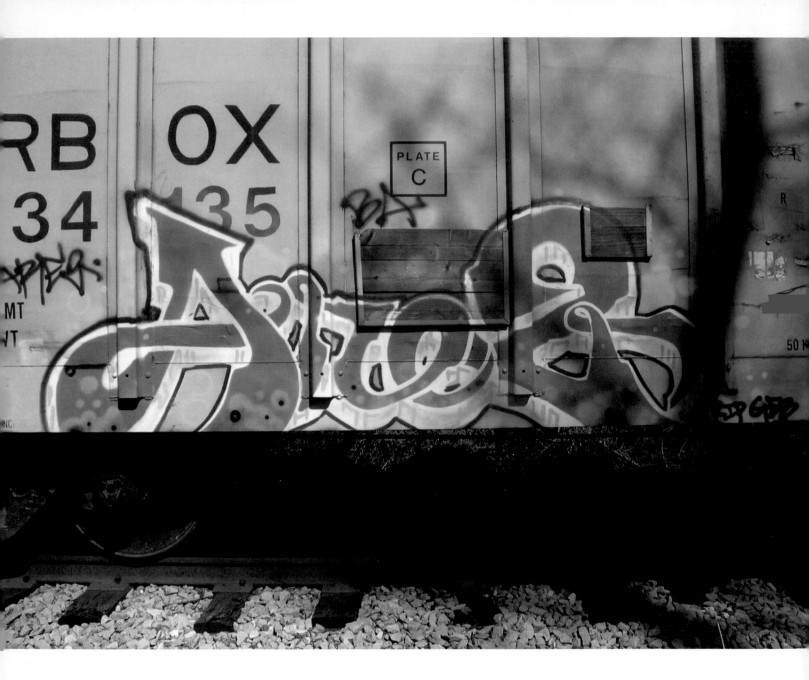

Are2

In 1993 East Coast spray artist Are2 started to sketch,
putting in the groundwork for her first piece, which she
didn't attempt until three years later. 'I like to express
abstract concepts of movement and change,' she says,
'but also just my own emotional release.'

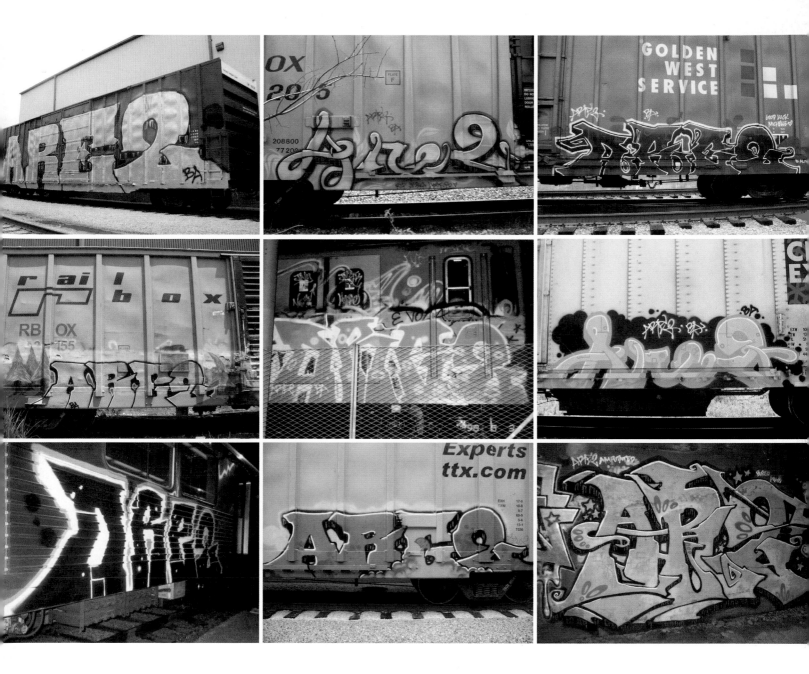

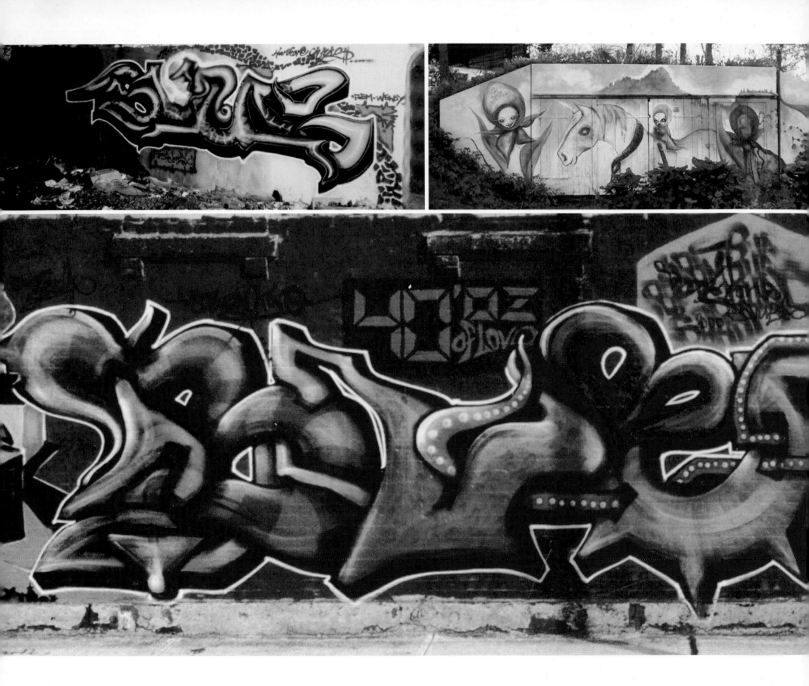

Blue

'I want to come up with a solution to make everything better and more beautiful,' says Blue, one of Sweden's longest-standing graffiti artists. 'More women are becoming brave. They have stopped listening to the media, which is trying to get them to obsess about their looks and fuckability. And also the unsatisfying nature of today's society is driving women to go out there and be a part of what's going on in the streets/visual politics. Women have always been in the streets...graffiti is just another way of advertising your soul instead of your body. I believe women, convinced of the possibilities of doing what they love, are extremely powerful.'

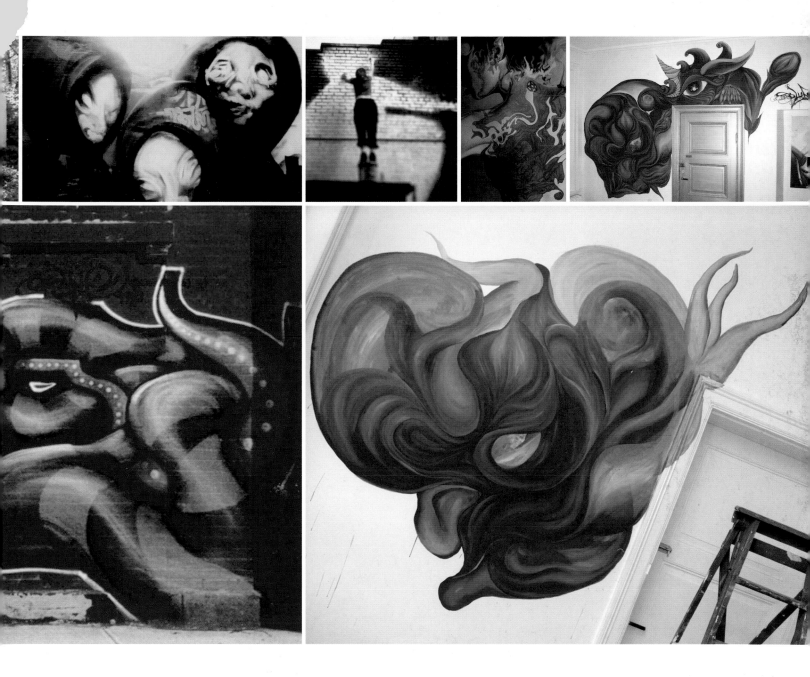

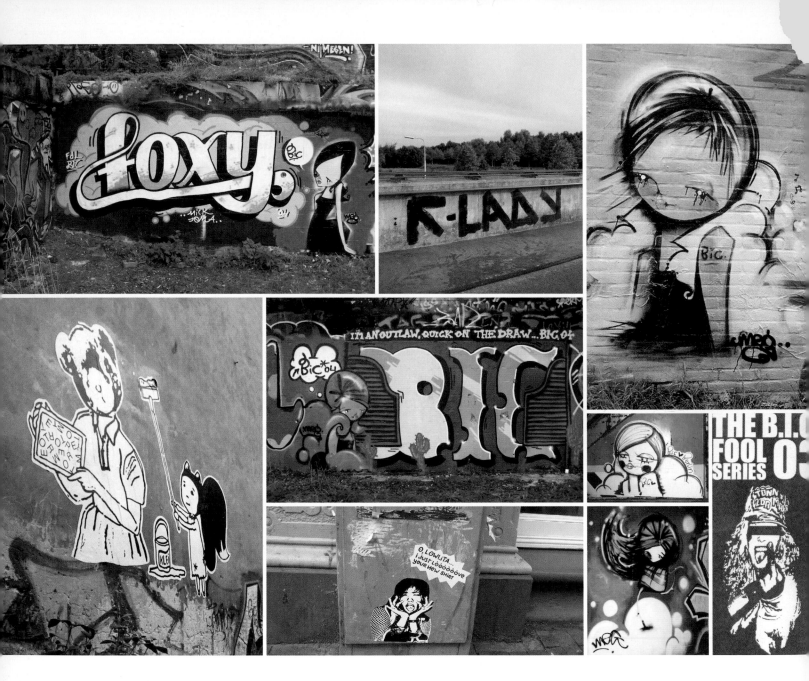

Bitches In Control

Bitches In Control crew was founded in 2003 and consists of F.Lady, Meg and Lowlita, who get up using every conceivable material and technique. F.Lady doesn't distinguish between men and women in the graffiti world: 'For me it's not about being a female who does graffiti, but about doing graffiti – period.'

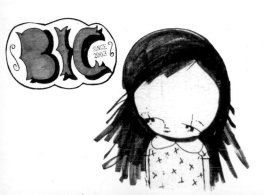

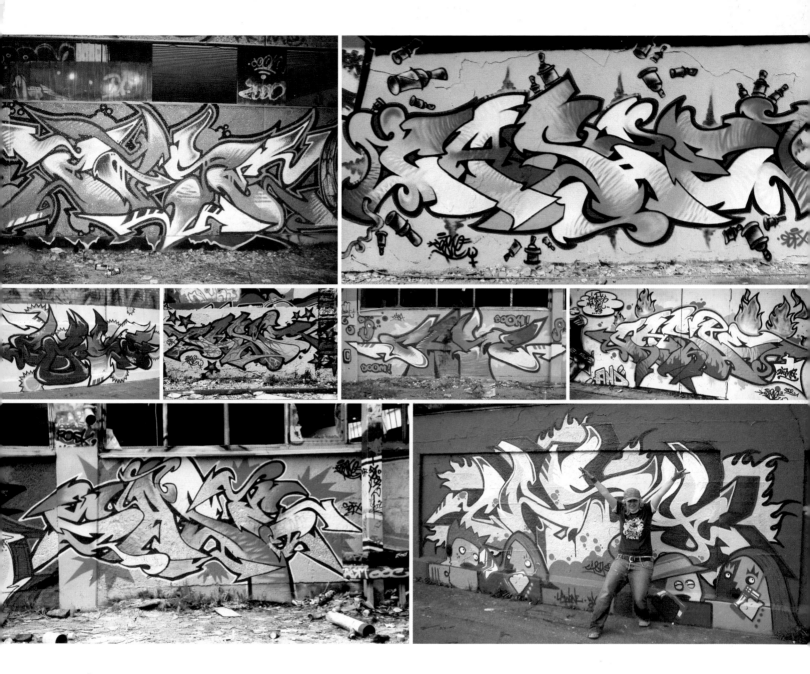

Casie

'My first pieces have pretty much disappeared,' says Munich-based Casie, who has been active since 1996. 'They were painted at night, when I could hardly see a thing, and they looked really bad when I went back to check them out the next day. It took me a while to learn the knack, but I didn't give up. Later, when I painted at the Hall during the day, everything went a lot more smoothly…. I really like lettering or characters to look like they have been done by a female hand, and every now and then I try to make my choice of colours more feminine.'

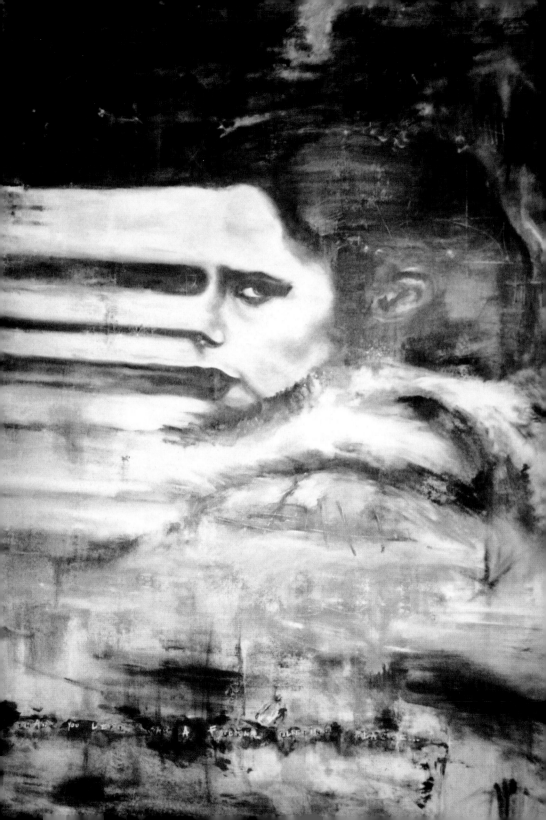

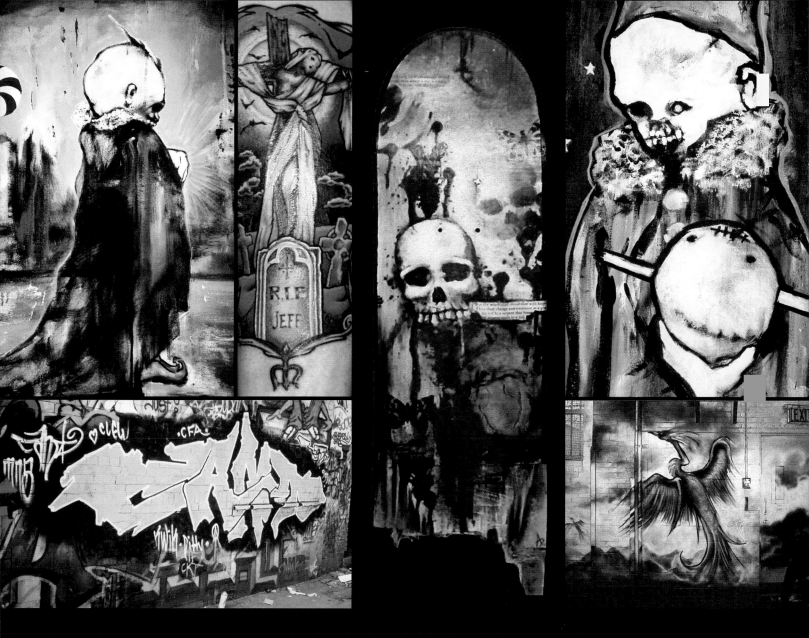

Cant4

Cant4 (aka Amanda D) comes from a graffiti background, with a focus on canvases and pieces, and also works as a custom tattooist in Toronto. She started off writing under the name Deses in 1995 but switched to Cant in the summer of 1997. In her images Cant tries to use versatile techniques to convey movement and emotions. She has also been involved with the CFA and MSN crews and now represents UCM.

'I am a tattooist by trade,' she explains, 'so skin as a canvas is always challenging, but my favourite material to work with has to be oil and acrylic paint. Process and experimentation are very important to me as an artist and I love the way paint acts on and reacts to different surfaces. You can lay it on thick and rich, or fine and subtle. It's very expressive.'

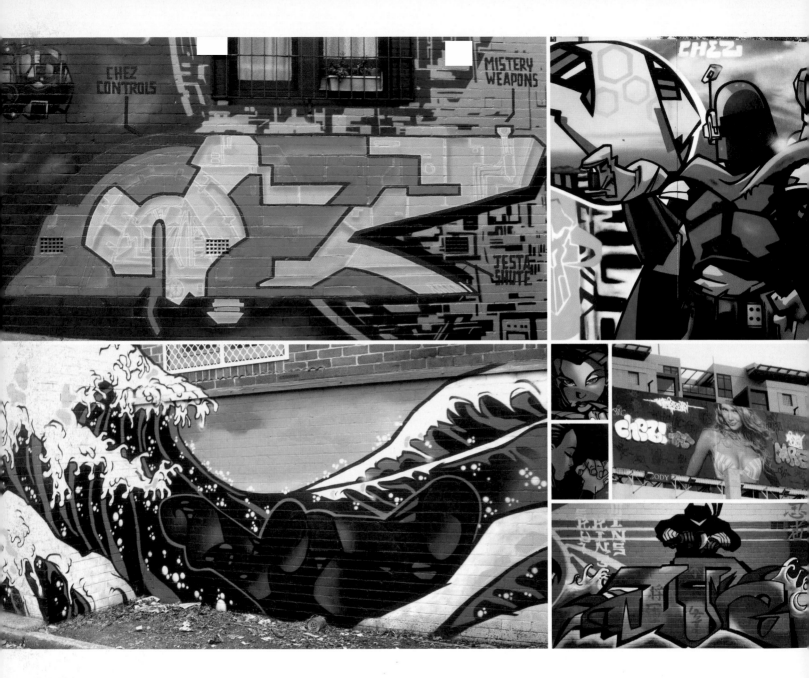

Chez

Chez was born in the beautiful Fiji Islands but has been living in Sydney since 1989, when she got to know the hip-hop scene. Nowadays she teams up with her partner Mistery and generally keeps her graffiti legal, with workshops and commissions.

'I paint what I feel like painting at the time,' she explains. 'If I'm in a dark mood, I'll do something dark. Graff is an emotional outlet for me, and life is a roller coaster, not a sunny walk in the park. I also prefer doing characters with a bit of attitude (the whole b-boy tip), whether it's male, female or cyborg.'

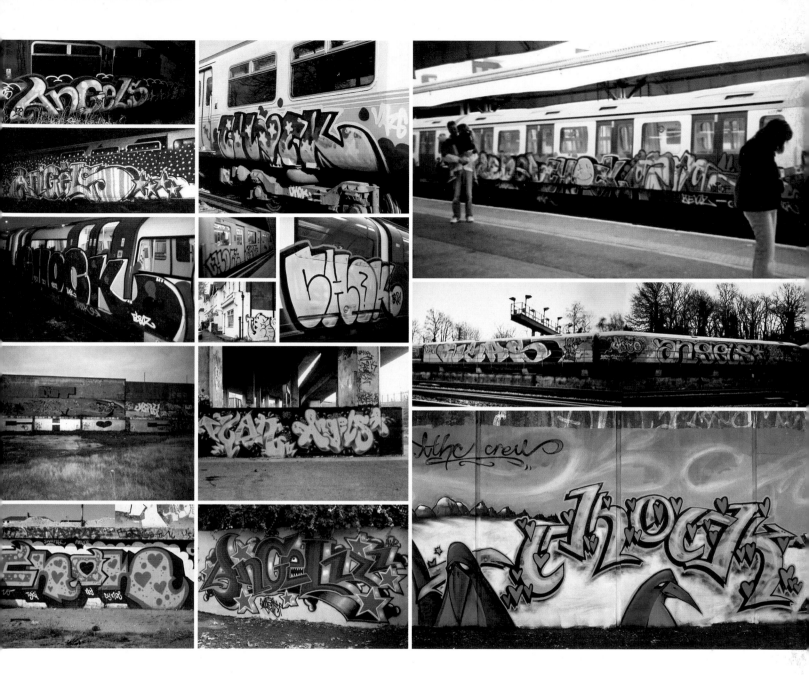

Chock

English artist Chock (aka Angels) got into graffiti in the late 1990s and is still very active. She says: 'I want to express lots of things that I find difficult to verbalize. Graffiti has also been a good way for me to channel my anger and aggression. A lot of positive things have materialized as a result of me painting in this way. I'm known for my illegal graffiti trains and tracks mainly, but these days I'm working on my style more so I'm doing more walls than trains. But I still do my bit illegally and I love it just as much as I always did!'

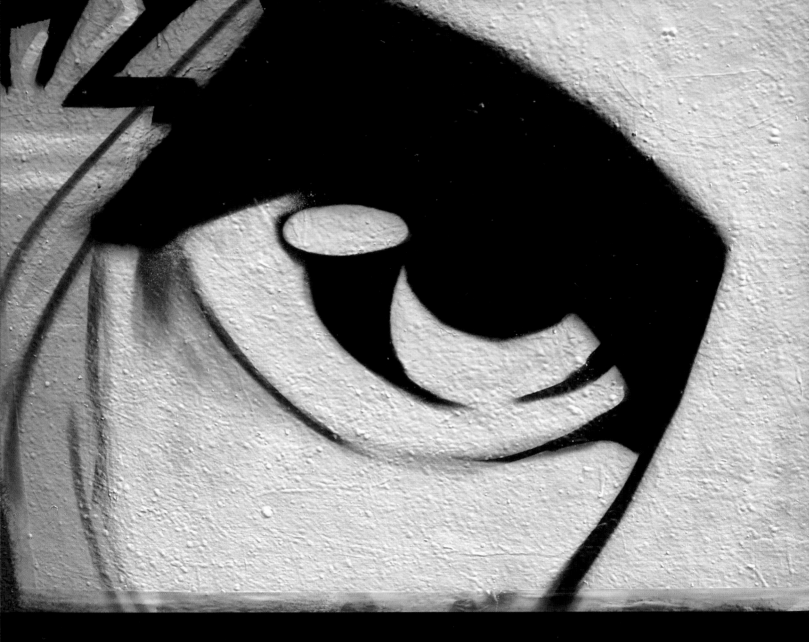

Chour

French-born Chour paints in an array of different styles and uses various techniques, including stickers and the spraycan.

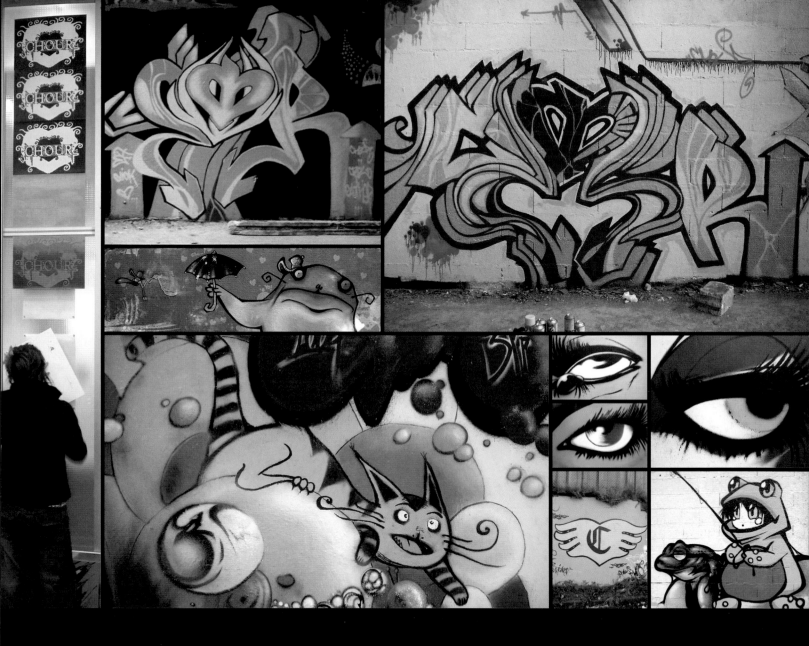

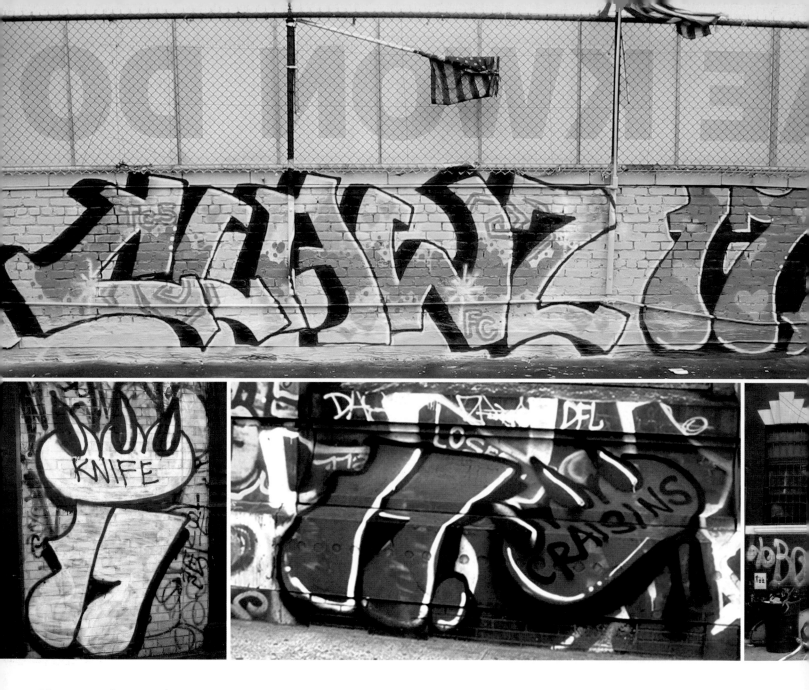

Claw & Miss17

Claw and Miss17 are the female 'Dynamic Duo'. This graffiti tag team, reppin' the PMS crew, are the most badass of NYC bitches. With Claw's mysterious talons, which have been popping up all over New York's five boroughs since the early '90s, and Miss17's prolific bombing over the past decade, these two femmes fatales have earned the respect and admiration of writers everywhere. Power, money and sex make the world go round, and these two – whether on stealth solo missions or double-teaming the streets – make it their mission to keep reminding us of that, in their incomparable, renegade way.

Minya Quirk

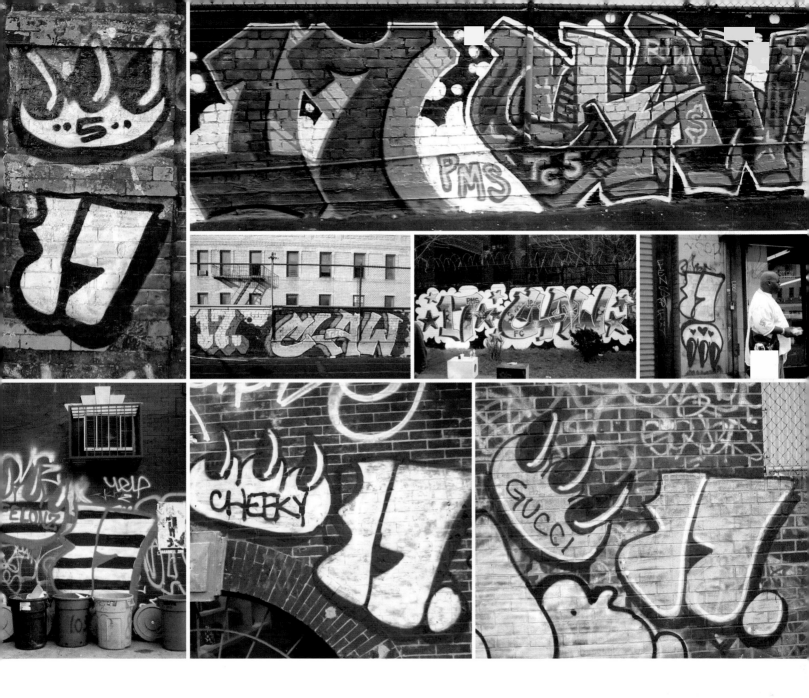

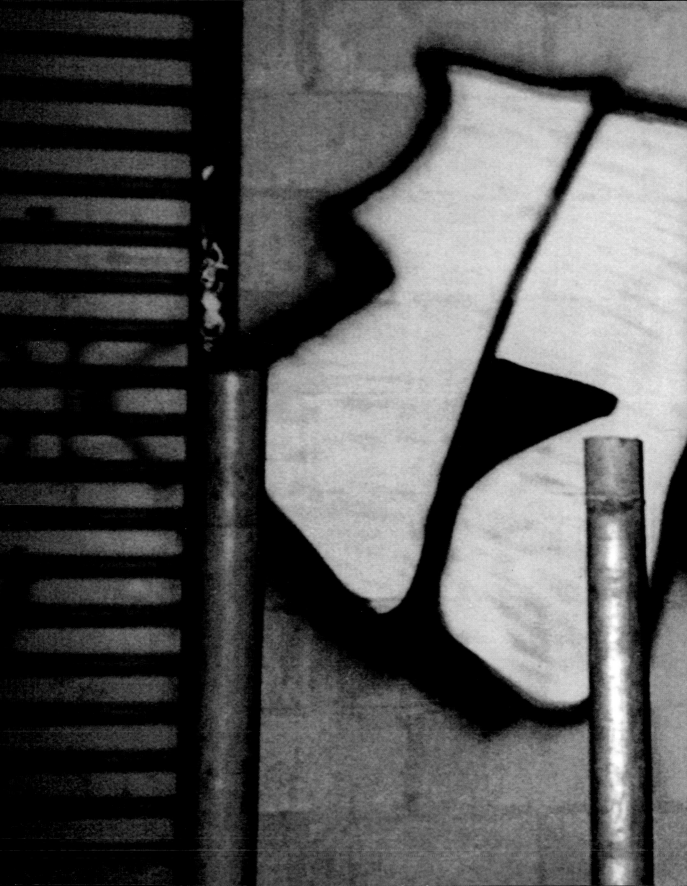

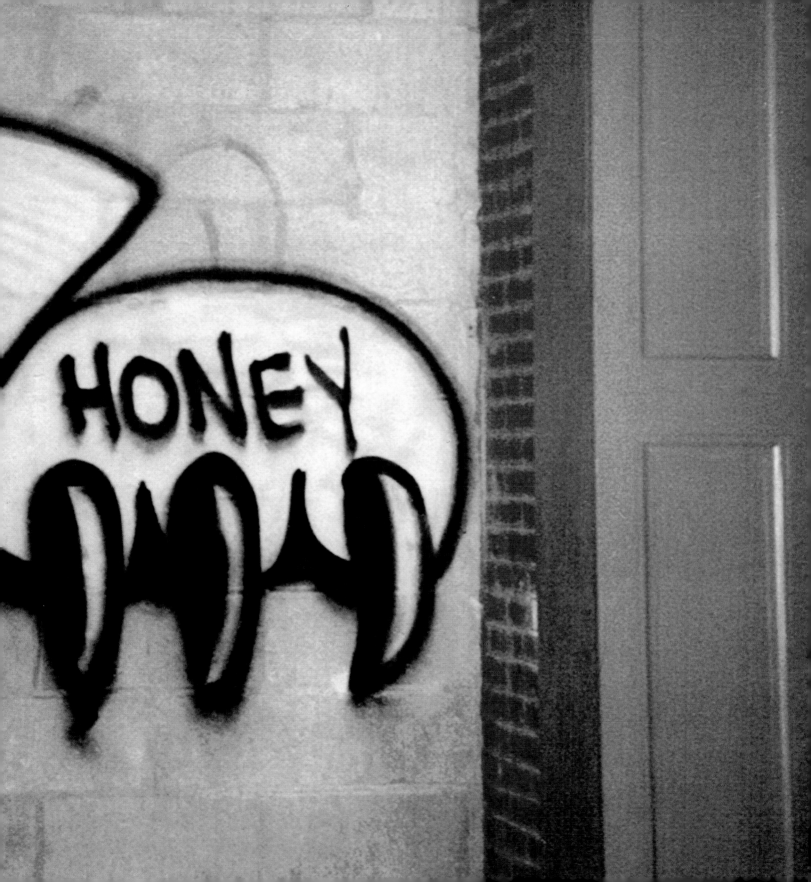

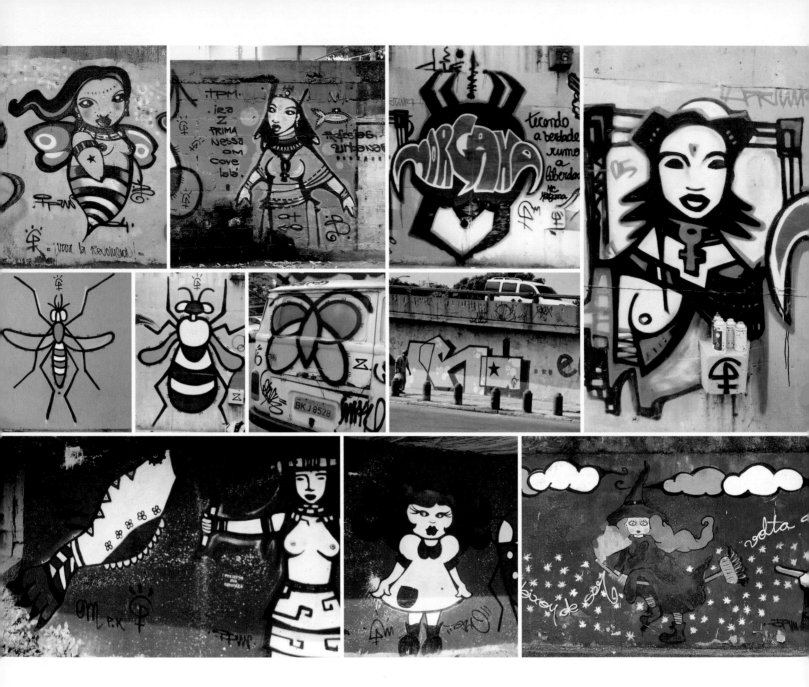

Coletivo TPM

Rio de Janeiro-based Coletivo TPM was founded in 2004 to unify and empower women and now boasts five members: Ira, Morgana, Om, Prima Donna and Z. TPM stands for a number of things, including 'Transgressão Pelas Mulheres' (Transgression for Women).

   'I want to open people's minds, make them review their conception and test their soul,' says Om, one of Rio's first female spray artists. It's a notion that's backed up by Prima Donna: 'We're always expressing something. I want to show things that are part of my routine, my reflections. I paint female characters most of the time, characters I've invented, but in some ways they exist. Sometimes I also do abstract drawings.'

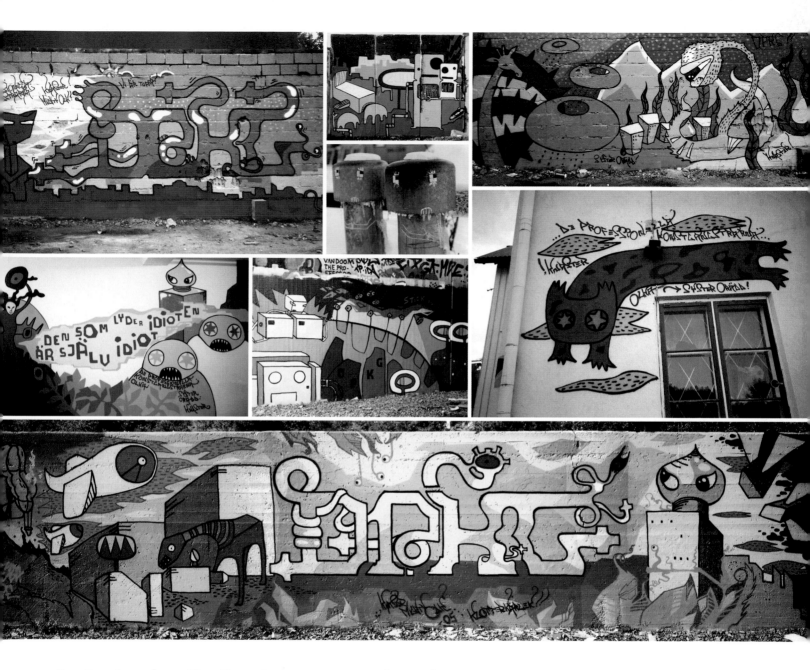

De Professionella Konstgangstrarna (DPKG)

De Professionella Konstgangstrarna is a collective of Swedish artists who are involved in various different projects. One such scheme involved installing yellow benches for lonely people to sit on. 'The significance is that De Professionella Konstgangstrarna create their own rules. Our goal is to let the future into the world and create reality the way it really wants to be…. It's our duty to make the surrounding environment more interesting to the rest of humanity.'

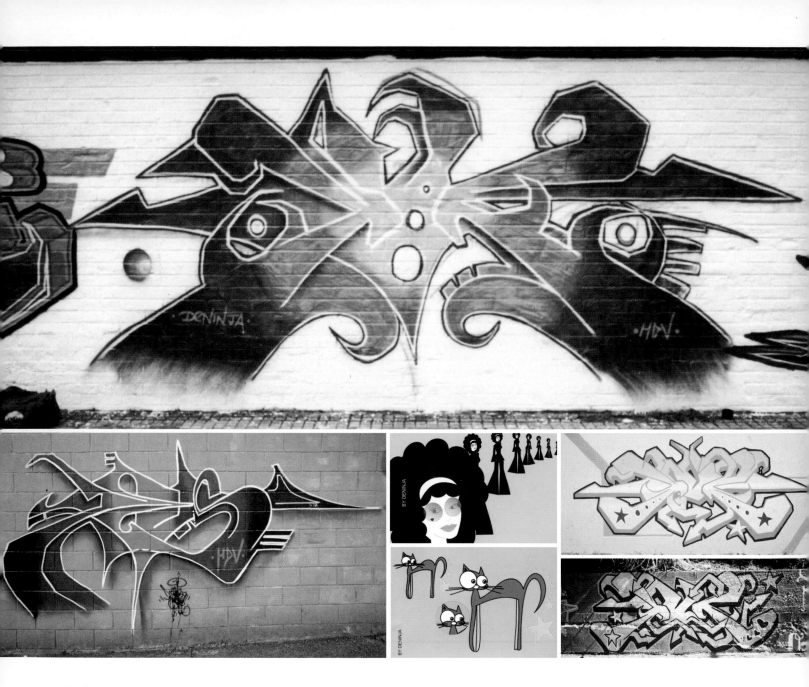

Deninja

Deninja has dreamt of being a writer since the mid-1990s, but she only got into the scene in 2001. Her first works included stickers and pieces on cargo boats, for which she got a lot of support from her husband, Does. She has since trained as a graphic designer and works on digital images, although she still spray-paints her distorted letters on the street.

'To me graffiti's art,' she explains. 'Not a hypocritical art, like a lot of (although not all) the stuff you see in galleries, but something that we do without the hope of getting anything in return. To paint out of the simple desire to express oneself. An art that is there in the street for those that don't have a culture, don't understand art but like it for what it is...for the beggars, poor children, prostitutes, lunatics and drunks of the streets; at least, here in Brazil they adore it and always stop to chat with us.'

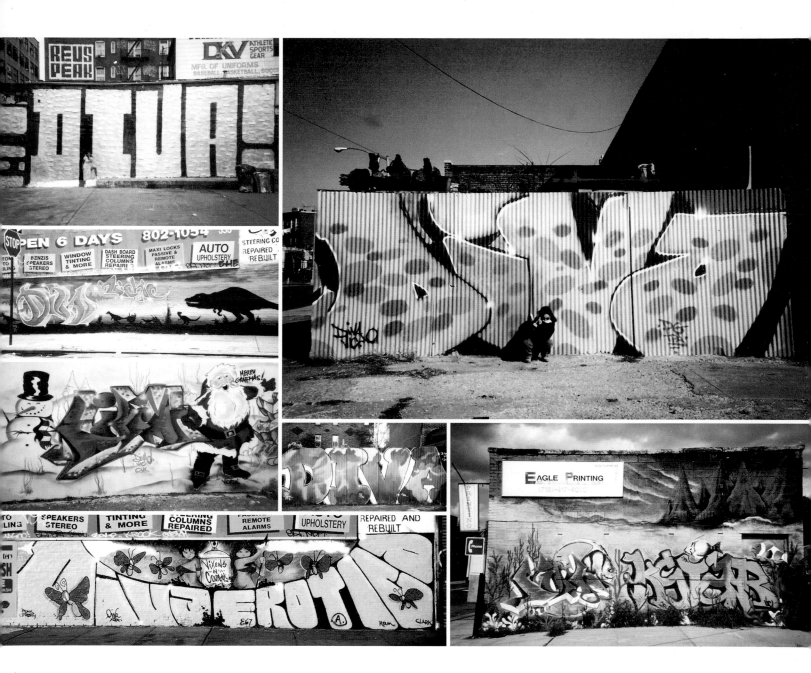

Diva

Brooklyn-born Diva caught her first tags and pieces in *c*. 1984–85, going by the name of Tabs or Tabz. She didn't write under her current name until 1996, after a long break from the scene.

'I don't find what I do to be feminine,' says Diva. 'I think we're all doing pretty much the same shit – some people are into drawing girls, others are into making political statements, some concentrate on lettering styles, while others just hit shit up. I can't speak for anyone else, but so far I haven't encountered anything I would consider to be a problem. You're always going to have someone talking shit or going over you. I don't see that as a problem, just part of the game.'

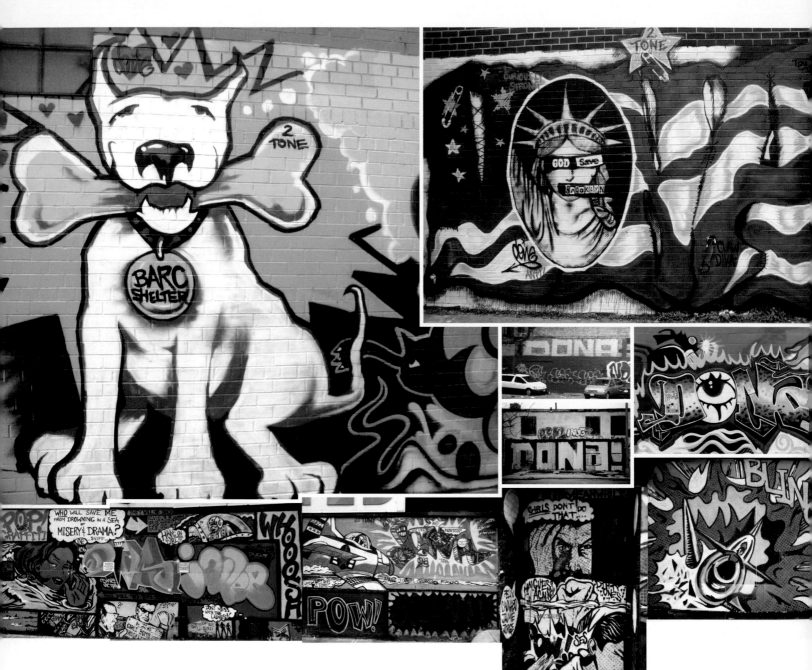

Dona

Dona lives in an illegal loft conversion in Bushwick, Brooklyn, with her fiancé, two dogs and two cats. In the early 1990s she squatted in houses on 13th Street, where she found inspiration in political graffiti, as well as a love of punk, hip-hop and reggae.

'Art is one thing, graffiti is another,' she says. 'I'm a writer who happens to be an artist. I keep them separate, although at times they will correlate, and jump into bed with each other. People only knew who I was after I was slapping the sides of buildings with 20-foot blockbusters, not 'cause I could draw pretty things and hang them in galleries. The high art thing hasn't really ever happened for me.'

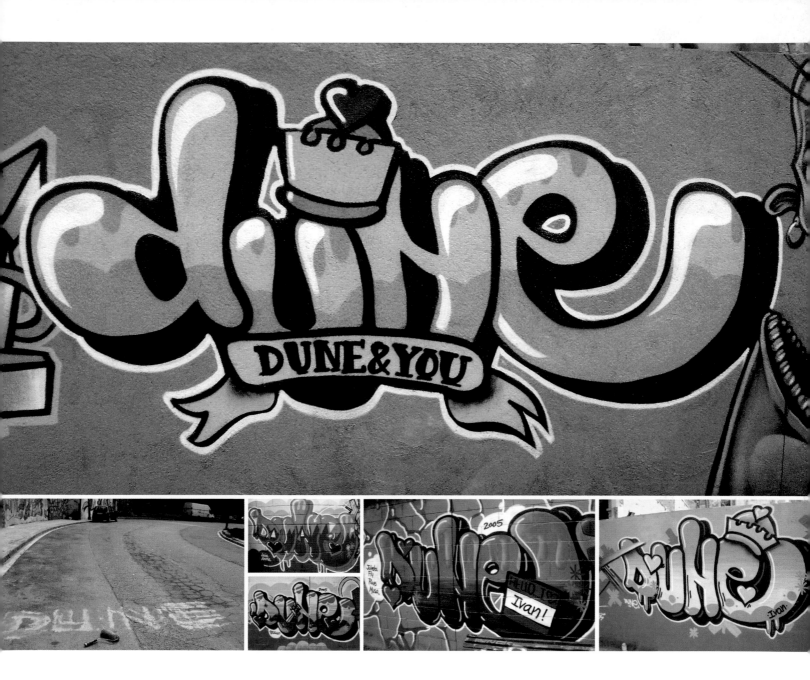

Dune

Barcelona's Dune did her first piece in 2002. The active artist is part of a lively female scene that has developed in her home city.

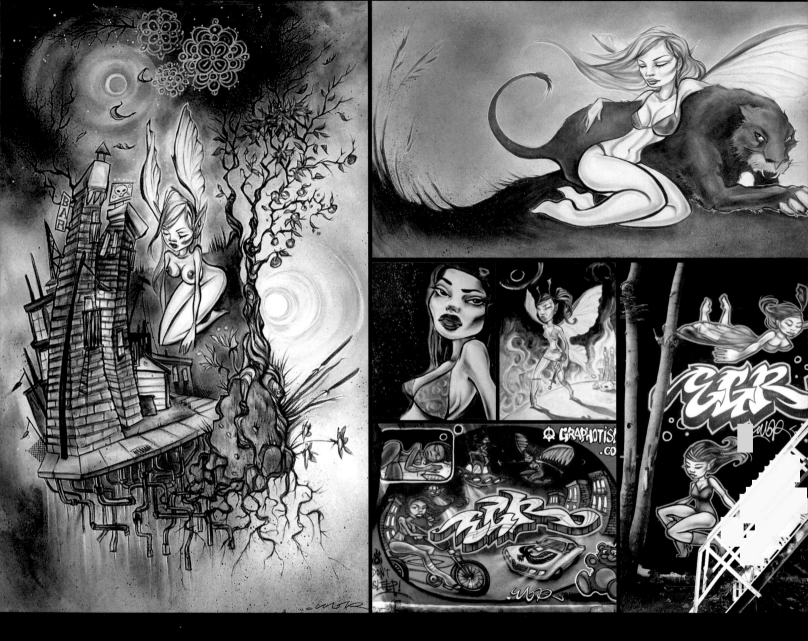

EGR

The 'E' and 'G' represent EGR's initials; the 'R' is dedicated to her late sister, Kristen Rose (1980–82). When she first got into graffiti, in 1996, EGR needed to work up the courage to paint in public. She initially concentrated on her blackbook and stickers, and did her first piece in a hidden spot under a bridge in the city's suburbs. Now EGR uses a variety of techniques and surfaces – large walls, oil on canvas and wood, or mixed media.

'What I would like to express with my art is the endless possibilities of ideas that we can all share, learn and grow from. I would like to strike a chord within mass consciousness, to lift our minds higher, beyond prejudices or misconceptions. I would like to communicate on a positive level for women, and to surpass any expectations or limitations the world may put on us. Painting is also very therapeutic and often helps me to realize my place in the world.'

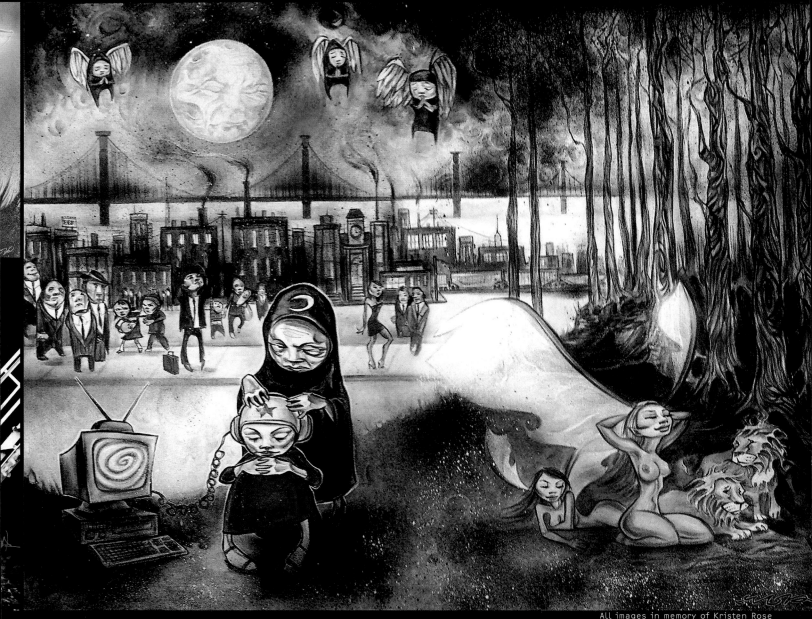

All images in memory of Kristen Rose

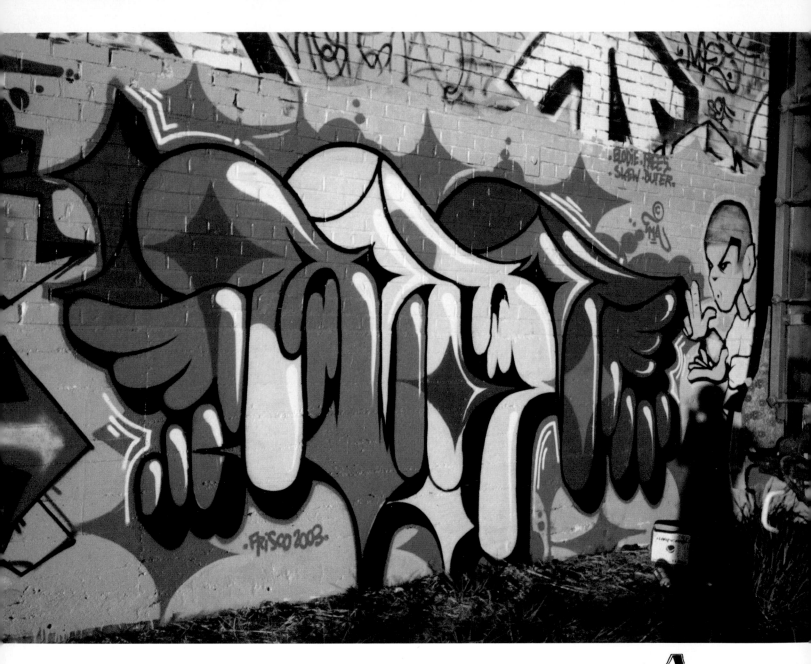

EMA

Montpellier-born EMA has been living in New York for some time. She bombed a bit in 1991–92 but didn't do her first real piece until February 1996.

'There are different ways of doing graffiti,' she explains. 'Me, I started graffiti because of the peaceful hip-hop culture, listening to music like A Tribe Called Quest, De La Soul, The Goats, The Pharcyde…. I evolved in the culture of living with style, where whoever you were, wherever you came from, you had to have style. Even if you were a thief, you had to steal in style!

46

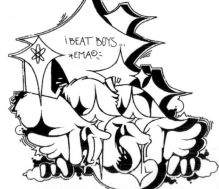

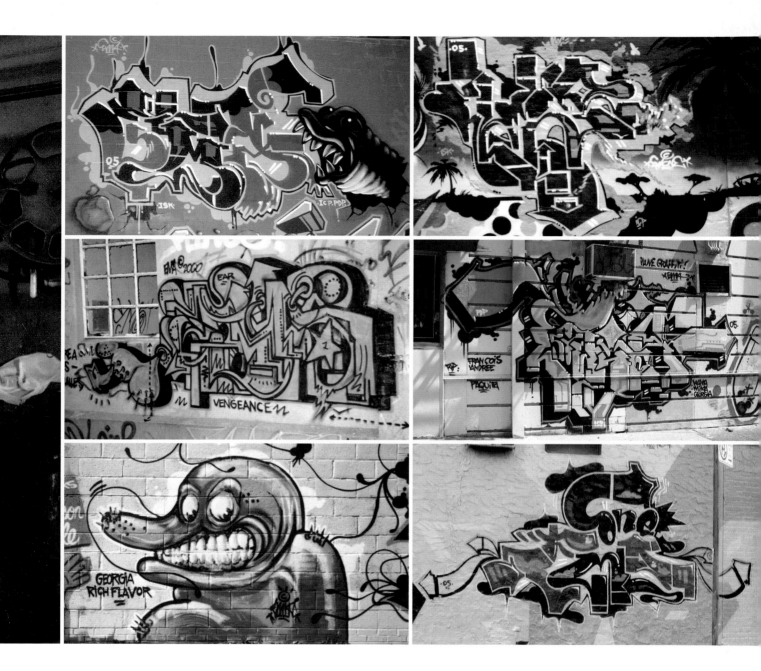

'Not everyone sees the hip-hop culture the same way, because they take the game too seriously and start ego-tripping too much. Generally, they are the ones that cause trouble, for everybody, and especially for women who try to be part of this culture. Also, mainstream culture goes against this idea of battle of skills, and tries to put hip-hop in a category that doesn't suit the majority of women. That's why I think there are so few. They get brainwashed by what is said on the radio and on TV.

'I had the chance to grow up at a time and in a place where hip-hop was ultra underground. If you wanted to listen to rap, you had to struggle hard to get mix tapes. If you see hip-hop the way I see it, there's no room for a gender issue, it's all about love and peace!'

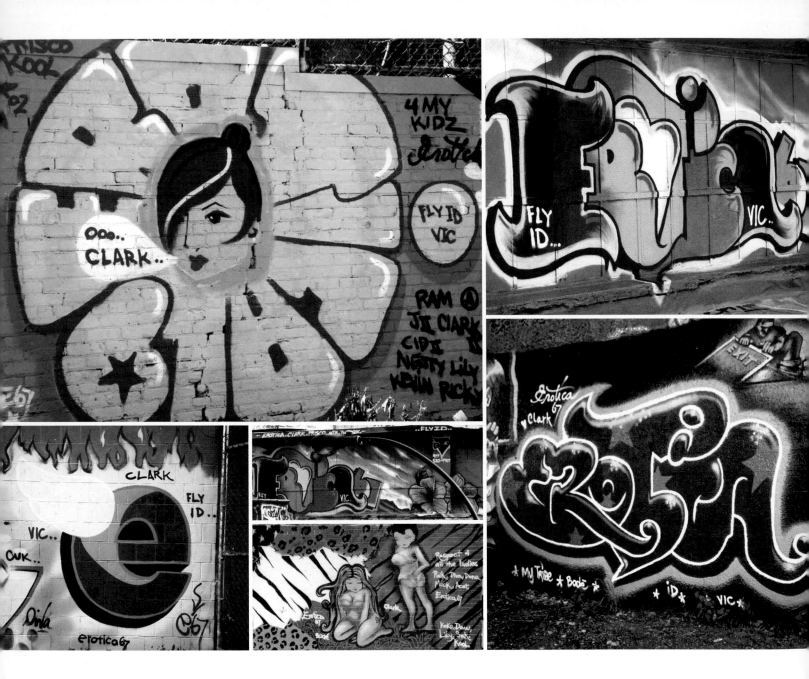

Erotica67

Erotica67 reps the Bronx. In 1977 she started to sketch under the name Kitty in order to compete with her male counterparts, but by 1986 she had settled on her current name, inspired by cartoonist Vaughn Bode's Erotica figures. She didn't pick up a spraycan until the early 1990s, bombing Queens and the Bronx, and a couple of years later she did her first piece with future husband Clark.

'It's a great experience to be involved in what Eva62, Barbara62 and everyone before and after did in representing women in graff,' says Erotica67. 'Thanks to Nicholas Ganz for his energy in organizing the info and documenting us around the world. Big ups to all the female writers!'

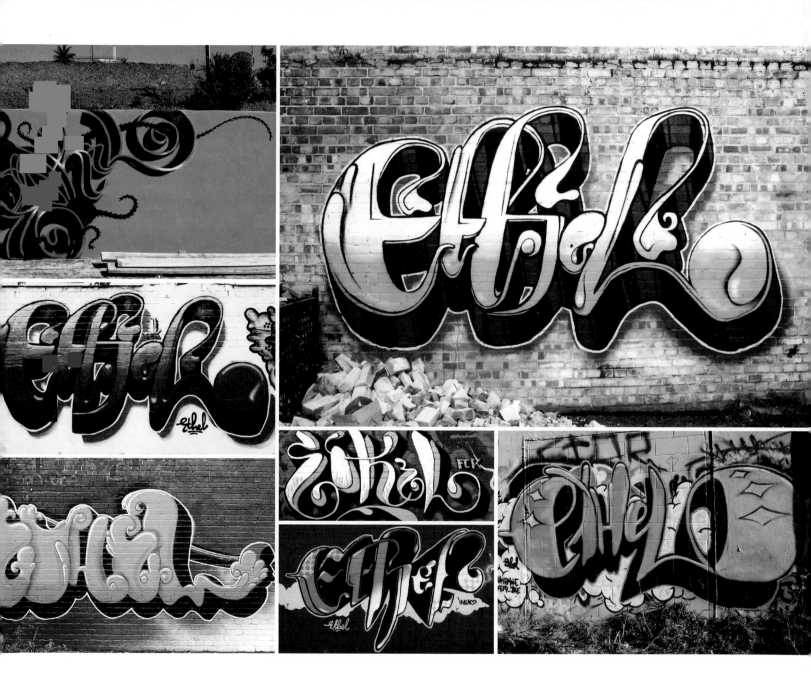

Ethel

Ethel grew up in southern England, where graffiti was
sparse. Her life changed when she moved to London
and got to know Insa and Astek, who taught her a
great deal and enabled her to develop her own style.
In her pieces she likes to include inspirations from
books, films and lettering.

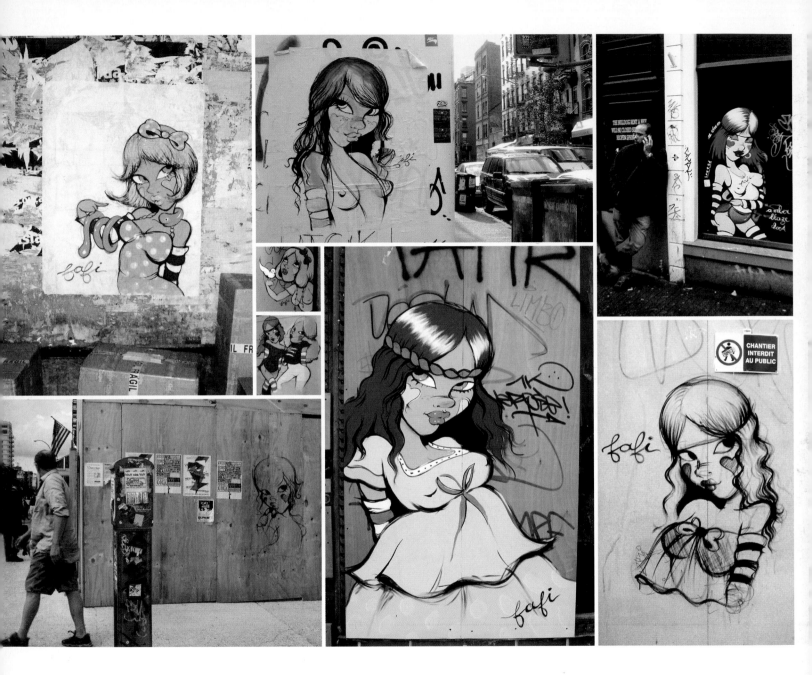

Fafi

Fafi belongs to a particular group of graffiti artists who use a brush to paint figures on walls – a style that emerged from Toulouse independently through the work of Kat and Miss Van. She started out back in 1994 and has concentrated on female figures – known as 'Fafinettes' – for many years. 'Fafinettes' are reminiscent of Japanese manga comics, with strong colours and sexy poses; they beautify dirty places, and Fafi tries to show her respect for the neighbourhood by connecting them to the surroundings. Of late, in order to move away from drawing just women and to be able to express her personality fully, she has been experimenting with other creatures such as Hmilo and Bitrak.

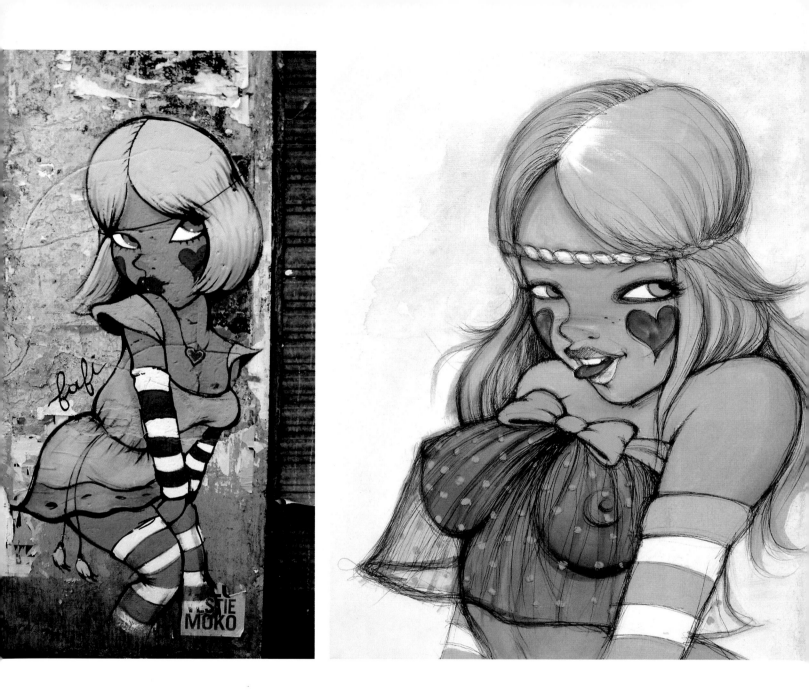

'I find I have two distinctive states of mind,' she says. 'Most of the time, it's all very spontaneous and instinctive. I think most of us don't know why we do it – it's like a calling. We want to be remembered. Then, sometimes, if I stop a little bit, take a moment of reflection, I see a place in a different light – not just as a target for one of my characters, but like a big canvas, of which my character is just one part...she stands there with traffic lights, trees and moving passers-by. Now I want to create my own world where my "Fafinettes" will be among the characters.'

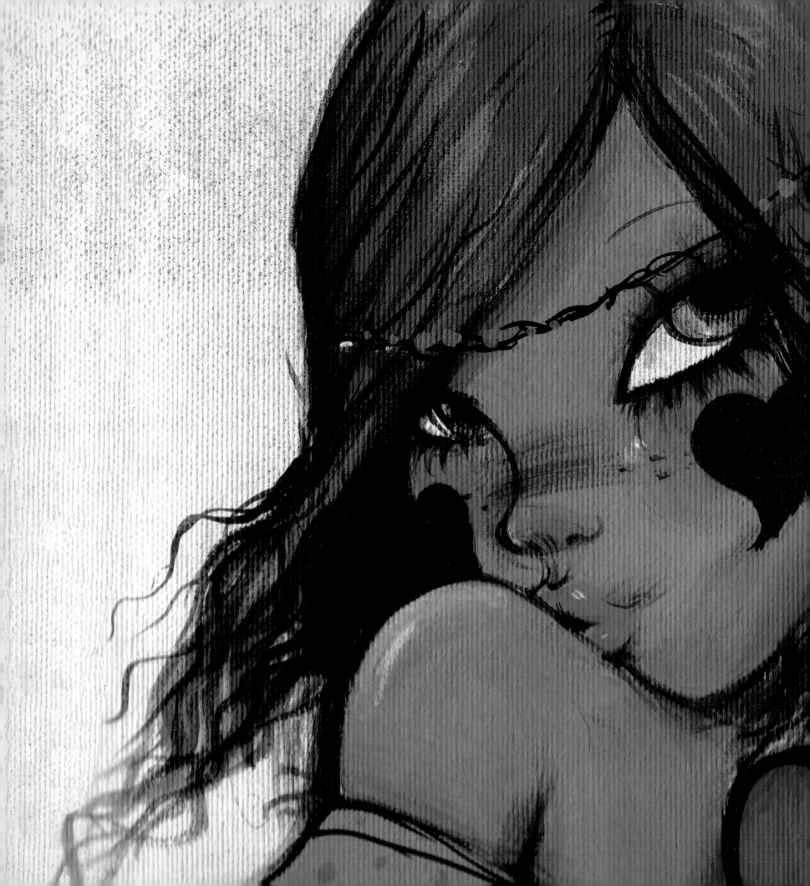

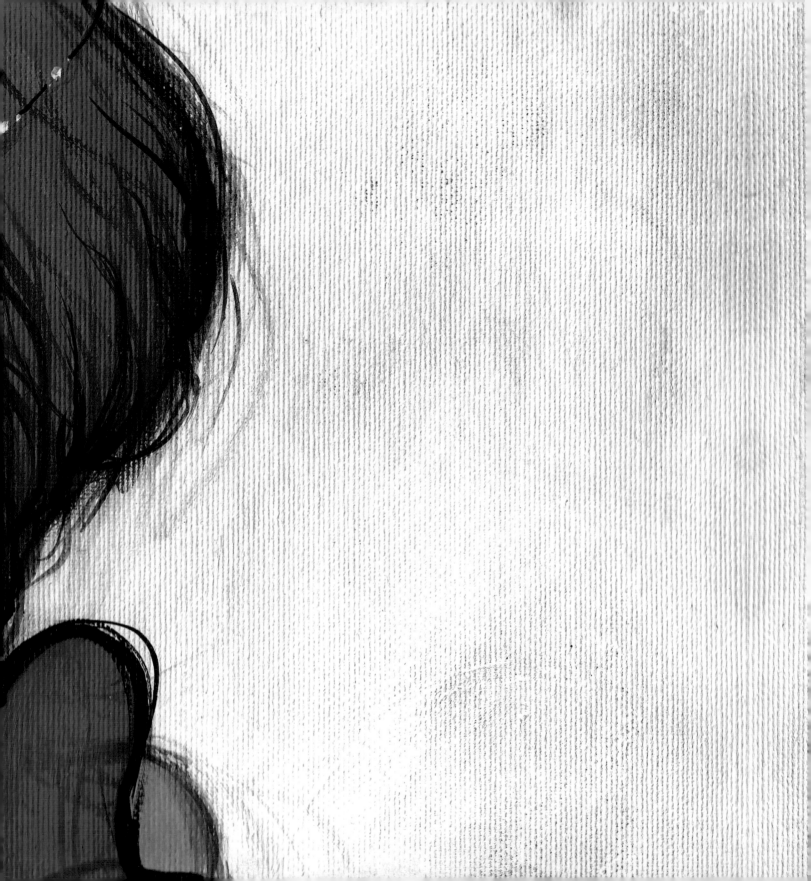

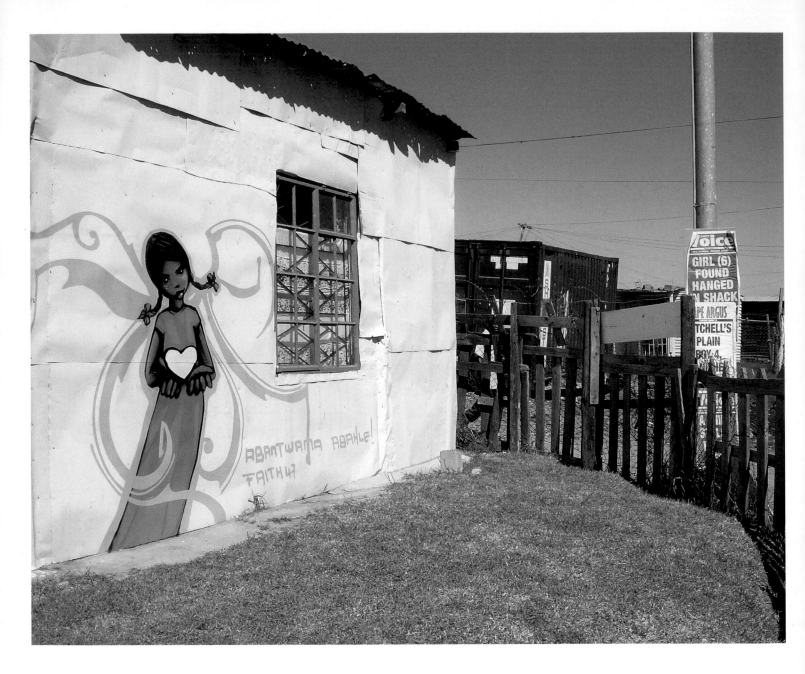

Faith47

Cape Town-based Faith47 was introduced to graffiti by Wealz130 and the YMB crew. Today, using her surroundings as her gallery, her work includes graffiti, graphic design, illustrations and canvases.

'Female empowerment is one of the issues I explore in order to inspire and provoke response,' she says. 'This is due to the fact that I can relate to female issues, identity and emotions. Promoting female empowerment is something I feel strongly about. In South Africa there are a lot of women who are subservient, disempowered and/or live in abusive environments. The rape statistics are one in three. There is a definite lack of constructive role models in the media and this is something we need to approach progressively and change.

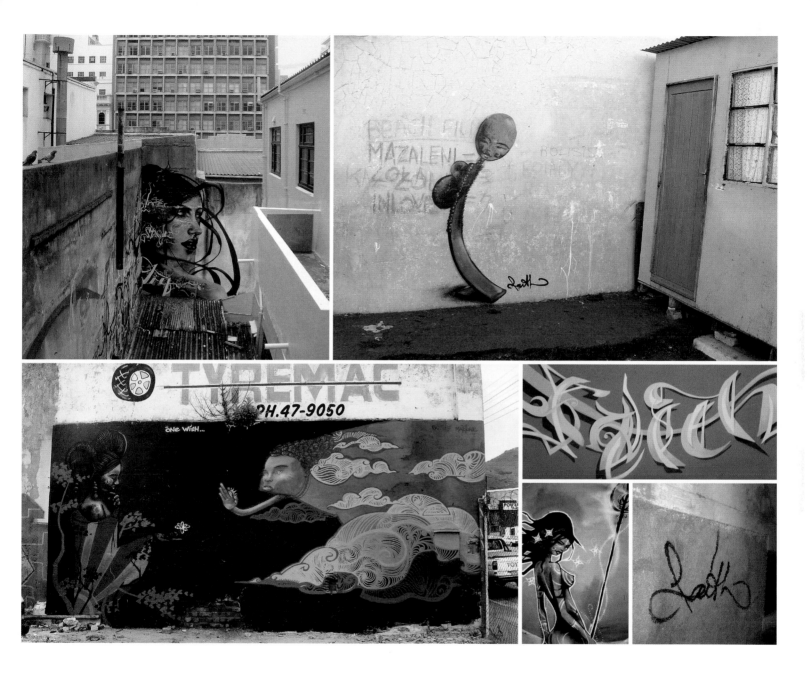

'Women have the potential to be extremely strong characters. We are the ones who bring children into the world, and teach them about the world. If we are not well adjusted and educated, then it's reflected in society as a whole.

'There is so much mass-media input, propaganda, loud, glossy desire, want, need, dramatization, bright colours and obvious human emotions. We become distracted from the subtle movements, intricate details, gestures, feelings and truths that give life its substance. I like my work to suggest something more than what you see, something that can't necessarily be put into words, something subtle yet strong.'

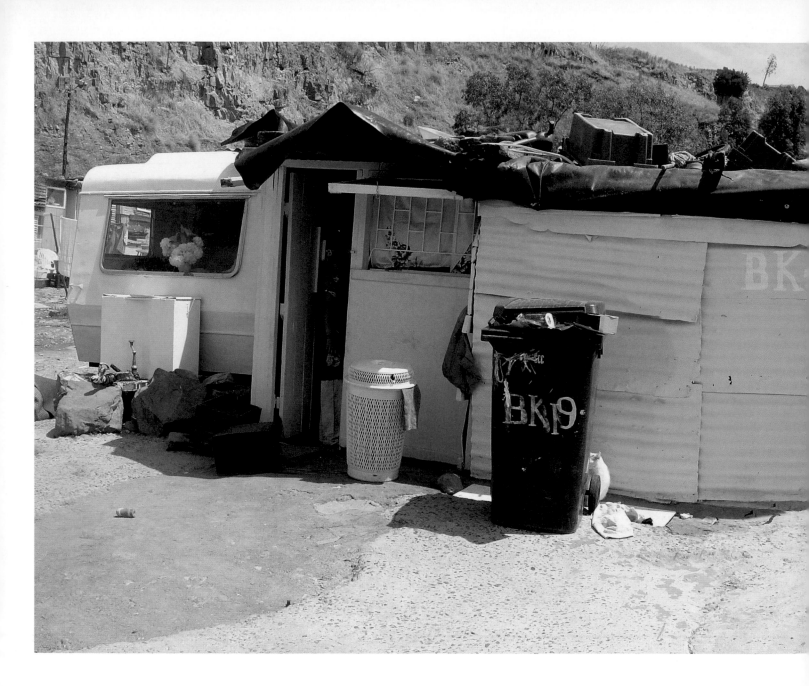

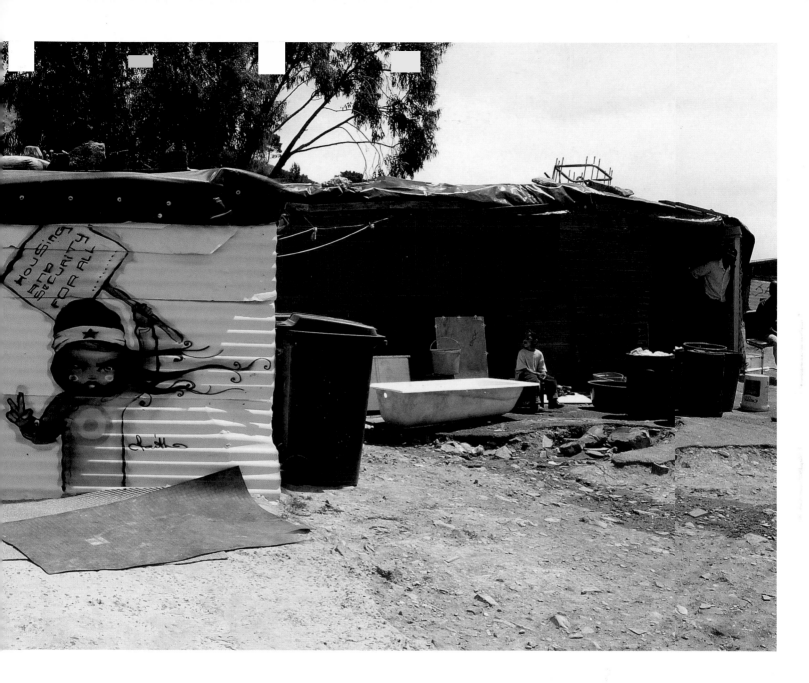

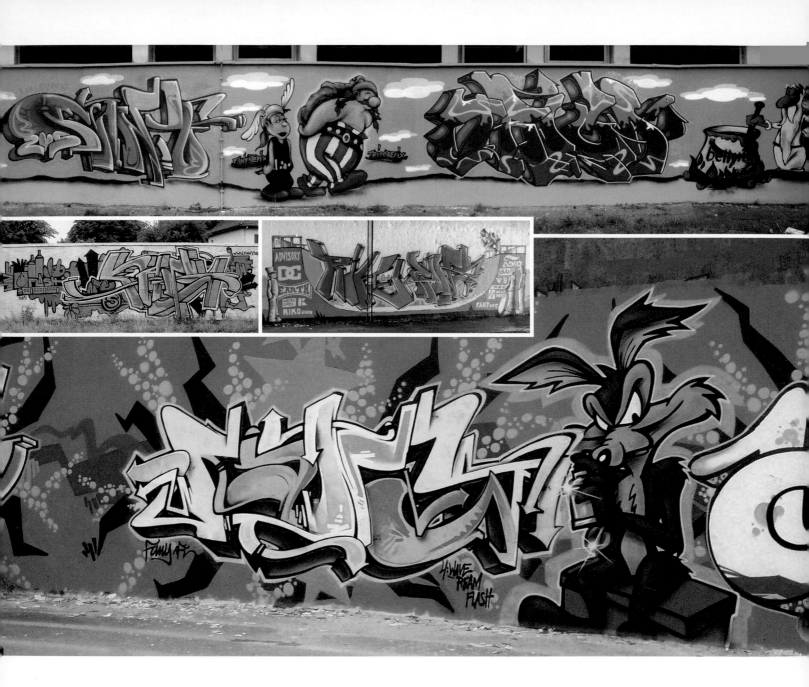

Fany

'I would say my pieces look quite neutral,' says Fany, who also reps the AFC crew. 'To me this is very important as I don't want people to necessarily know that I am a female writer. Quite the opposite in fact — as a woman in this game you're often marvelled at, and you get comments like "You write pretty well for a woman". I think it's key that my work isn't compared to pieces by other female artists but is judged or valued from an entirely neutral perspective. Also, I don't want to achieve fame just by virtue of my gender. Obviously I could use it to my advantage, but I want to avoid doing that as much as possible.'

For Fany, painting is a philosophy that defines her life, a way of thinking and feeling: 'A sphere that just belongs to me, in which I am able to be self-confident. When I go through the streets, I scan my surroundings, paint what's in my inner eye. To me it's important that the picture and environment merge: both must embrace and abandon themselves to one another. That is passion and love, never just "scrawling".'

58

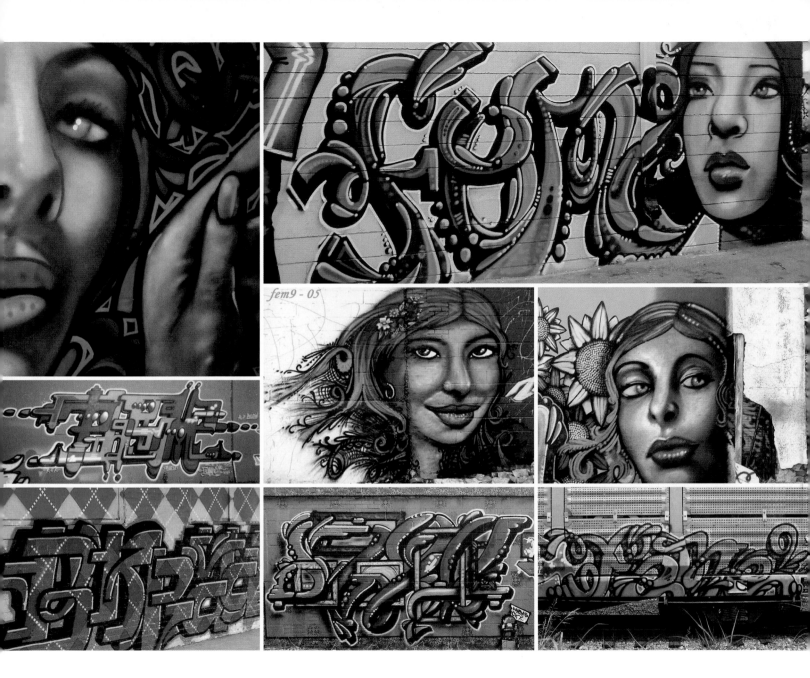

Femme9

'In everyday life there are women who act masculine and there are men who act real feminine,' says American graffiti artist Femme9. 'Some have suggested I write a more masculine name to level the playing field I suppose, but I say no way! I wanted a name that hinted at gender! I wanted to inspire other females. As men and women we put all our attributes into our work and I'm no exception. I remember I would always catch Hope4, a freight writer from the Midwest. I was inspired because I was sure this was another female. When I met him we had a good laugh about it. He said he often painted in pink and sort of girly to get more attention. Hey, it worked. He painted simply to paint and never came across as gangster, like many writers do. It sucks when people feel they need to play a part and they can't just be themselves. That's an unfortunate thing in this stain game and in all walks of life. We all want to be so different in our little categories. While often hiding under an alias, in turn creating more division and confusion, many lose sight of self.'

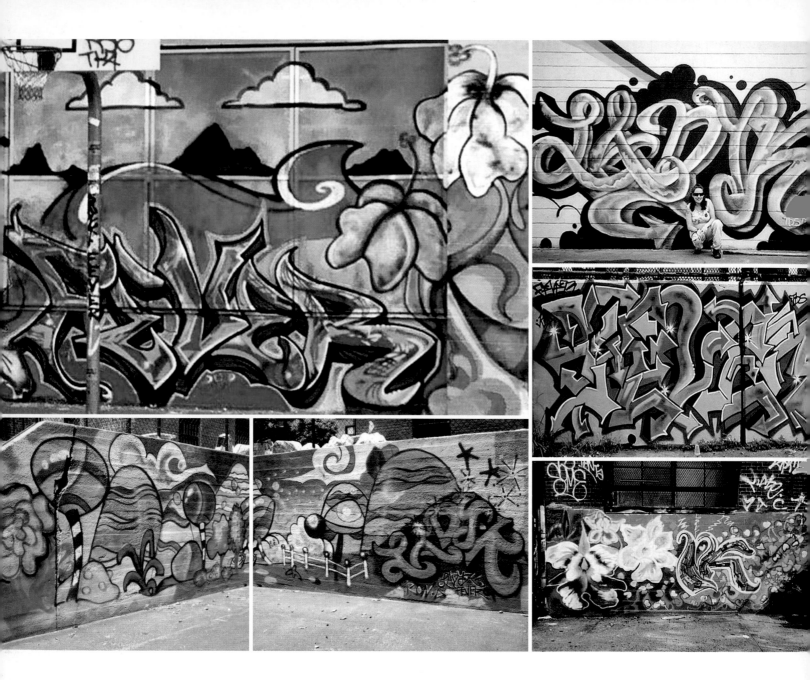

Fever (Lady K)

'I got into graffiti through being a skateboarder,' says Lady K-Fever. 'All the parks had pieces and I wanted to see my name there too, but ironically I started doing more art than piecing through "Riot Grrls", a youth feminist movement that was happening across North America in the 1990s.'

The Canadian-born graffiti artist lives in New York and is involved in many different fields, including film-set design. She also used to write for German magazine *Backspin* and has founded her own company called Lady K-Fever: Words. Images. Art & Design.

'I feel that I express myself through the experience of painting. The challenge for that day or the design: balancing styles. I like to paint the abstract moments in emotions with experimentations of colour and can-control techniques. The femininity, fierceness of fonts, or soft purring of imagination. Each time I paint, something new inspires me to paint what I paint. I've always been dedicated to creating my expression in my style, whether I'm painting Dora The Explorer in an uptown sneaker mural for four-year-olds or a door with a hundred dollar bill for a millionaire.'

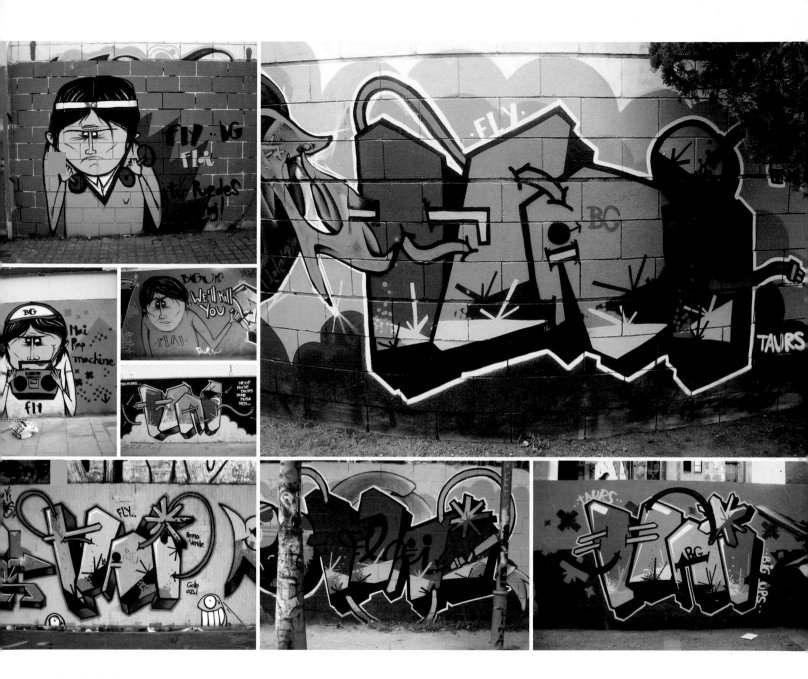

Fly/Flai

Spanish-born Fly, a young artist from Barcelona, initially painted predominantly on paper. Although she started off working alone, her later involvement with the BG crew proved a turning point, encouraging her to become increasingly active.

'I've seen that graffiti is something that becomes a part of your life,' she says, 'and if you're really into it, you won't be able to let it go, because it isn't just about putting paint on a wall. The relation with people is a very important aspect of graffiti, and this is the reason why it's a way of life. It's more than I ever thought possible when I first started out.'

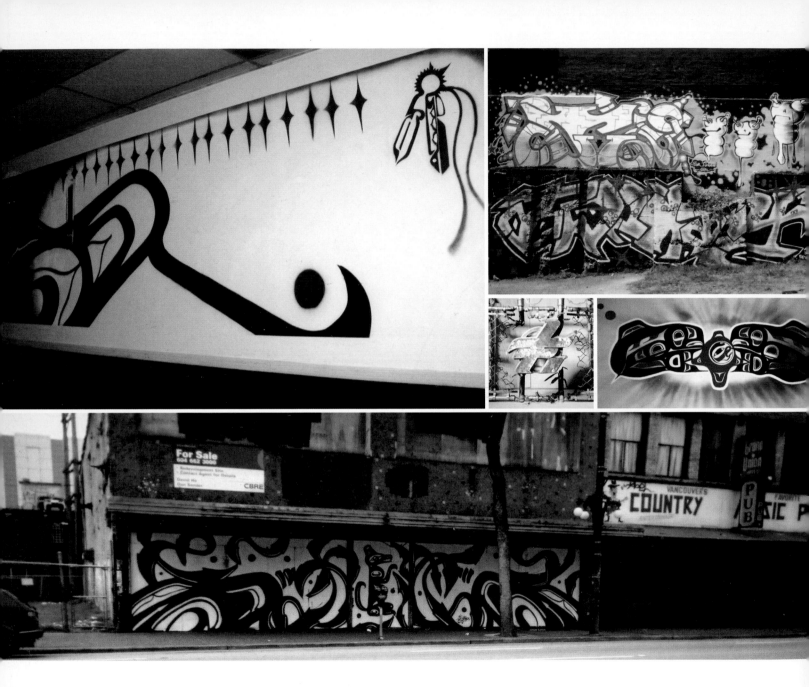

Girl23

First Nations graffiti artist Girl23 lives in Vancouver, Canada. 'In the end is the beginning,' she says.
'Love and courage to all my native sisters and brothers!'

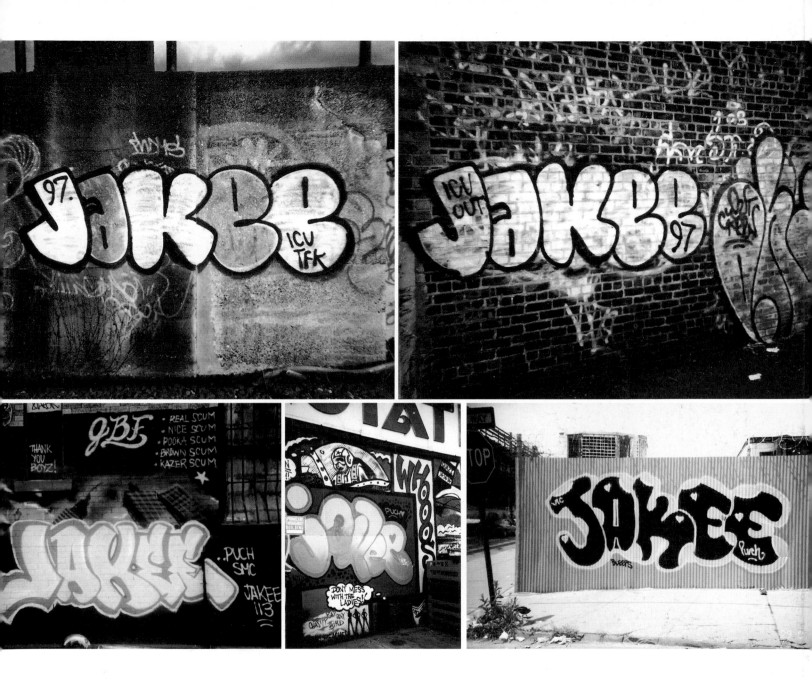

Jakee

Jakee's a New Yorker, from Queens, and is known primarily for her throw-ups, which she has been spray-painting since the early 1990s.

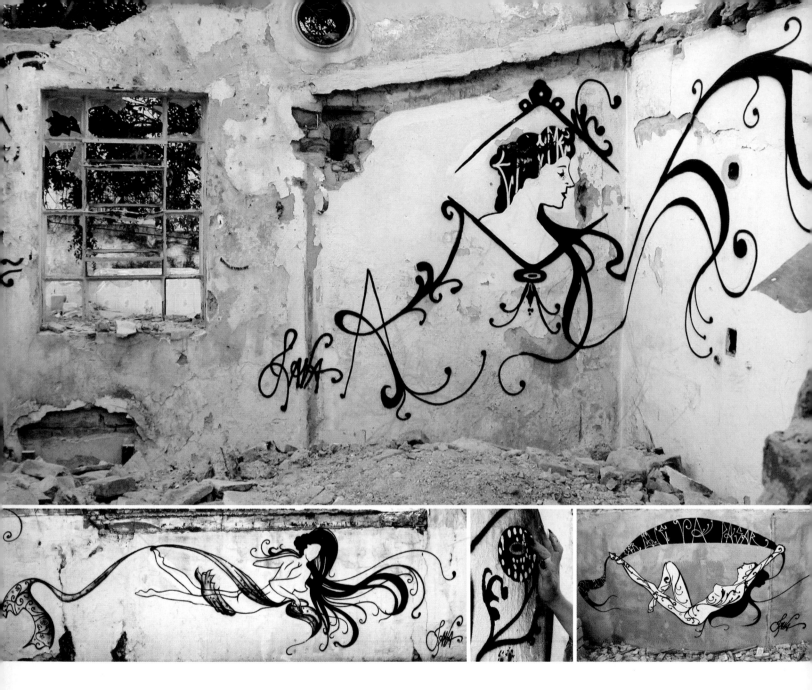

Jana Joana

Jana Joana has been enriching São Paulo's vibrant graffiti culture since 1998, and takes Brazil and women as her inspiration. She has used her smooth style of painting to create urban art interventions, developing different and delusive projects associated with the life experiences of city women. Her broad artistic remit also includes expositions, scenography, illustrations and lithographs.

'I would describe my work as social, female and poetic,' she says. 'I've always wanted to interact with the city. I try to show women – so that it can be a starting point for those who look at it. Freedom, motherhood and women's dreams can be interpreted in different ways…. We wear different clothes to men. We have different bodies and ways of thinking. It's natural that my interest in characters, colours and themes is to do with the female universe. I like working on feminineness in my drawings and the sensitivity that every woman has, and I seek the valorization of women as singular productive and creative human beings in society.'

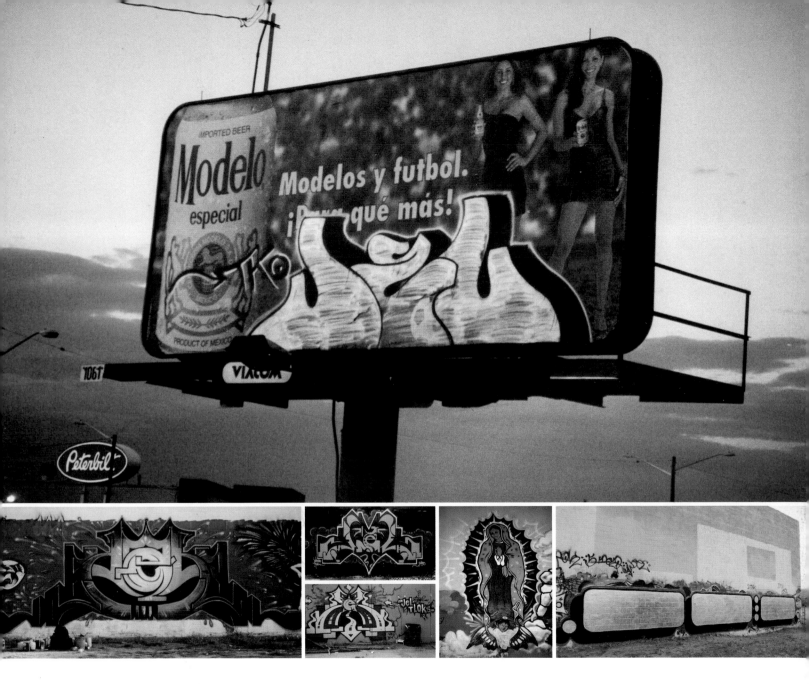

Jel

LA graffiti artist Jel says: 'It's harder to get away with graffiti out here, considering all the gangs we have that would jack or kill us over it, and then there are cops that will practically hang us with big fines, jail time, and slap us with a felony to go on our record to fuck up our future, like we're some hardcore criminal ready to hurt somebody. It's pretty screwed up! So naturally, after all the crap we risk and go through to catch a spot, we don't take getting capped lightly out here. I don't cap anyone unless it's really toy, on a fresh spot…. I think it takes a lot of heart for a female to go out at night to catch a spot alone. Guys only have to worry about getting arrested, jacked or killed. We have to worry about all that, plus more – like getting kidnapped or raped. I could look my crappiest, but perverts would still follow me around and not leave me alone. And, since I look like a little kid, old people and cops wonder what I'm doing out on the streets at night alone. So we definitely get harassed a lot more in every direction.'

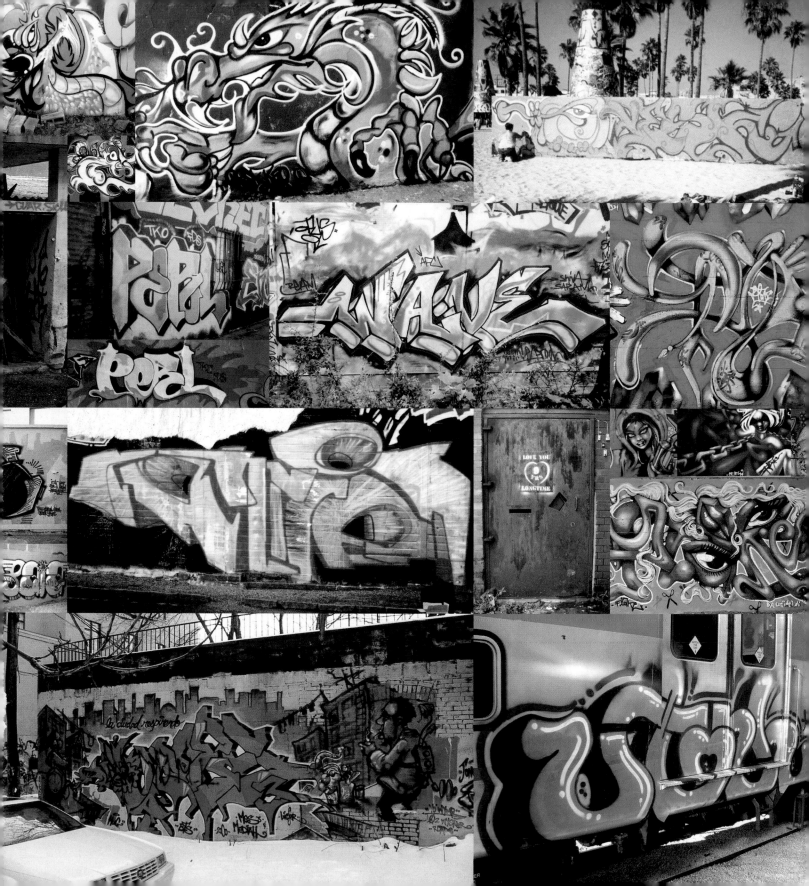

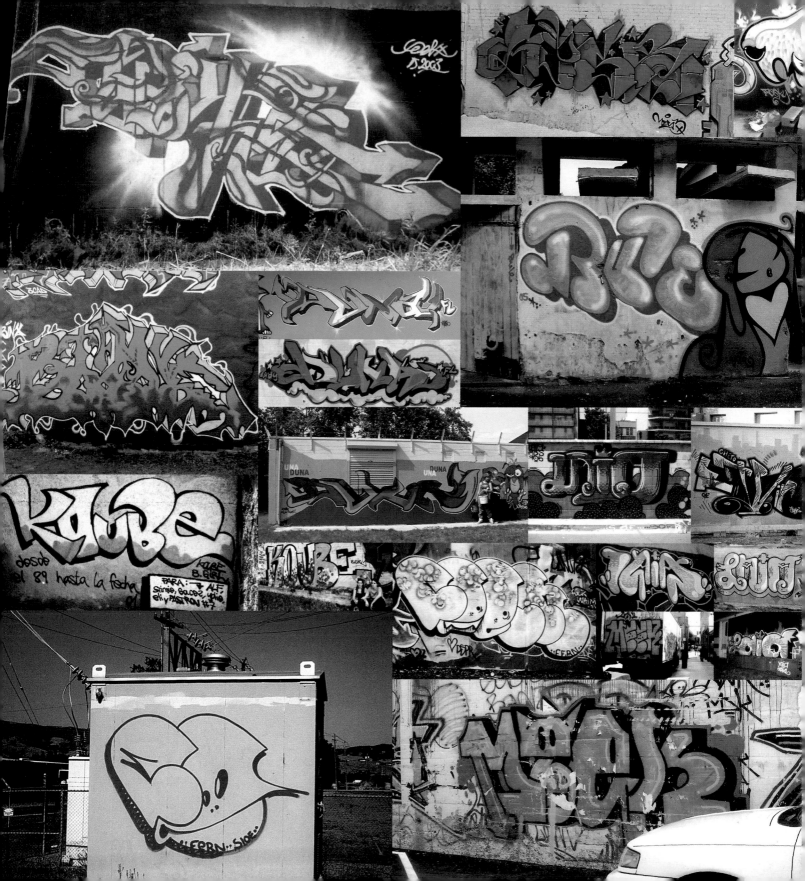

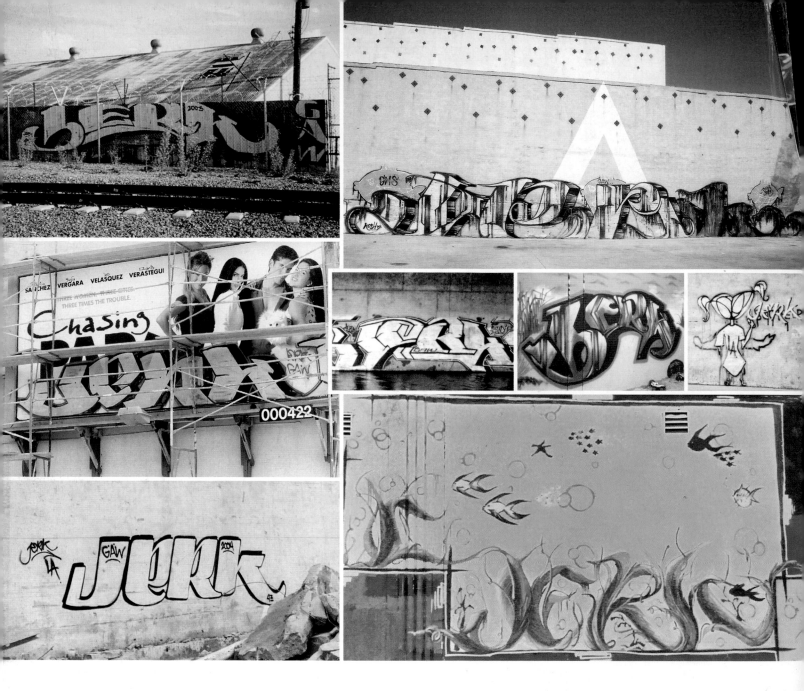

Jerk

LA artist Jerk got into graffiti in 1995–96 and is of Latin American origin. She works alone, in the city's side streets or along the LA River. Like Jel, the numerous gangs in the suburbs pose the real threat to Jerk, rather than the risk of arrest. Recently, Jerk's pieces have made it into a number of West Side galleries.

'Graffiti is something that I grew up seeing,' she explains, 'and eventually it just became a subconscious act. Later, I began to learn more about graff and decided that I wanted to be known for more than just being a girl in the graffiti scene. I want to be known for having skills, and practice makes perfect. What I express in my art is what I want, whether it represents me, my culture, my surroundings or my opinion, even if it's offensive.'

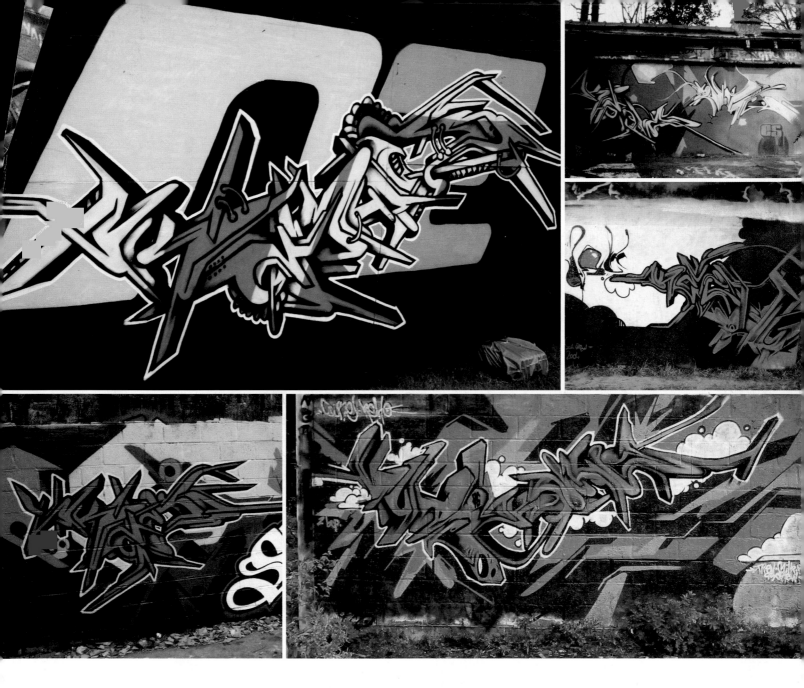

Keho

Spray artist Keho often teams up with her boyfriend, Durex, to piece in her home city of Brussels or further afield. Durex must take the credit for having kindled Keho's enthusiasm for spray-painting initially, and both artists get a lot of inspiration from graphics and mechanical design, but she has developed her own rich style. 'We search for a fusion between our work and life!' she says.

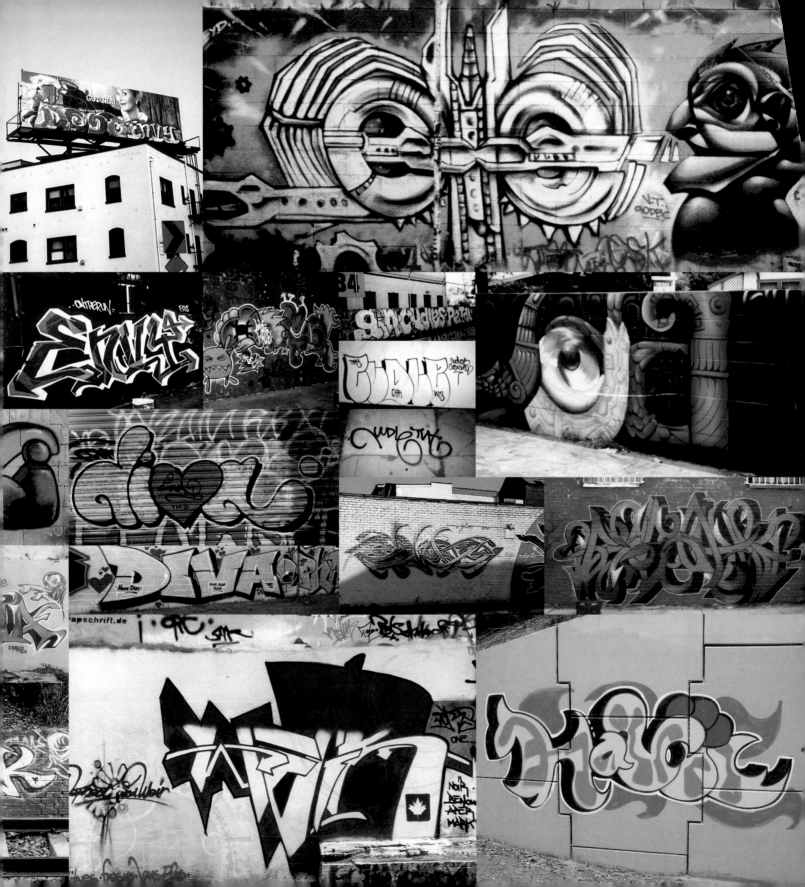

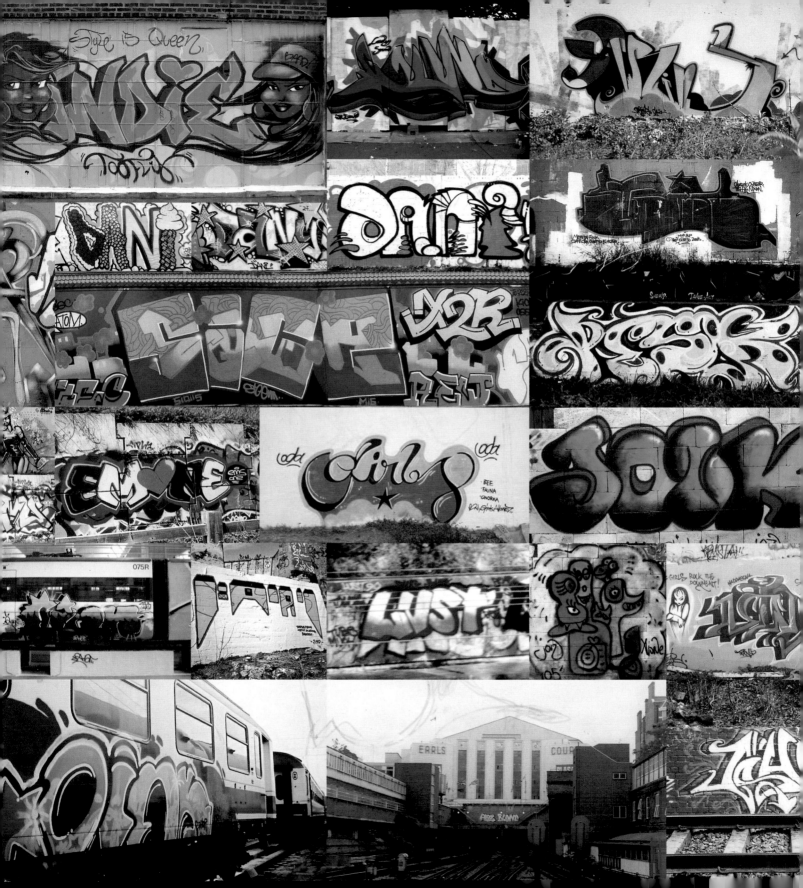

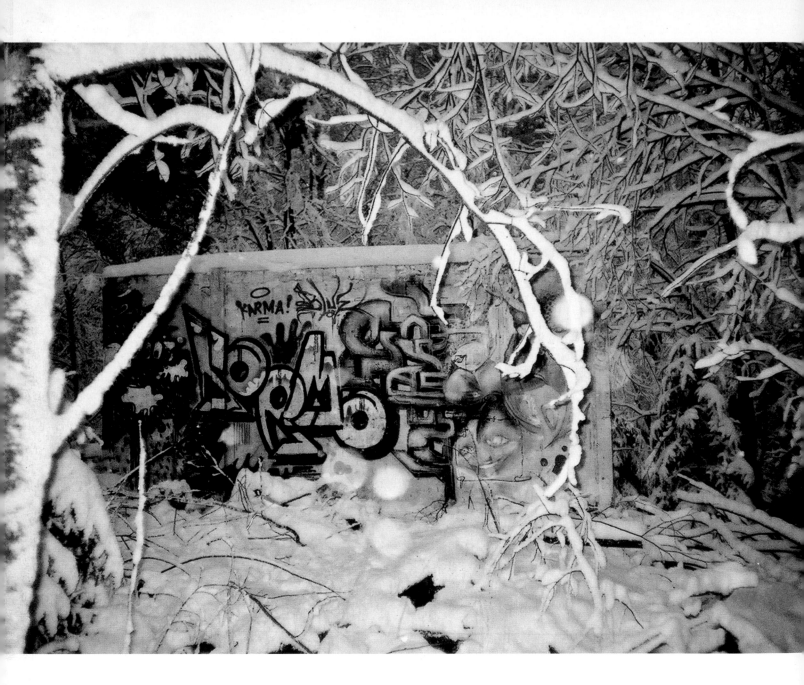

Karma

Massive Attack's song 'Karmacoma' inspired this artist to paint Karma on a piece of paper, and she takes the responsibility of where she catches tags very seriously as every action can bring good or bad luck. It was a fellow student in her art class that first made Karma aware of graffiti, but at that time it didn't make much of an impression on her. Later, when she did a piece with him, she became totally hooked. Having spent a long time focusing on letters, now she also does figures, which are reminiscent of street art.

'I think it's impossible as a human being to paint something that doesn't reflect what you're thinking and feeling,' she says. 'Your personality really shines through in the art you're making. In that way, you always express something, consciously or not. But in general the work often improves if you know what you're doing and what feeling you want to express.'

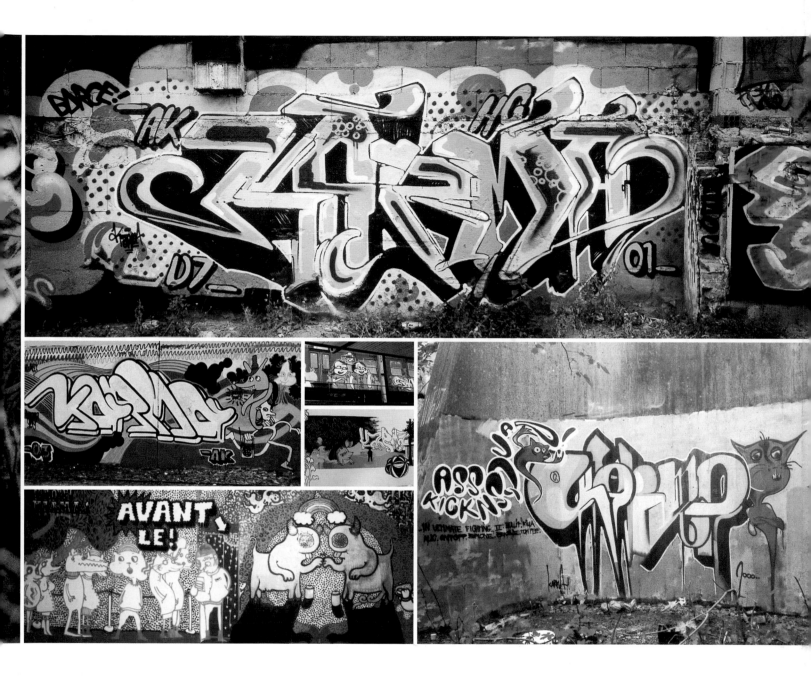

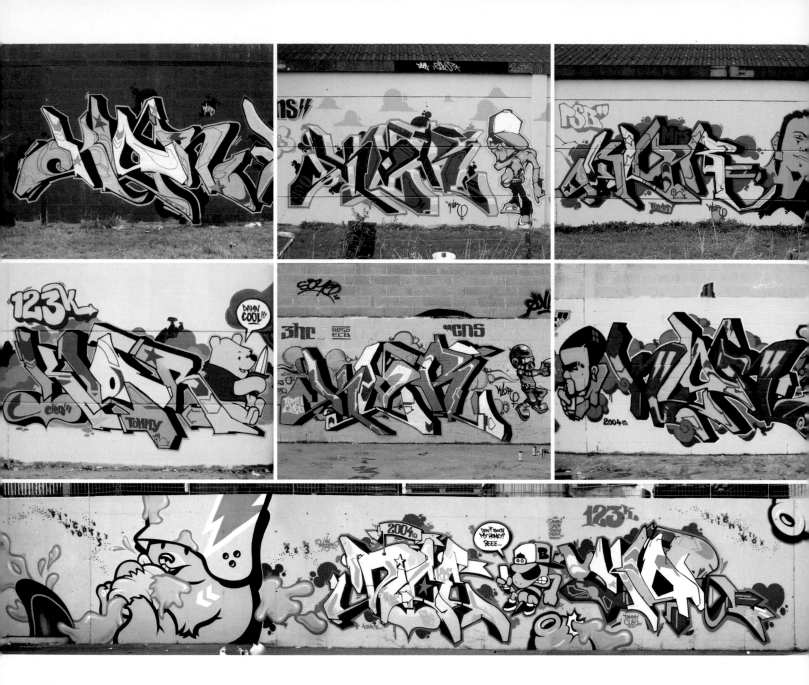

Klor

French artist Klor is a co-founder of internationally renowned 123 Klan, whose work has successfully melded design and graffiti to great acclaim. Her artistic talent has opened up exciting opportunities and enabled her to travel around the world with her husband Scien and their children, Tommy and Clèo, working on various commissions and design projects.

It all seems a far cry from Klor's earliest experiences of graffiti: 'It was 1992. All my crew went to Paris for a concert of Grandmaster Flash, but I was too young. Only one of us had a driving licence, and we had one car between us. There were only five places for six people. So I went out and painted my first piece alone.'

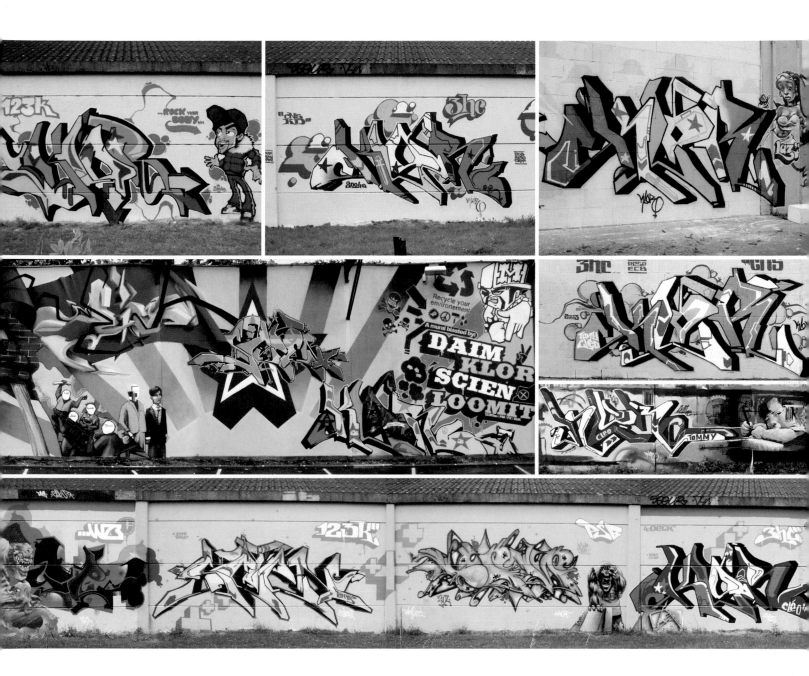

Klor sees the scene as a level playing field: 'When I paint I have no sex. I don't think that the fact you have a cock changes anything in your way of painting, 'cause for making a piece you just need your arms and a 400-gram spraycan…even a kid can do it! When I discovered graffiti, I totally fell in love with it just as it was, so I wanted to play the same game, with the same rules. I never need to add some pink and a butterfly to my piece. I really want to do the same kind of pieces. For me this culture is totally UNISEX.'

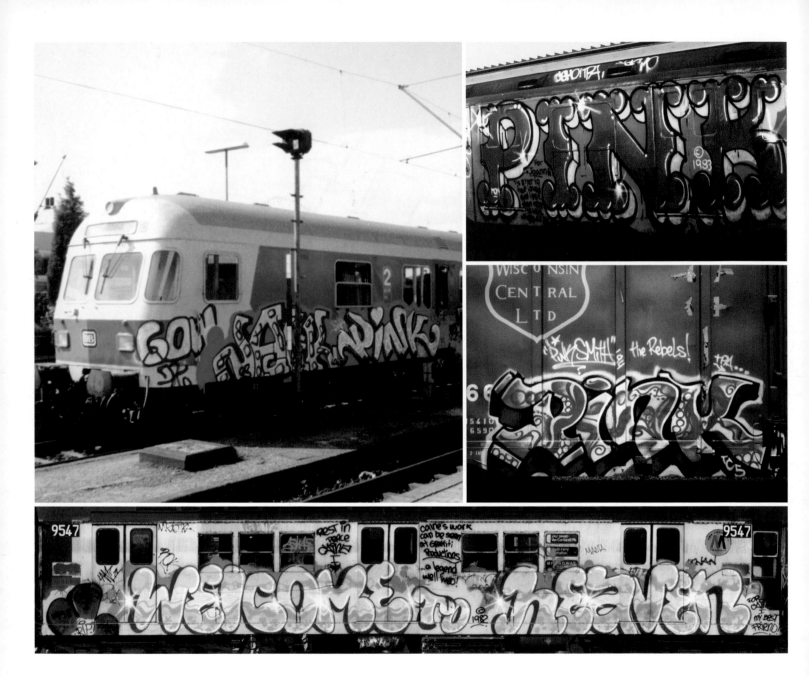

Lady Pink

Whenever you hear people talk about women in graffiti, the first person to spring to mind is almost always New Yorker Lady Pink, who came to prominence in the 1980s through her involvement in the book *Subway Art* and the film *Wild Style*. Seen TC5 gave her the name Pink, and together with Doze showed her how to get up on the subway.

'I was born in Ecuador but grew up in NYC,' she says. 'At the age of fifteen I started writing graffiti. At first it was to mourn the loss of my first love, so I wrote his name everywhere.'

The early days weren't always easy: 'I encountered a lot of sexism trying to paint with the boys…. When I came along, in the third generation, all those females had disappeared and there was barely any oral history left. I had a very difficult time convincing the guys to even take me to the train yards.'

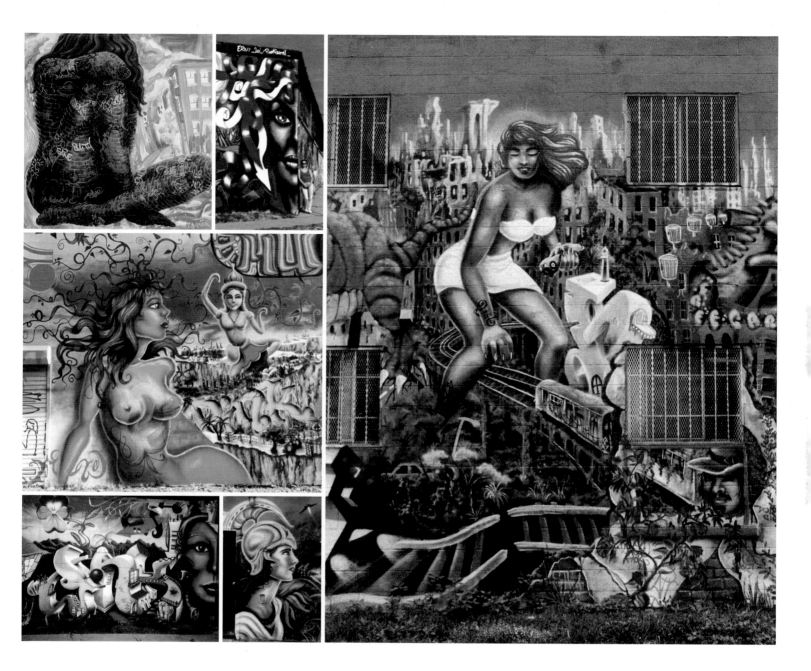

In 1980 she did her first piece on a subway train. At around the same time, Lady Pink and other artists started to sell their work in galleries, where they were able to make several thousand dollars for canvases of the pieces they painted illegally at night.

In 1993, after many years of gallery work and bombing the subway, she got to know her future husband, Smith. He inspired her to broaden her art, moving it away from its focus on the gallery scene. Together they organized numerous legal surfaces and held mural workshops to give teenagers a more creative and public forum for their art. Freights also became a vital medium for Lady Pink between 1993 and 1997.

'My greatest contribution to our culture has been the ability to inspire people and to have had a positive impact on their lives. Many young women look up to me as a role model, and that is not a position I wanted, but I do my best not to let them down. I expect great things from our future generations, so don't let me down!'

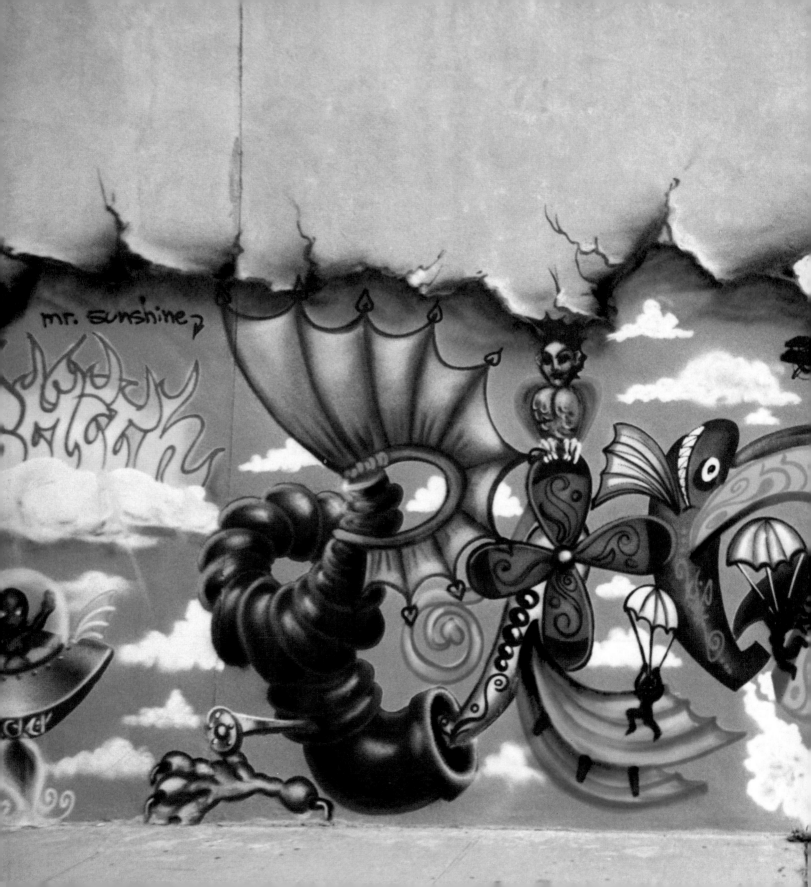

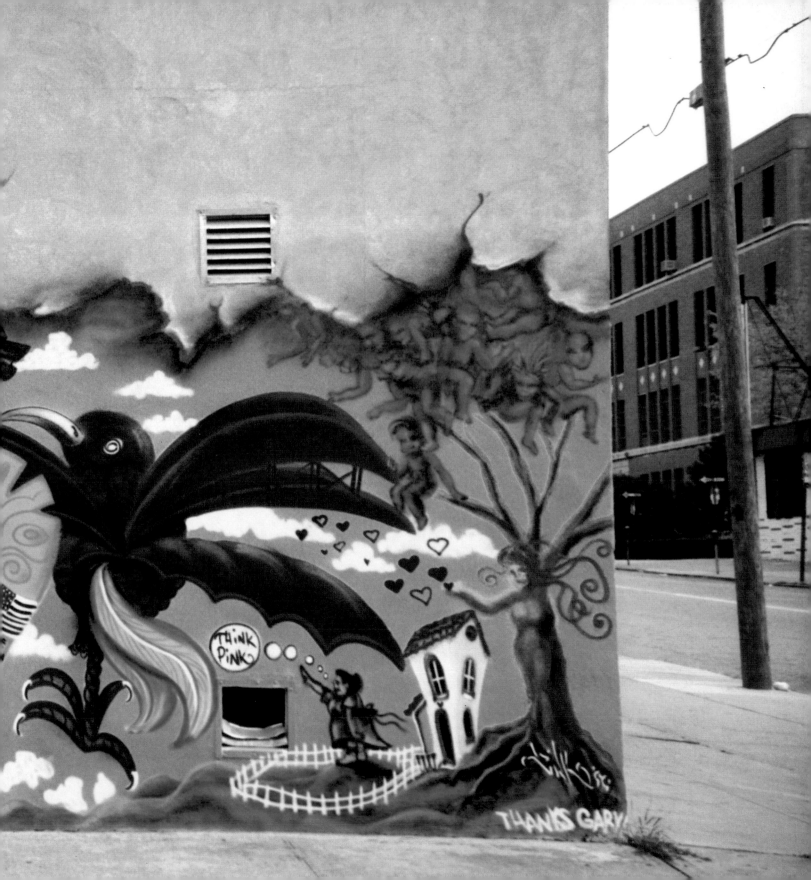

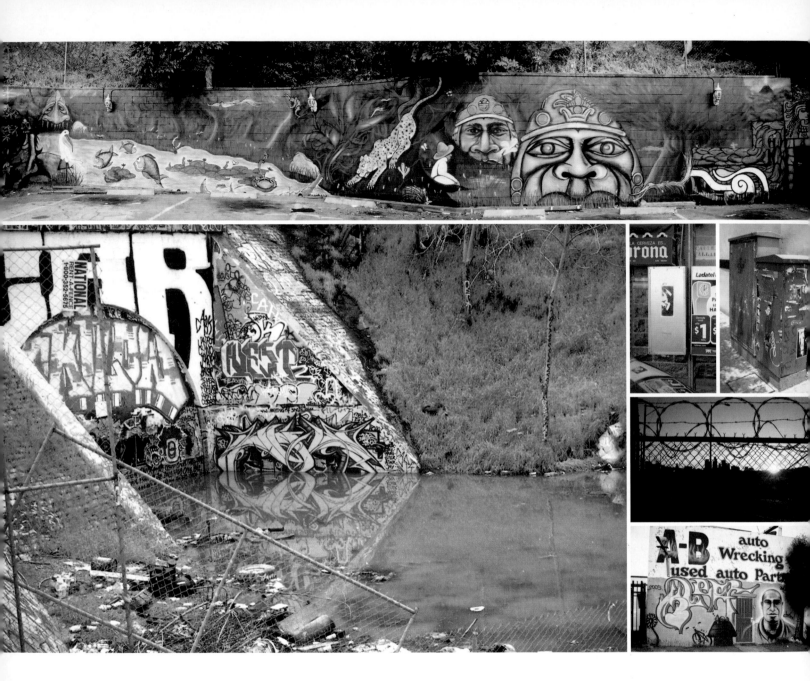

Luna

Mexican-born Luna has lived in Los Angeles since she was a child. She first became drawn to graffiti in junior high: 'Something about it appealed to me, and I guess you can say I've been hooked ever since. When I got to high school a friend of mine "borrowed" *Subway Art* from the library for me. I loved that book so much, it never went back. Since then I've experimented with spray-paint and other fun marking tools, but mostly I've spent my time documenting things – much of it graffiti – throughout LA (and wherever else I find myself) on good old-fashioned film. Every once in a while, I'll pick up a can or two for mural projects and other such shenanigans. I also love screen-printing, using my photos and tweaking them for posters, T-shirts, stickers, etc. I love it all…. My eye is very drawn to walls, bridges, trains, buildings, and the paint found on these surfaces. Because of this, I must give the writers whose work is often found in my pictures much thanks, props and respect for sharing their creations with me. Many thanks are also due to my family. Now, because words are rarely enough, I'll let the images speak for themselves….'

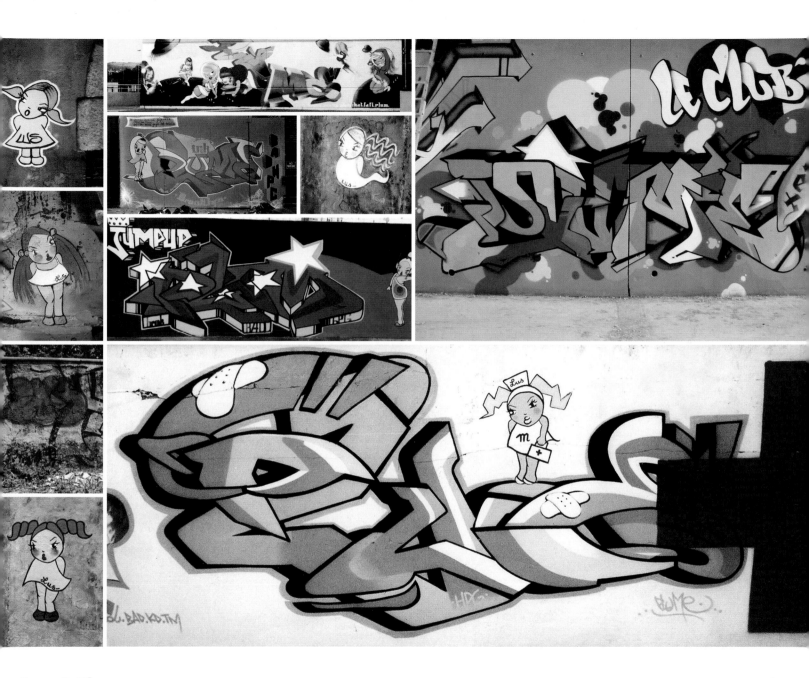

Lus & Plume

'Ever since I can remember, I have had a passion for graffiti,' says Lus. 'In my small city of Toulouse graffiti art is abundant and I wanted very much to be a part of it. I was friends with the local graffiti artists, but my biggest influence during this time and the person I credit with getting my art out in the world is Miss Van. Back in 1993–94 there were very few female artists. We would canvas the walls, proudly stamping our work with female characters, and we'd also make sure our tag was clearly female. Soon the women artists in Toulouse gained equal respect to the men.'

Plume is also part of the Toulouse set: 'I know that some of us paint to decorate streets or walls, but it never was my first motivation. Graffiti has a therapeutic or curative side, like an outlet, a need to express something that I can't explain or express in a different way, a need to create something that only belongs to me when I do it, and which afterwards doesn't belong to anyone. You have the opportunity to establish your own rules or no rules if you want! That's the dark side of a part of society – an outlaw place where you can play without doing something really bad.'

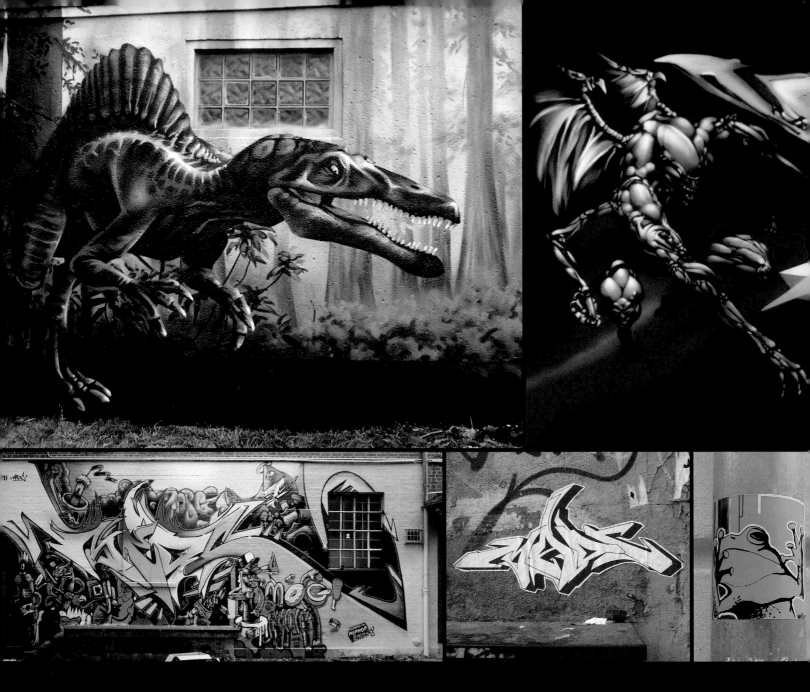

Mad C

One afternoon in 1996 German writer Mad C did her first illegal piece on a garage. Graffiti has since become a huge part of her life, although these days she generally keeps it legal.

'I have always seen myself as a writer,' she explains, 'rather than a woman who spray-paints. I don't see a male/female divide. Also, until now, a lot of people haven't realized that Mad C is actually a woman. I think that's good because it means that I'm judged objectively. The first four or five years were the hardest for me, and I came up against a lot of prejudice and disrespect. I don't have those problems now that I've been accepted and have earned respect.

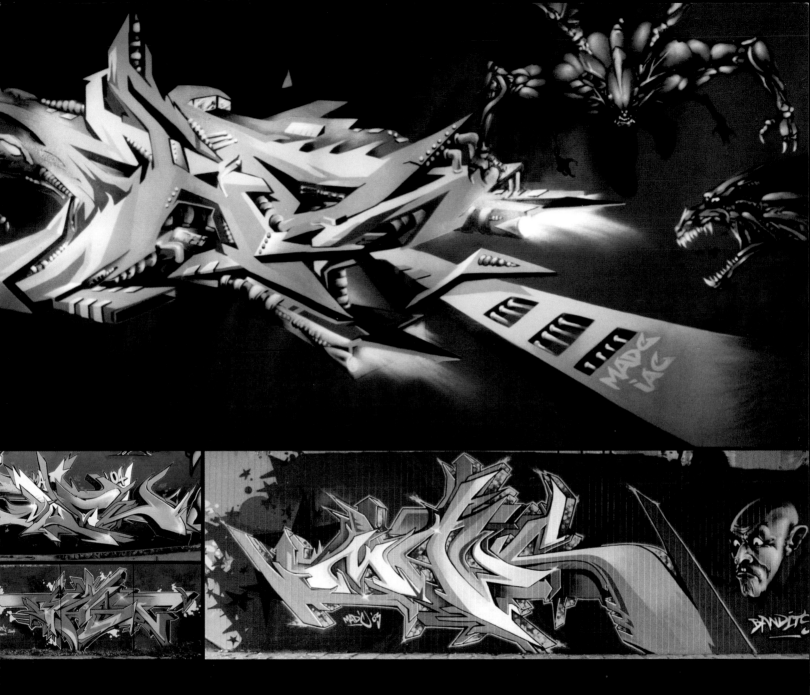

'I think that everyone in the graffiti scene has it rough when they're just starting out, and must prove themselves first. Of course there were a few sexist words and shitty moments, but I find the yammering of many women exaggerated and misplaced. You have to prove yourself overall and every day. Also, there are enough walks of life in which men have it tougher than women.

'These days there are just two things that really wear on my nerves and get me rattled: when a man tries to tell me how to hold a spraycan, even though I've been doing it for years, or when someone says something like "the best I've ever seen by a woman"....'

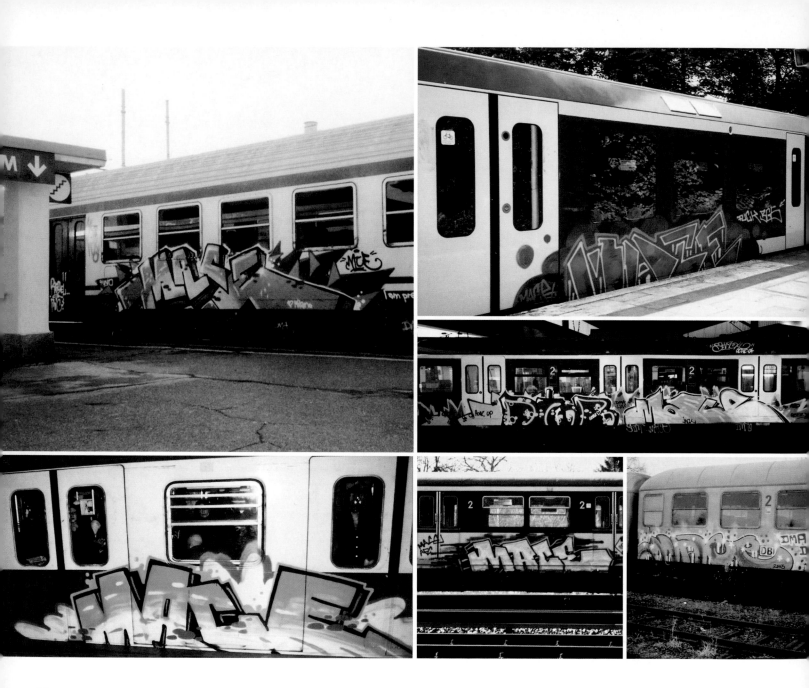

Mace

Mace is part of the DMA crew, which is active throughout Germany.

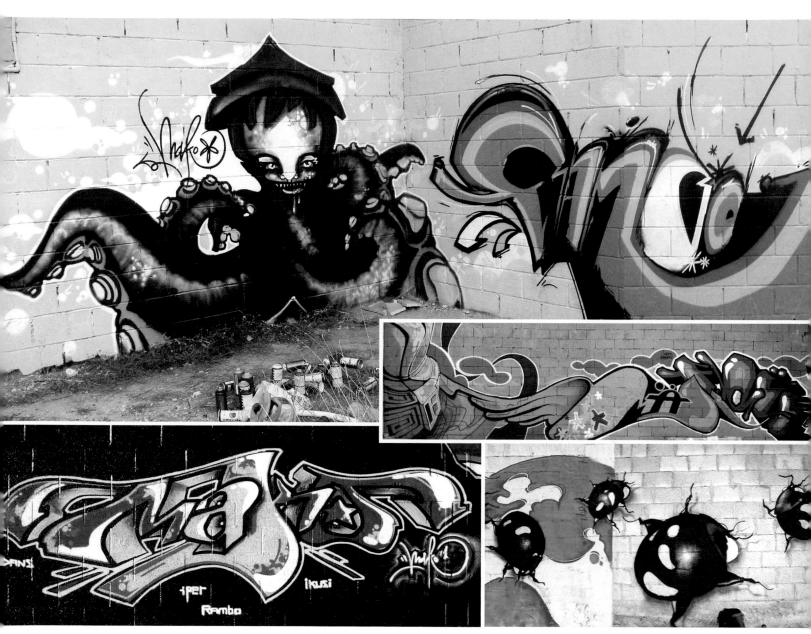

Makoh

Makoh first used a spraycan when she was fourteen and wrote her name in the streets of Alicante, Spain. She hasn't stopped since and spray-paints every week. Although Alicante is relatively small, it has many writers and the scene there is growing. 'My painting is a game between lots of people,' she says.

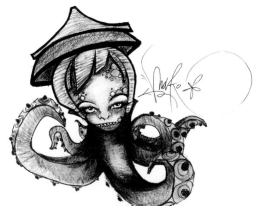

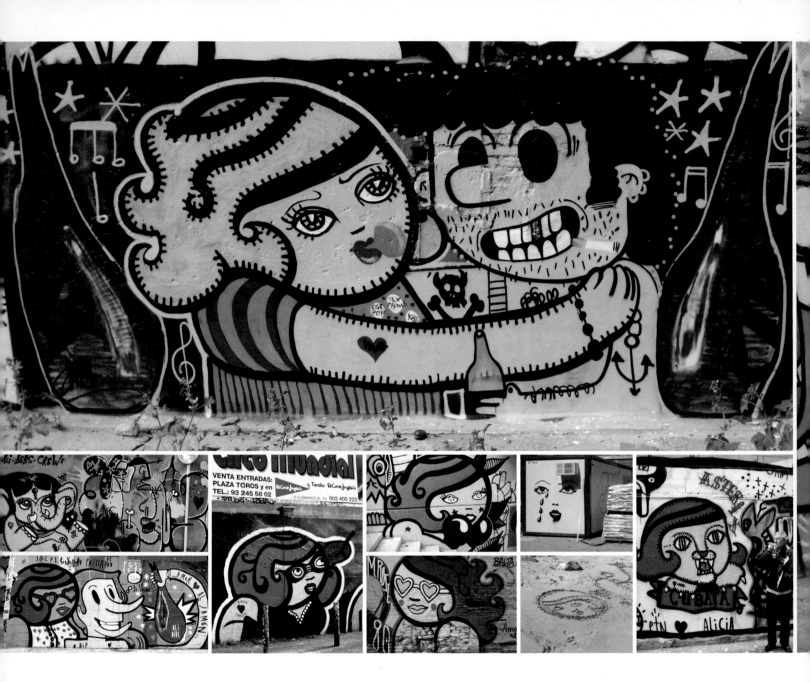

Malicia

Malicia is part of Barcelona's colourful graffiti culture. She started to paint after the death of her father, as she explains: 'Life became tough for me when my father died, and to cheer myself up I decided to paint one piece for him, in his memory. I bought cans and went to Valldoncella Square in Barcelona. People liked the piece and told me to paint more, and I haven't stopped since. For me graffiti is a secret, and only a small minority know about it. We have an argot among ourselves, doing art for our own benefit. People can like it but not understand why we do it, and it stays there in every part of the city.'

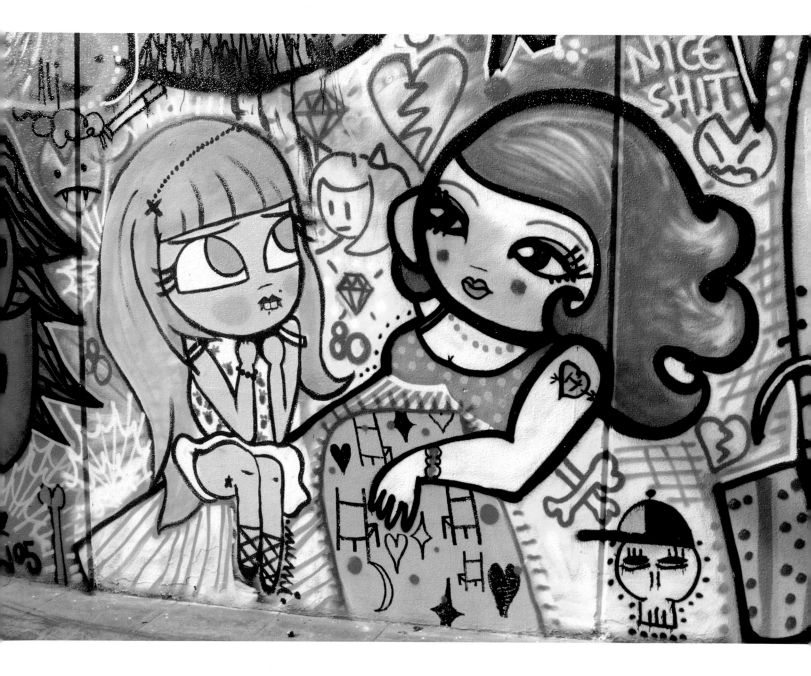

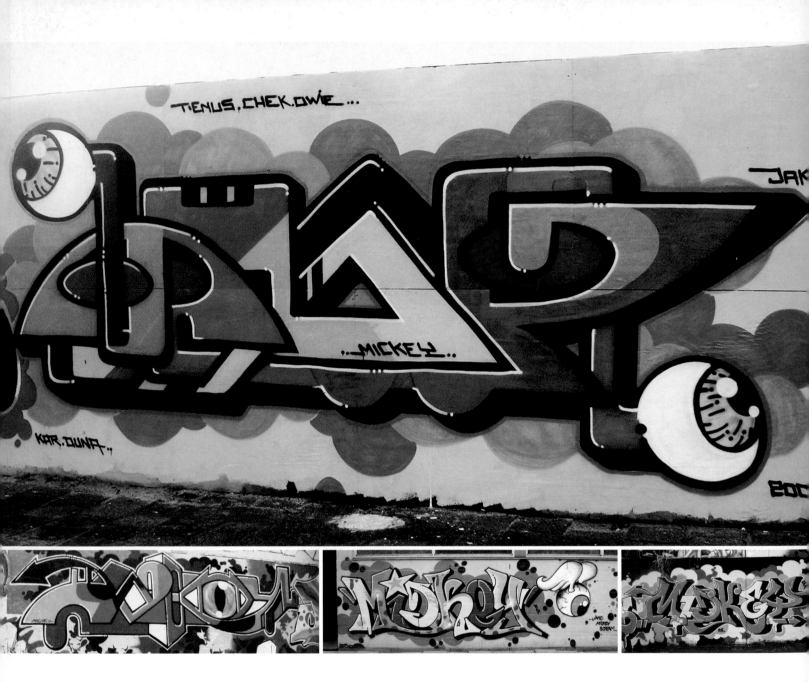

Mickey

Amsterdam-based Mickey has been active since 1983, which makes her one of the first female spray-painters in Europe. 'I was influenced by existing graff back then in all its appearances and I decided to do it too,' she explains. 'The first piece I ever designed had letters taken straight from the *Wild Style* wall by Zephyr. I twisted the "W" around to make it an "M" and tried to come up with a matching "C" and "K". That was my first graff letter study. Then *Subway Art* came out and my parents ordered it for me. I studied the outlines in it and from then on started to design my own styles. The next step was to get spray-paint and just do walls somewhere. I don't have much affinity with girly stuff like hearts, teddy bears, big-eyed characters, even though I have used them in the past. As a kid I never played with dolls – doesn't that say enough? I just want to rock my name in different styles.'

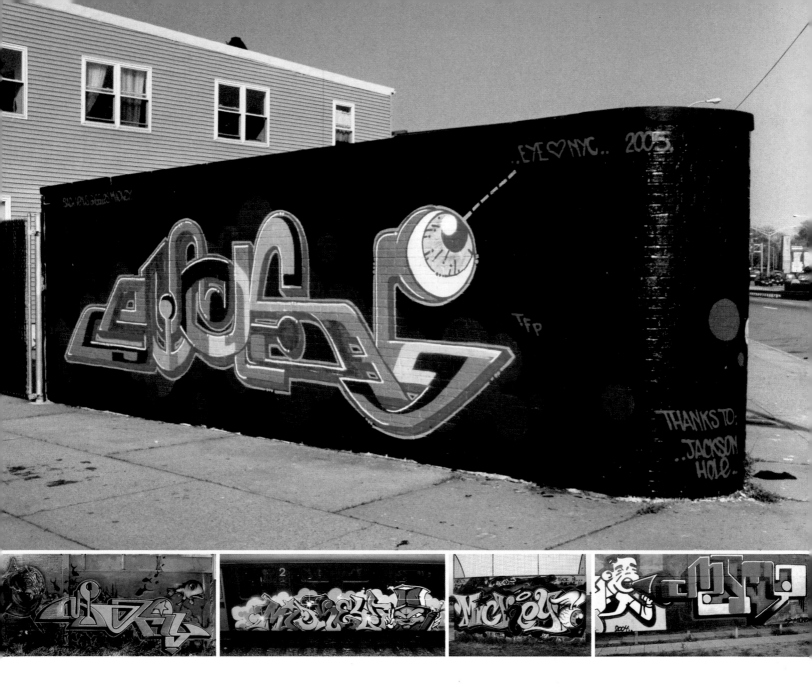

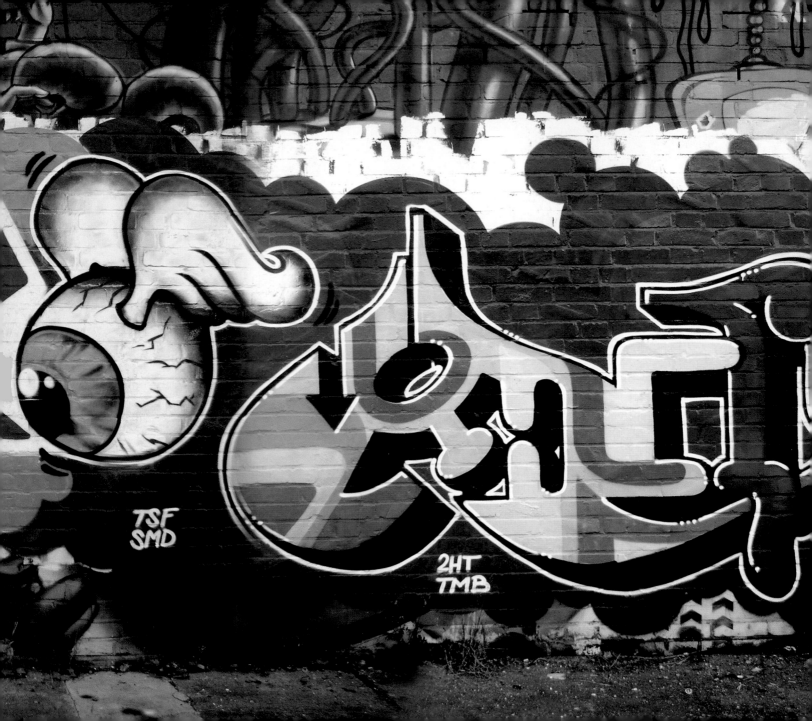

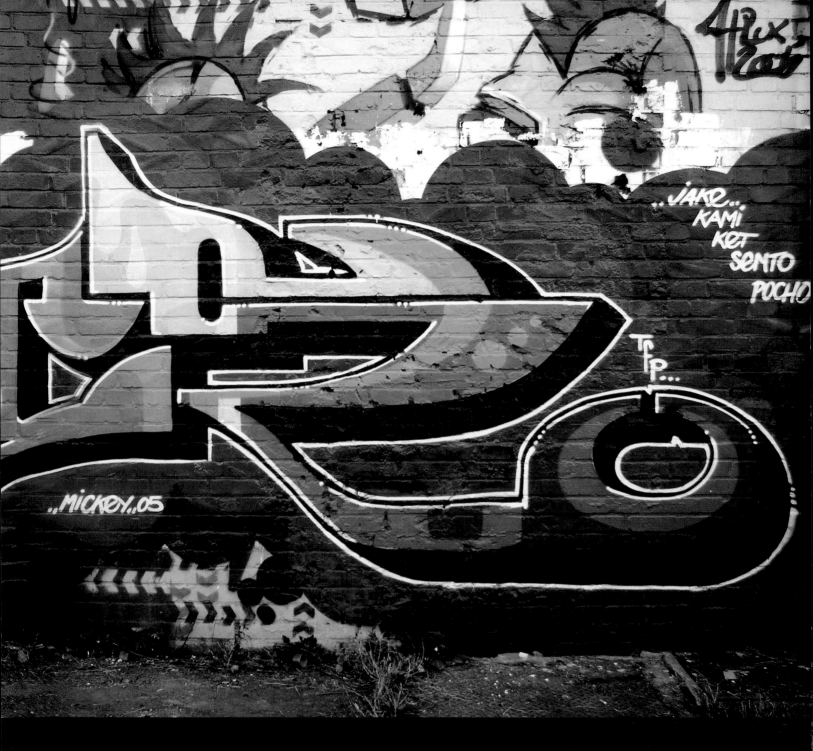

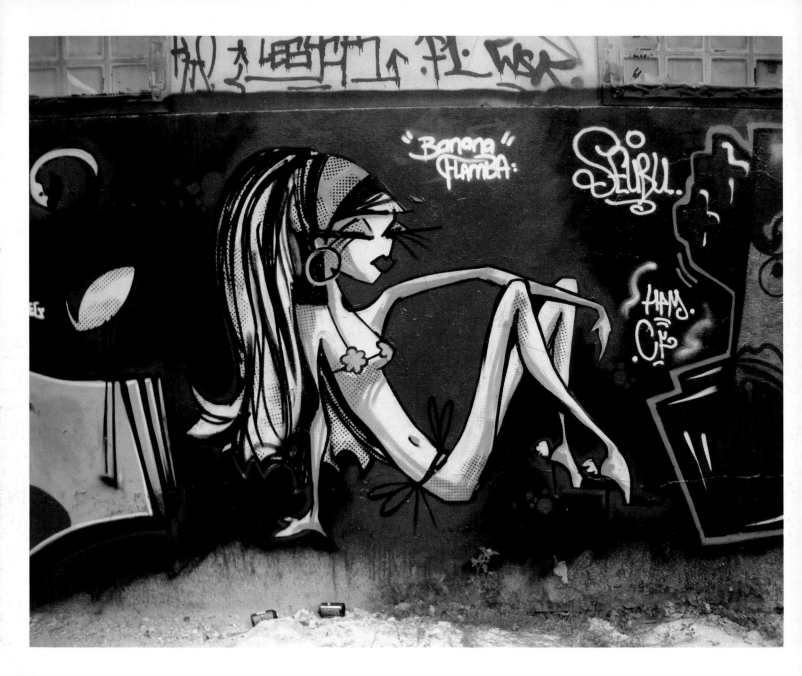

Miss Lili

French-born Miss Lili comes from Valence but has been living in China's Shenzhen since 2004. Her husband was really into graffiti and got her hooked in 1998. The artist's work features spray-painted women and letters, but she's also keen on using other materials in her pieces, as she explains: 'When I first started out, I liked finding "things" to paint on, to use in my painting. I mean, if I find a holey piece of metal, I can play around with it to get more of an effect. It's my favourite material.'

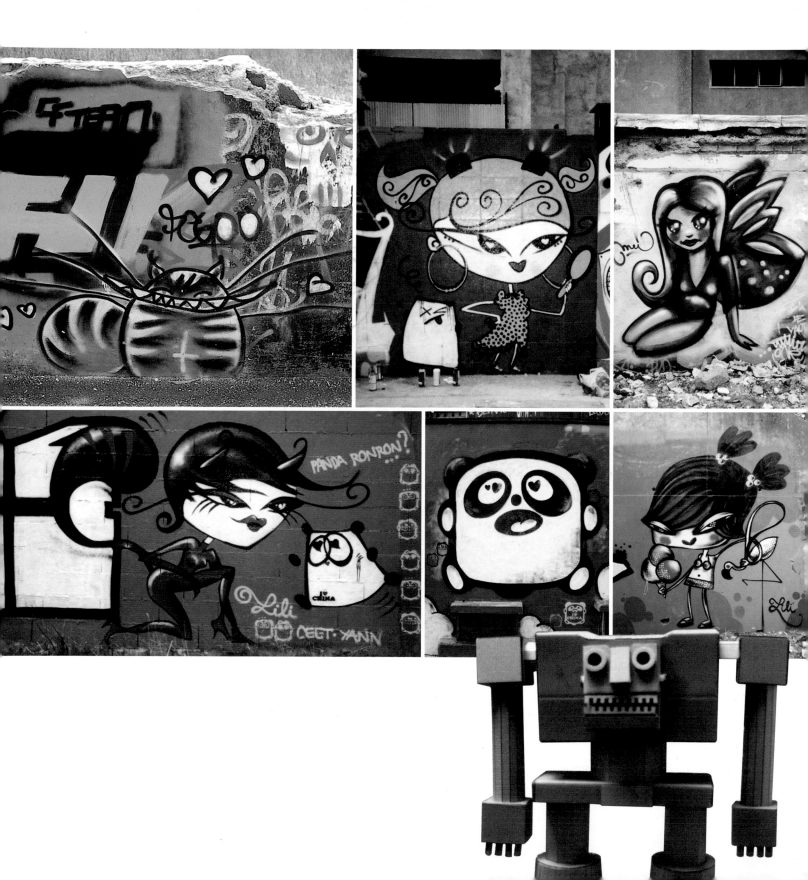

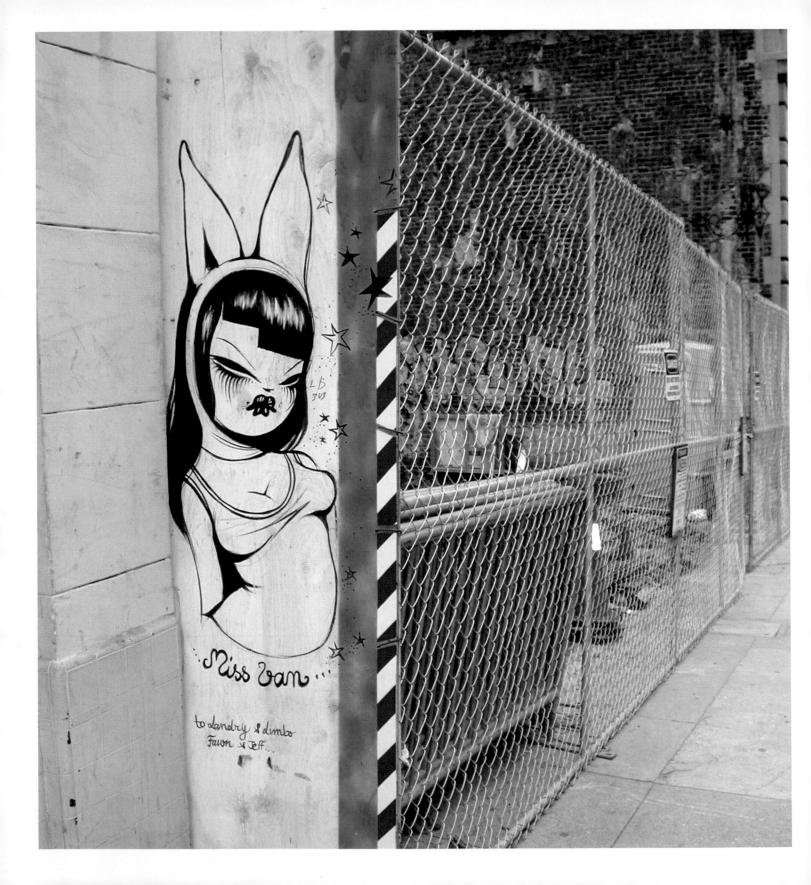

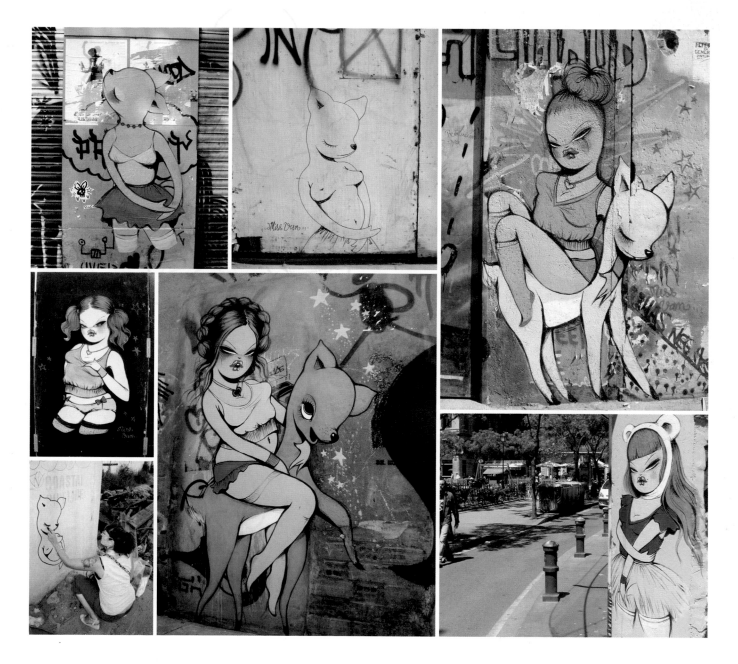

Miss Van

Throughout history, artists have joined and furthered artistic movements. And yet it is extremely rare for an artist to actually change the direction of that movement. French painter Miss Van is one such artist. Before Miss Van hit the streets of her home town of Toulouse, a female graffiti writer was extremely rare. While many would have tried to hide the femininity in their work in an effort to become accepted by their male counterparts, Miss Van did the exact opposite. She stayed true to herself,

embraced her female sensibilities to the fullest, and used them to define a style that today – years later – is often imitated, but never matched.

When you see a Miss Van piece on the street you know immediately that it was painted by a woman. Why? Miss Van's exquisite taste and her impeccable sense of style let you know that this work was done by a woman's hand. With each piece, she deftly balances the playful and the alluring with

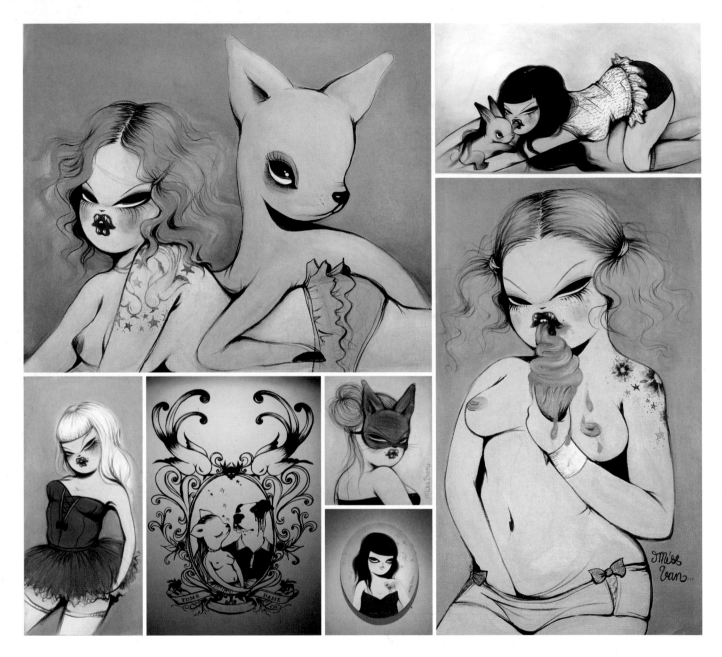

a precision and skill that allows her characters to be insightful, multi-dimensional and fully realized.

Each girl Miss Van paints is unique. Each one has a different story to tell. And like any great storyteller, Miss Van leaves it up to the viewer to fill in the history and back-story. It's up to you to determine how you want to interpret them. It is precisely this aspect of her work that makes Miss Van's art so interesting. A man may see Miss Van's girls as overtly alluring, sexual and erotic, while a woman may see them as playful, sexy and sweet.

When you come across one of Miss Van's girls on the street, they can literally stop you in your tracks. They linger with you on the street and then follow you after you pass. It is this internal energy that Miss Van infuses into her characters which marks a Miss Van piece and sets it above all of the rest. Her girls seduce you in such a way that can completely transform the way you look at the city. Suddenly the city itself, like Miss Van's characters, becomes sensual, sweet, alive and full of mischief.

Sara and Mark Schiller, Wooster Collective

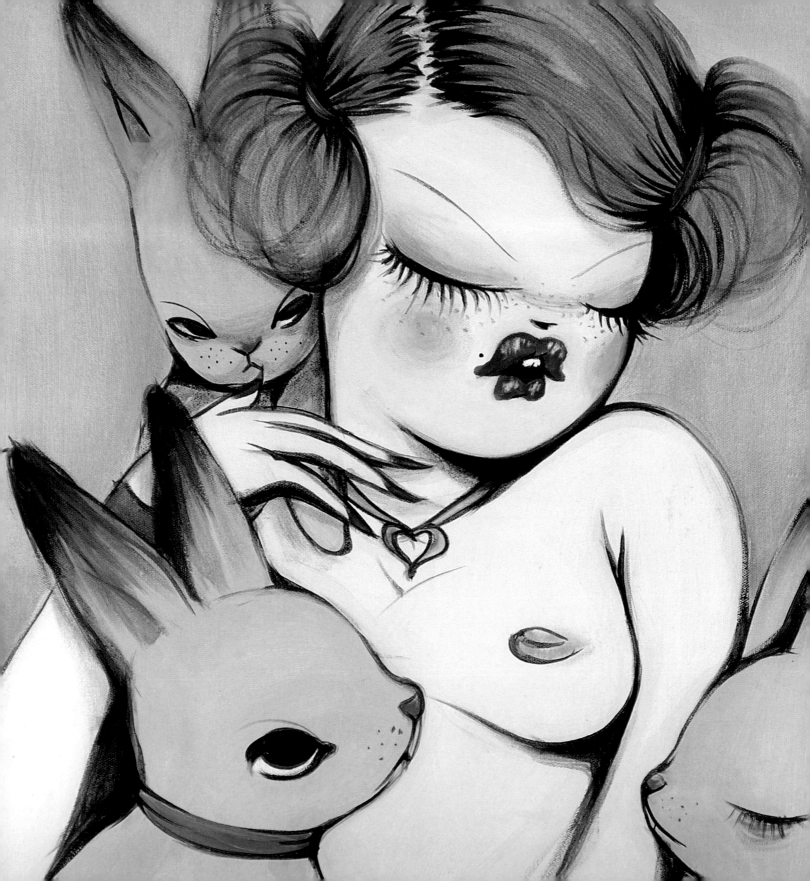

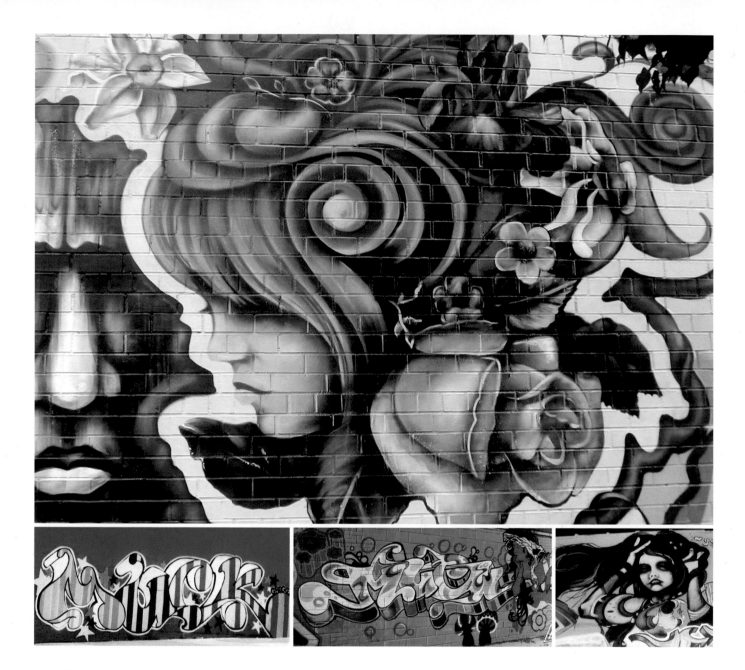

Muck

English-born Muck first wrote 'Mucky Pup', a nickname she had picked up as a child, in 1994 when she was staying on the Greek island of Lesbos. Later, after moving to the Bronx, she shortened it to Muck. Since painting her first illegal pieces, she has moved on to legal surfaces primarily, either on her own or, preferably, with large groups of artists.

  'Graffiti started out for me as a protest against private property,' she says. 'It has since developed into an art form for me, and Lady Pink taught me how to live off my art. At this point in my life I feel I have completed my cycle. I live to paint and paint to live. I will continue to do so until my demise.'

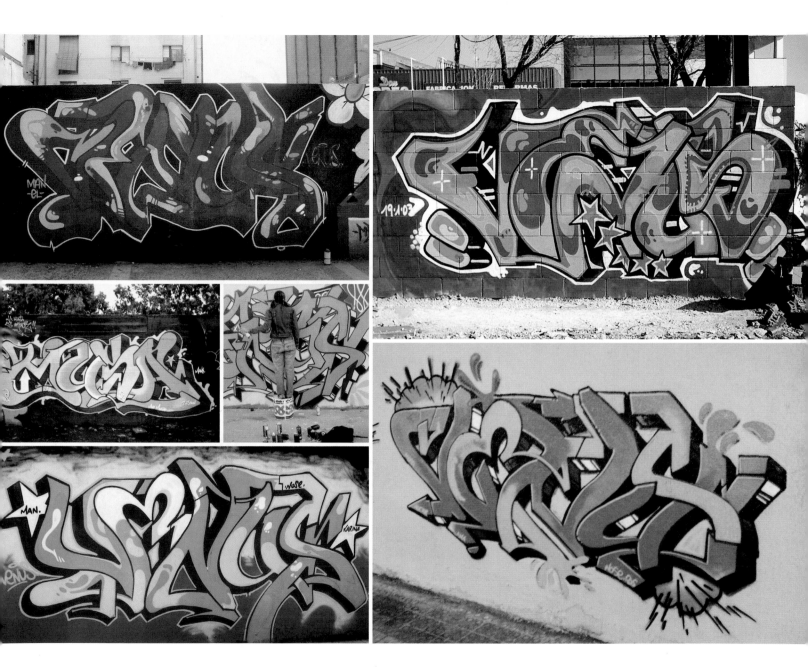

Musa

Musa (aka Venus/China) is one of Barcelona's longest-standing writers and is still active today. Her pieces bring out her sense of humour and key influences in her life.

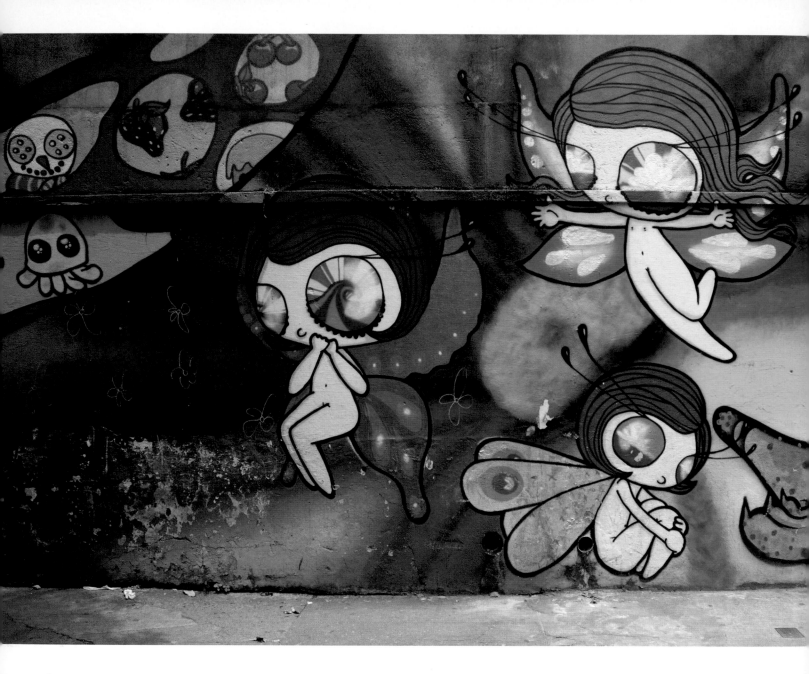

Nina

Nina is credited as São Paulo's first female spray artist and has been active since the mid-1980s. She has captured a worldwide audience with her wide-eyed figures and animals, and travels extensively in order to present her work.

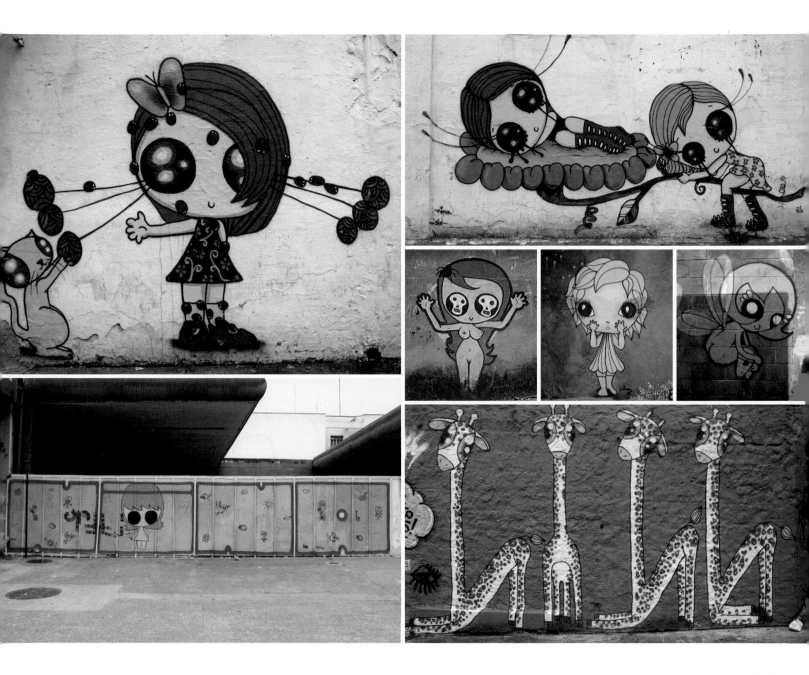

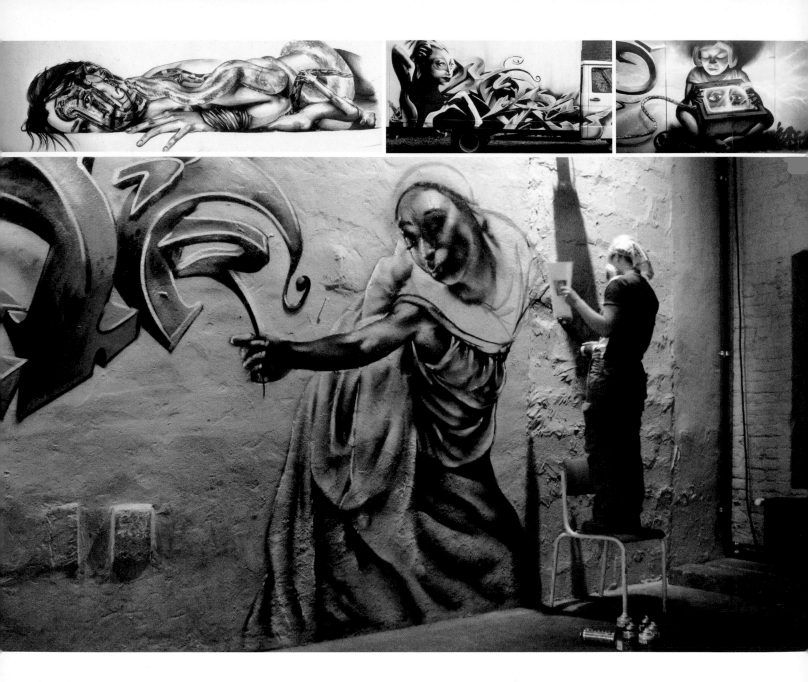

Omri

Omri lives in Aalst, Belgium, where she has dedicated her life to graffiti. She got into the scene through her friend Waf, and tends to concentrate on figures and portraits.

'I worked in a hospital with coma patients and saw a lot of people of my age living like a plant 'cause of a stupid car accident,' she explains. 'So for me graffiti means that I have only one life and that I want to use this life to realize my dreams and express myself.'

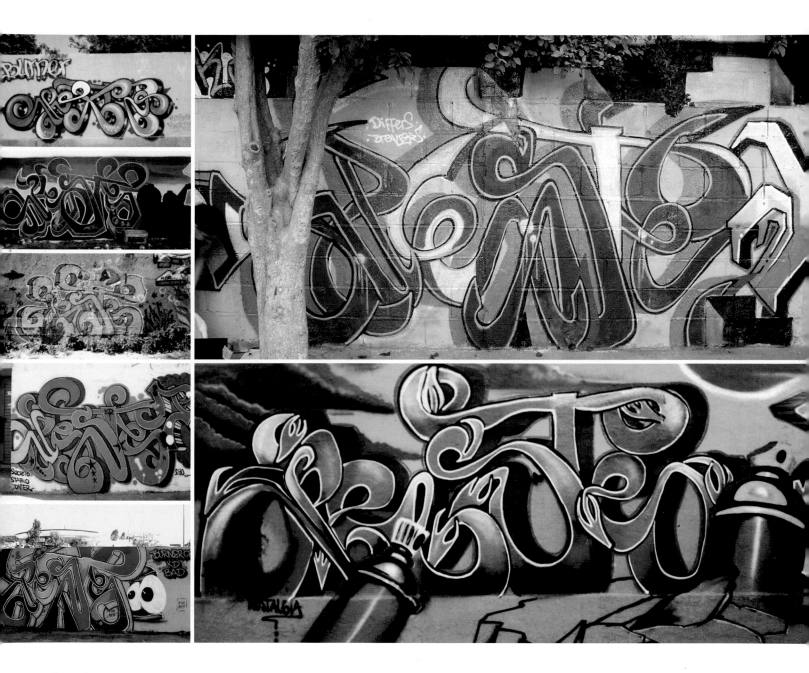

Peste

'I take equality as my ideology,' says Mexican artist Peste. 'You gotta aim for equality in every aspect of life, and you should never forget that everything has its place. I feel really sad when I see people selling themselves short, especially women. It gets to me when they use their beauty to stand out at the expense of their intelligence, although not a lot of people value this. I also think that we girls, with this state of mind, have got to show and prove that we can do everything ourselves, without a boyfriend or a pretty face.

'Let's stop thinking that we're fairy-tale princesses. I'm happy as I am – I love working, I wanna do a lot of things, and I'm always battling against time. I thank God and life for my ability to think, and for my health. I don't know what is going to happen. I only want to paint, that is the only thing I want to do.'

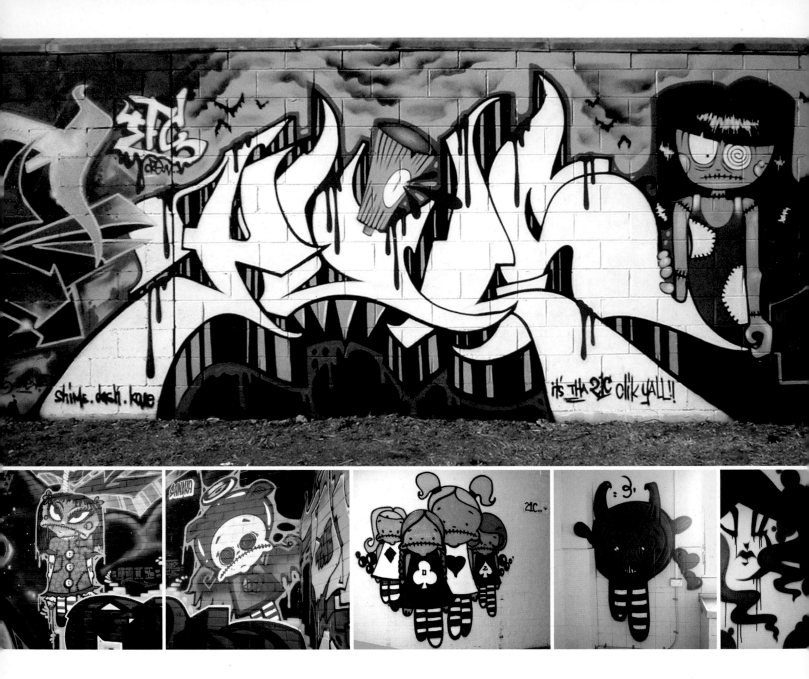

Poise

Poise got into graffiti in the late 1980s, when she was living in Western Australia. Her work reveals a variety of different influences, although 'more so in canvases than pieces as canvases have more thought put into them and pieces are about getting up, and I suppose it's more of a reaction from people than it is me expressing myself'.

'I've always had an unusual interest in death and the macabre. I'm fascinated by books about serial killers, ghosts and the supernatural, so I suppose an edge of evil is always lurking in what I draw or paint, especially the female characters I draw. There's something so alluring about an evil woman.'

100

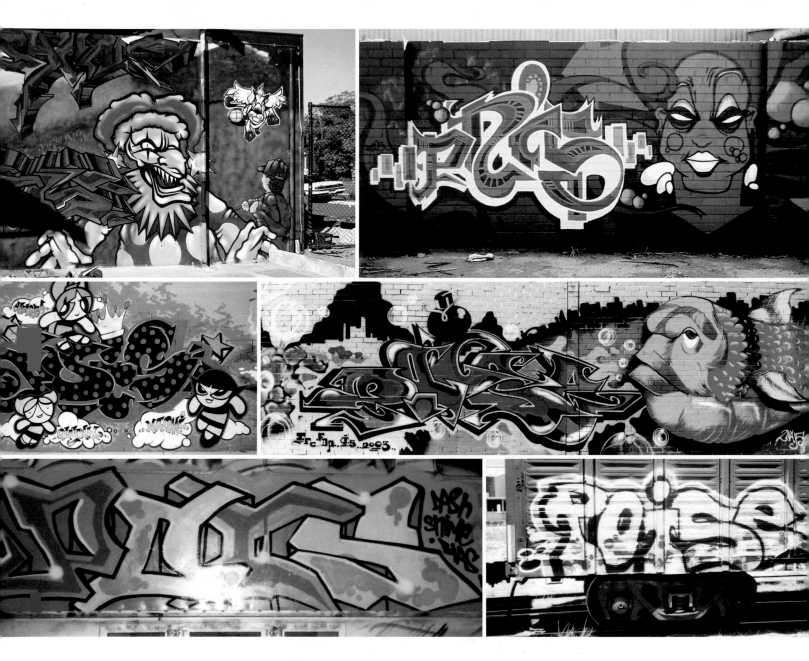

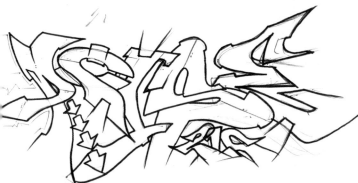

'With pieces, it's getting up, it's just too much fun for words. And I still love working on my lettering too, though nowadays I don't do as many outlines as characters. The two still get combined regularly though. I do rock girl characters most of the time, just because they're fun! I always tend to make them cute, but a bit evil too. Women doing bad things are hilarious. People just don't expect that shit!'

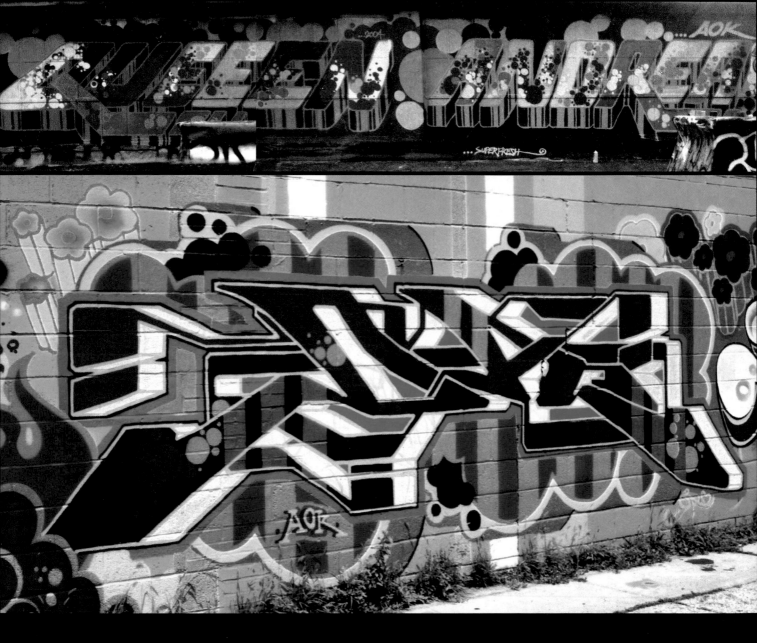

Queen Andrea

'I got into graffiti in 1992 when I was fourteen,' says Queen Andrea. 'It was always appealing to me, even before I learned about the history of graffiti and met legendary graffiti writers. I was attracted to the bold, free and daring aspects of graffiti and urban art, especially since I grew up in a vibrant, expressive downtown New York City neighbourhood (Manhattan).'

Later, Queen Andrea got to know a few hardcore bombers and was given a direct route into the graffiti world. Her portfolio is extensive: legal walls, the odd illegal piece, canvases and graphic design.

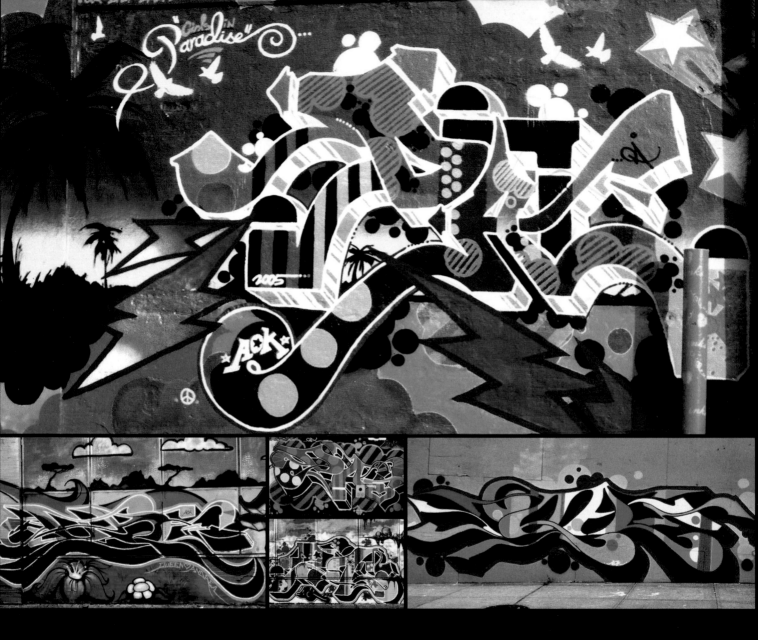

'I learned from early experiences as a young female graffiti artist that I was given a lot more attention than male graffiti artists. Often I was protected and perceived as "unique". There are very few female graffiti artists compared to the number of guys, so sometimes I felt entitled to be a somewhat rare type of artist. However, I recognized that deliberately using my gender to get more "props" and attention was shallow, so I avoid promoting my gender in the context of being a graffiti artist. I have a genuine love, respect and passion for covert urban art itself and I undermine what the general public thinks of it!'

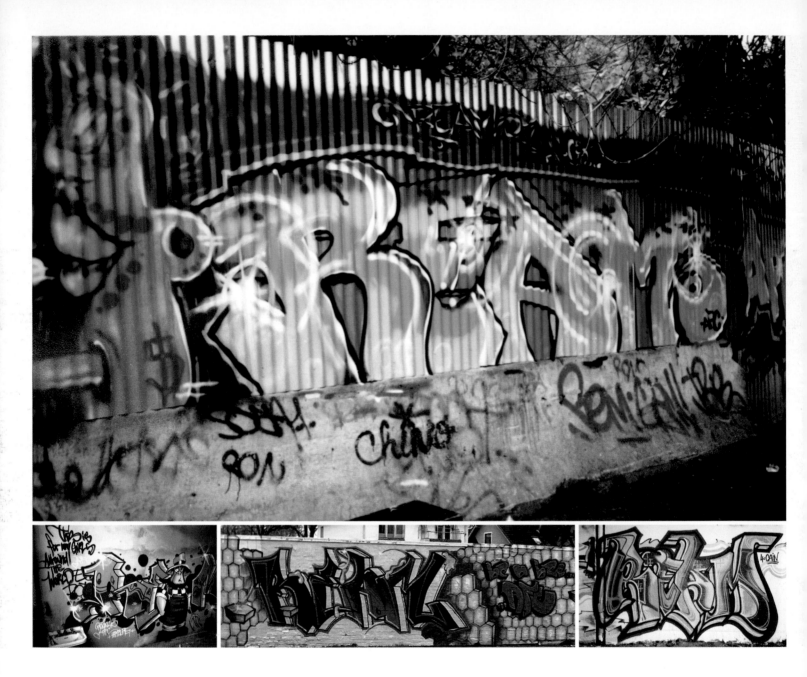

Ream

Hamburg-based Ream is a member of the AFC crew and has been active since 1996. The spraycan is her primary tool, but she doesn't shy away from using other materials and styles of graffiti or street art.

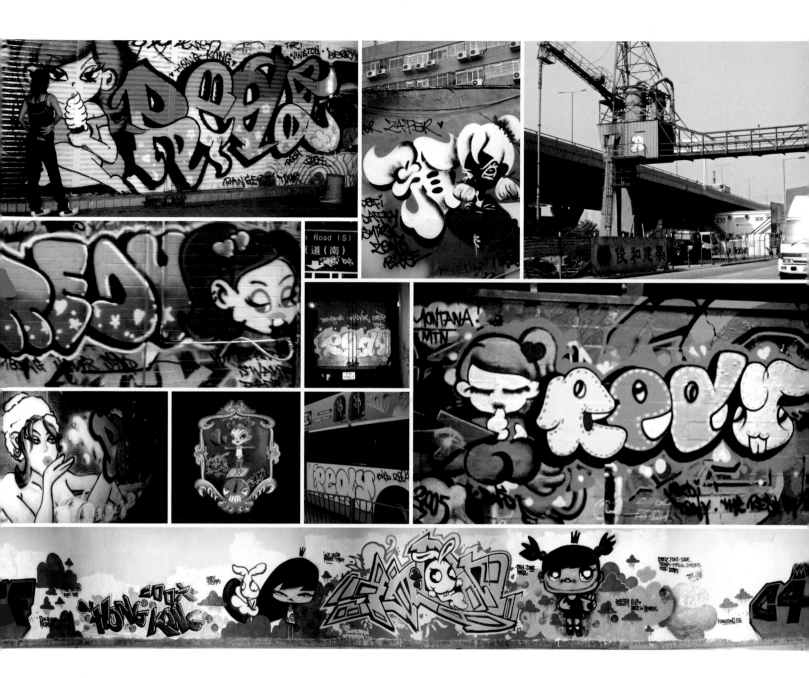

Redy

Under the joint name of BNS (Bombing Never Stops), Redy has been painting with her crewmate Smirk in Hong Kong with different influences. She says: 'LOVE! You can't live without it! Love for friends, family, life, boyfriend/girlfriend, nature, your culture, interests, food, the world…. My festival sticker is a way of showing everyone my love, even if they are passers-by in the street, and I use the poster and stencil media to reflect what's wrong with society, in my personal opinion. Do everything straight from your heart – that's one of the reasons I paint lots of hearts in my pieces. If it's a choice between the two, I prefer graffiti to street art. It's much more exciting! I like to paint with girly colours and styles as I think it's rare to see female stuff in the street. I particularly like to paint my "Babe" girl character. It's not because she's cute, but Babe's mind is the purest, simplest and most direct. There are a few domestic writers that I always see in books or on the Internet – I'd like to give a big shout-out to them!'

105

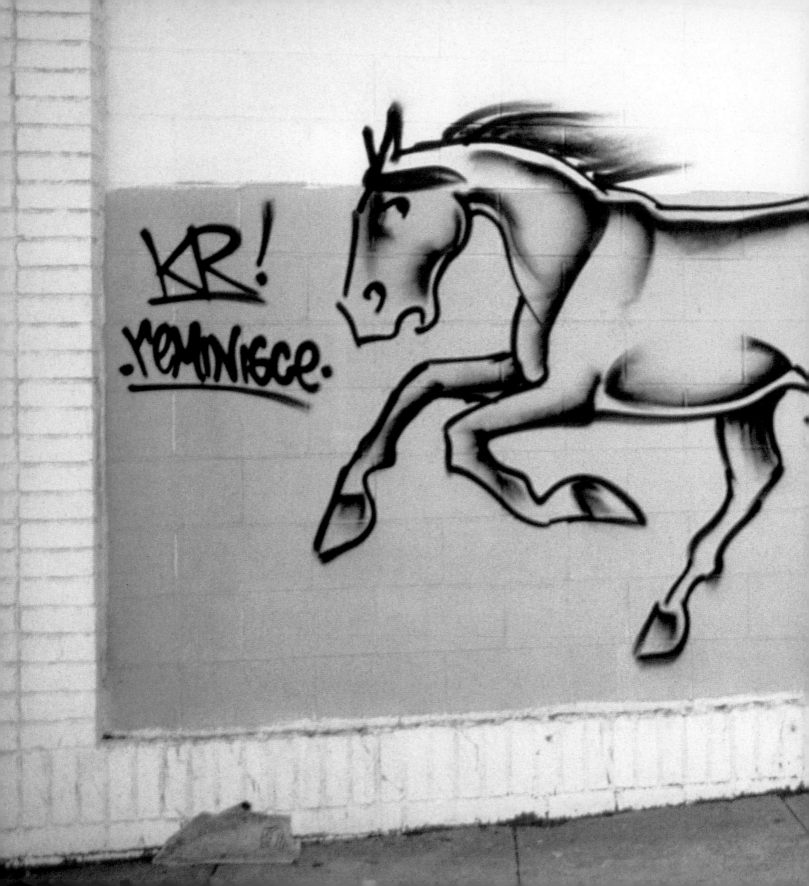

Reminisce

Reminisce (aka 'The Horse Lady') was active in downtown San Francisco in the late 1980s and early '90s, spray-painting alongside renowned artists such as Twist and KR. As well as tags and throw-ups of her name – or REM for short – Reminisce is known primarily for her horse pieces, which were often spray-painted with only one or two colours. Now she works as a freelance artist, having abandoned piecing altogether.

Photo © Jim Prigoff

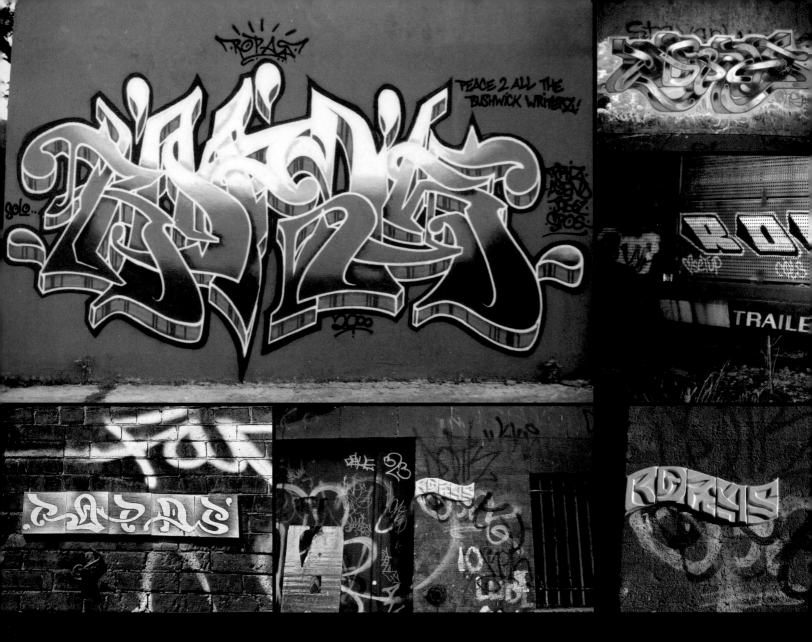

Ropas

Ropas spray-painted her first pieces in *c.* 1993 in Columbus, USA, and in 1997 moved to New York to study at the School of Visual Arts. Over the next few years she used the streets as her canvas, to achieve recognition. As the risks associated with getting up increased, she switched to working with ceramics.

'After some time studying Islamic art and taking a trip to southern Spain to visit various Moorish sites, I began working on a series of ceramic tiles with a relief surface and colourful glazes bearing my name, which could be affixed to walls around the city. Now, I much prefer this kind of intimate and pedestrian "street art" which whispers to passers-by rather than competing with all the advertisements, billboards, signs and other

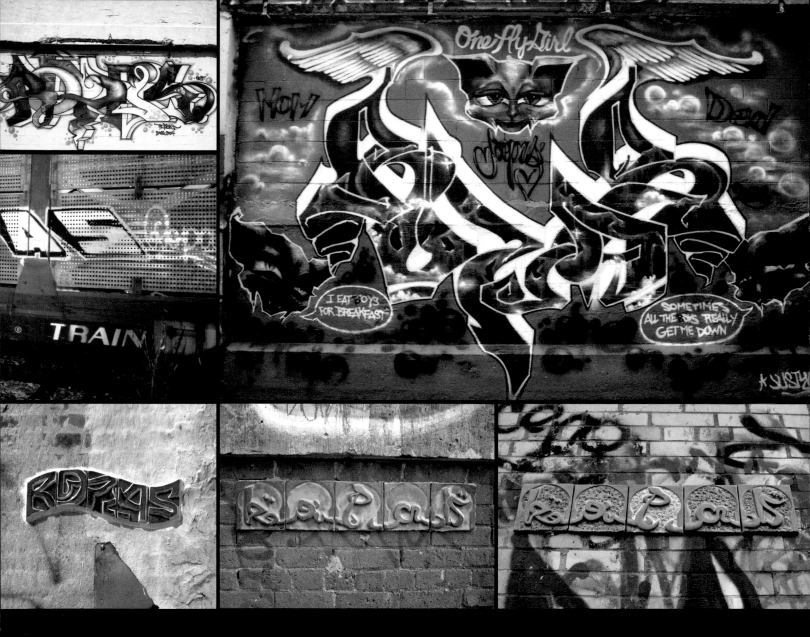

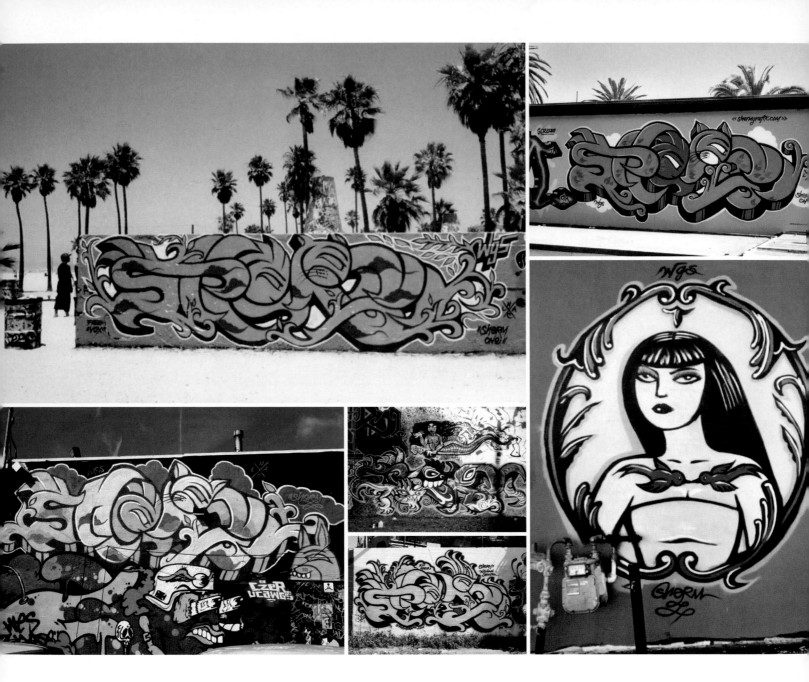

Sherm

Sherm got into graffiti in 1994 when she was sixteen years old. Although she did not paint her first real piece until four years later, she often drew in her blackbook and caught tags and scribes mostly on the bus. She is currently focusing her energy more on painting quality pieces and creating artwork during her free time.

'I'm older now, so I definitely find myself painting more legal spaces, but I always try to find a balance between the two – otherwise I get bored,' she says. 'Nowadays, almost every painting spot I can think of has either been demolished or replaced by businesses, homes or apartment buildings, or the spot is just no longer active due to too many writers going there and making themselves obvious by being in large groups, telling all their friends and leaving dead cans and trash.'

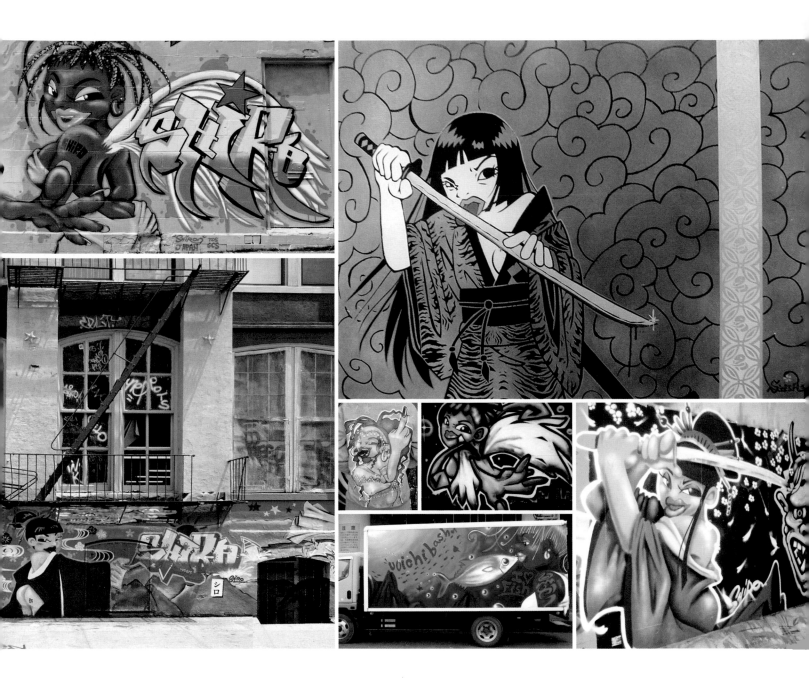

Shiro

Shiro is Japanese for 'blank canvas' or 'pure mind'. Born in the Shizuoka province of Japan, where she still lives, Shiro took up the spraycan in 1998 after doing a piece with fellow artist Clunch on a huge wall by the river in their neighbourhood. Between 2002 and 2004 she lived in New York, which had a profound effect on her, and she views art as a boundless medium through which to meet friends in Japan and further afield.

'I think I've been expressing another self who lives in a virtual world,' she explains. 'I wanna be like that other self, or something like that. Also I get to express my dirty side through my painting. I'd like these things to fuse, to reflect a deep world.'

111

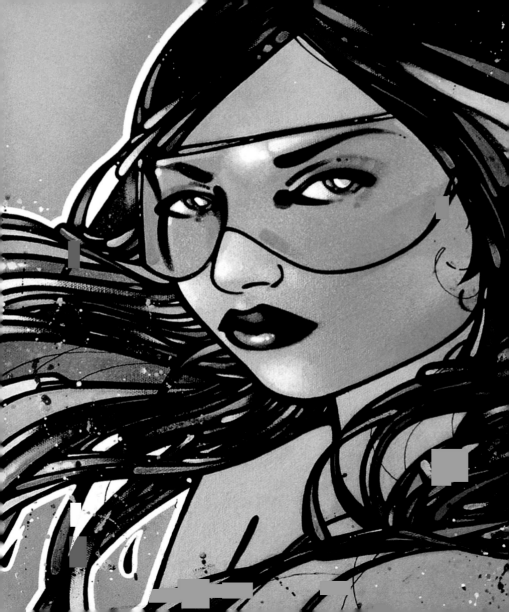

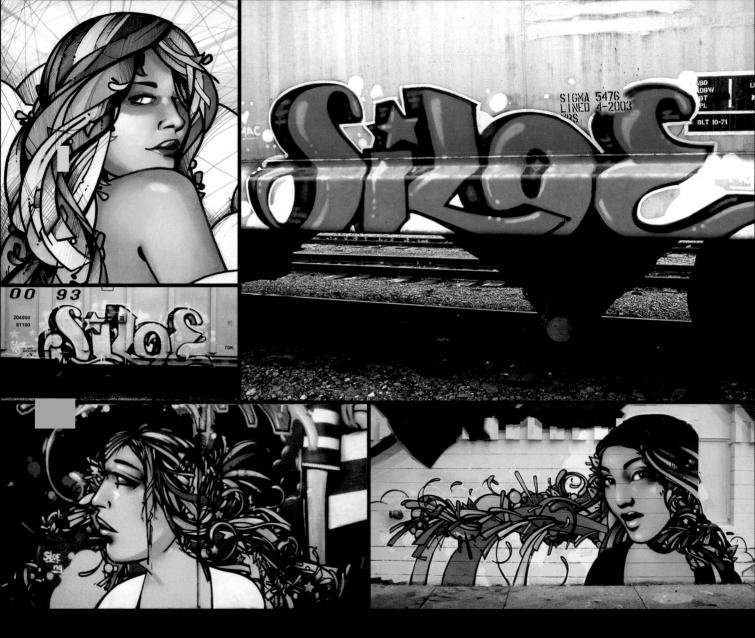

Siloette

'In my opinion there has to be a fine balance [between legal and illegal],' says American aerosol artist Siloette. 'I try to keep it separate, but push both elements equally. I love painting freights just as much as a nice wall, but for different reasons. I don't pretend to be some crazy bomber – never have. But painting freights with your crew or getting up in some random spot makes it all feel worthwhile at the end of the night.'

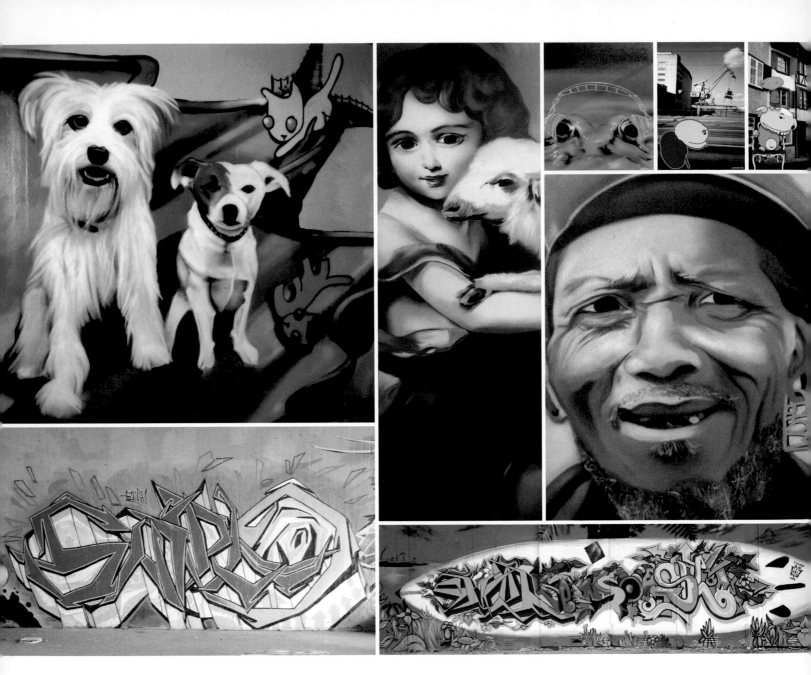

Smirk

In 1996, when she was still living in Switzerland, Smirk and a friend dragged themselves round town one night in freezing temperatures of -10ºC. Artistically, what emerged from that night was a yellow and violet cow in stilettos. Since then, she has made ample use of the spraycan and developed her art further. These days, she lives with her husband, Sky189, in Cape Town and calls both places home – torn between the lions of Africa and the cows of Switzerland.

   Smirk tends not to search for a particular message in her pieces: 'I'd like to make the onlooker react. I don't offer clearly defined messages, for two reasons. Firstly, I think that it's much more fun to provide the onlooker with a pleasant space in which to let his or her imagination run wild. Secondly, I'd like to create something for myself that is aesthetically beautiful. Sometimes, however, depending on where I find myself, I also paint socio-critical pieces.'

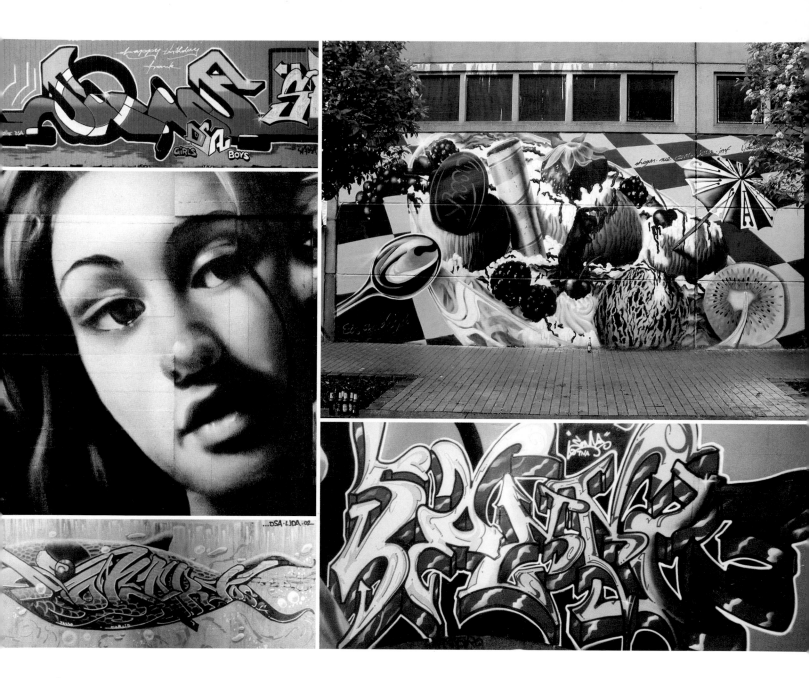

Sonne

Sonne's artistic streak shone through at an early age, when she was growing up in the German town of Chemnitz. 'I picked up my first spraycan when I was twelve,' she explains, 'and used it to paint my old skateboard. By the time I was fifteen I was catching my first tags.' By 1999 Sonne – whose name means 'sun' in German – had started spray-painting seriously with Cayn.

'You should seize the day and enjoy everything life has to offer,' she says. 'Life's knockdowns are just part of it. What I'm trying to say is that there's nothing more beautiful than life's opposites. That's why I spray-paint both styles and characters, why I like drawing but also using a brush. It's just like nature: sun and rain, wind and calm, entirely conflicting but rich in contrasts. I generally try to reflect the key influences of my life in my pieces – graffiti, sex and funk music!'

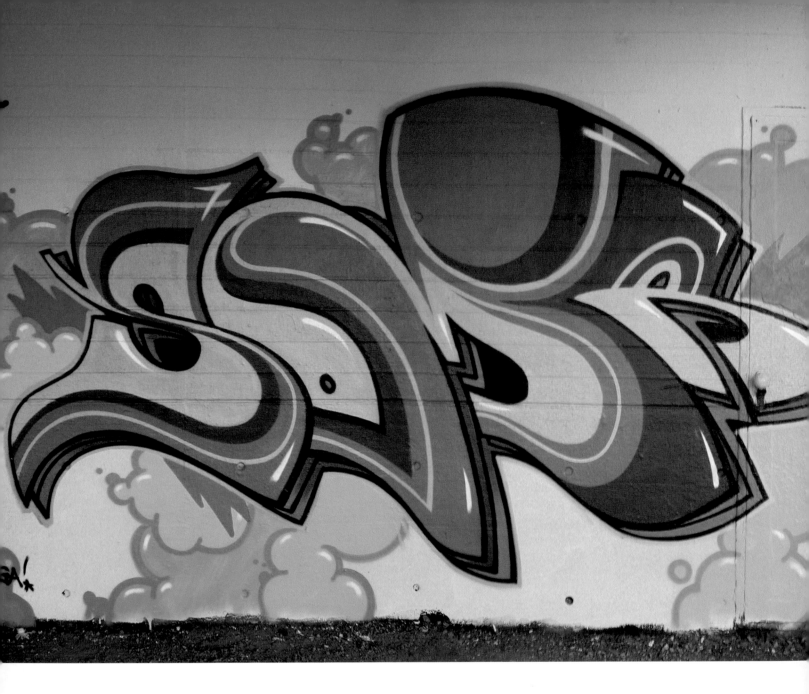

Soma

Soma comes from Switzerland and has been spray-painting since 1999.

116

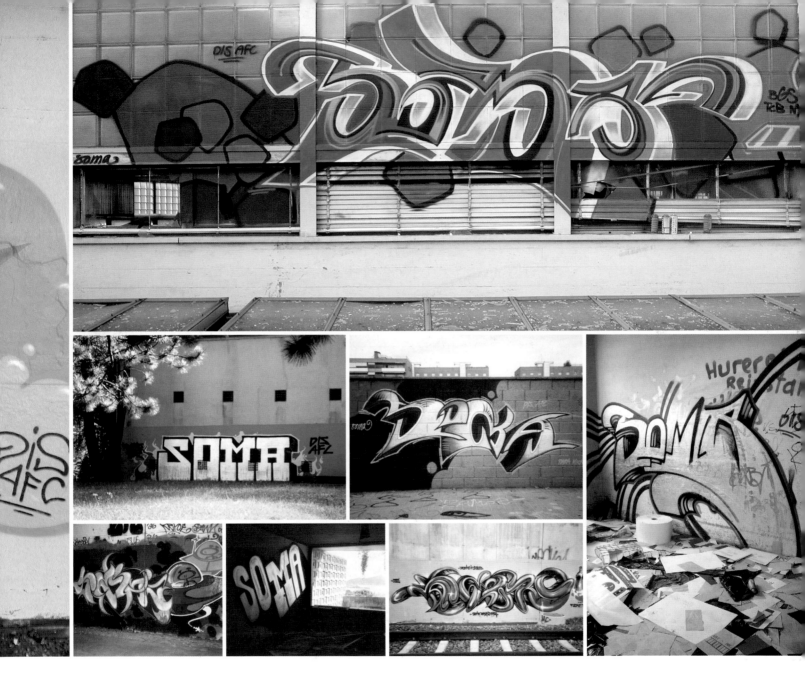

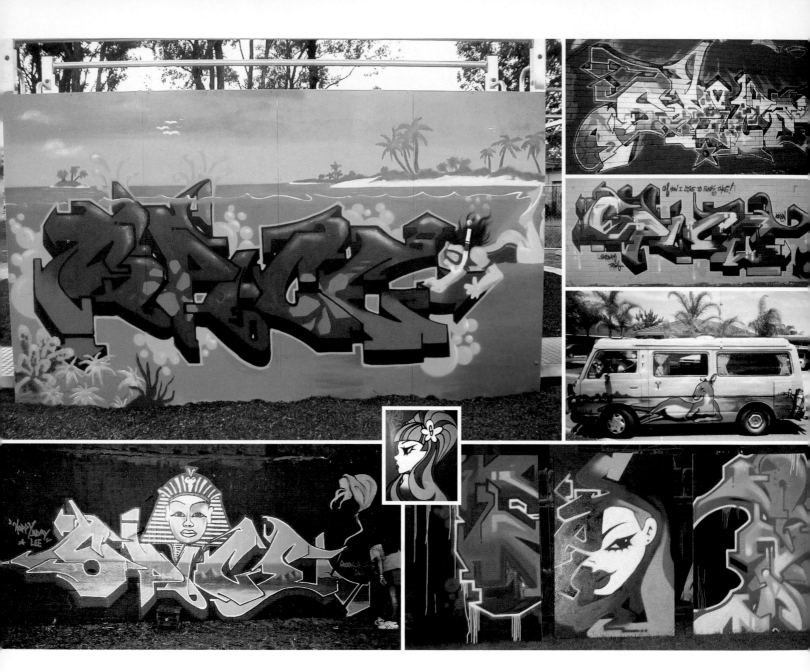

Spice

Maltese-born Spice lives in Sydney, Australia. 'I suppose overall I would like to express something with my art, but I don't think it really shows in my graff,' she says. 'It's more an expression of my mental state as I paint or, more so, of when I sketch. Sketching always clears my head of negative thoughts, and I'm never more confident or at ease than when I'm painting. Usually I write a few simple words next to my pieces – most of the time some lyrics from a song that I may have been listening to. Music is still my biggest influence. If my graff really showed what I felt inside and was put into a song or image, it would consist of George Clinton, Prince, Afrika Bambaataa, Looptroop, Cee-Lo Green, Dungeon Family, Al Naafiysh, Cameo, Rick James, and much, much more. Image-wise, it would be broken hearts, eyes (the journey to the centre of the soul), tattoos, UFOs and Egyptian artefacts.'

118

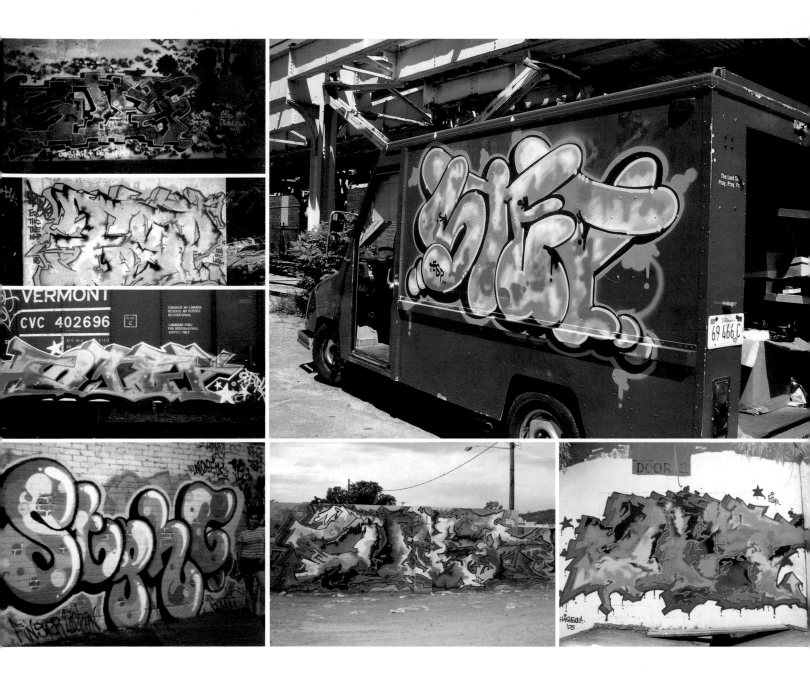

Stef

Chicago-based Stef has been active since the early 1990s and is an artist, producer, muralist and instructor. 'I teach art and ceramics for the park district here,' she says, 'and am currently working on canvases and shows, but I still have the most passion for busting tags and burning trains, any kind of trains, anywhere in the world. And trucks – I love trucks too.'

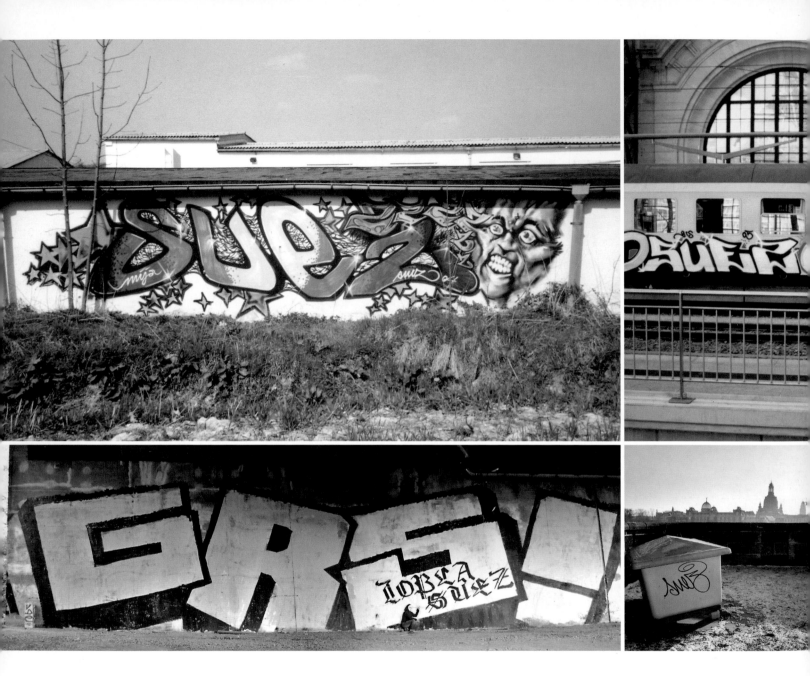

Suez

'Graff makes me feel alive!' says Dresden-based Suez. 'By going out and painting, I can cross over boundaries and really feel myself. I'm able to change the world every day and night! My experience is that a lot of women/girls only define themselves by having a boyfriend and looking beautiful, but I don't find that satisfying. I'm not a passive person who just accepts. It is often difficult to reconcile graff with "normal life", which means that I spend my time living in different worlds and in very different roles. But one world could never exist without the other! You could compare the whole thing to an iceberg: there is the small part that you can see above the surface of the water, and the rest, the huge part, lies beneath, out of sight. Both belong to the iceberg; I am both.'

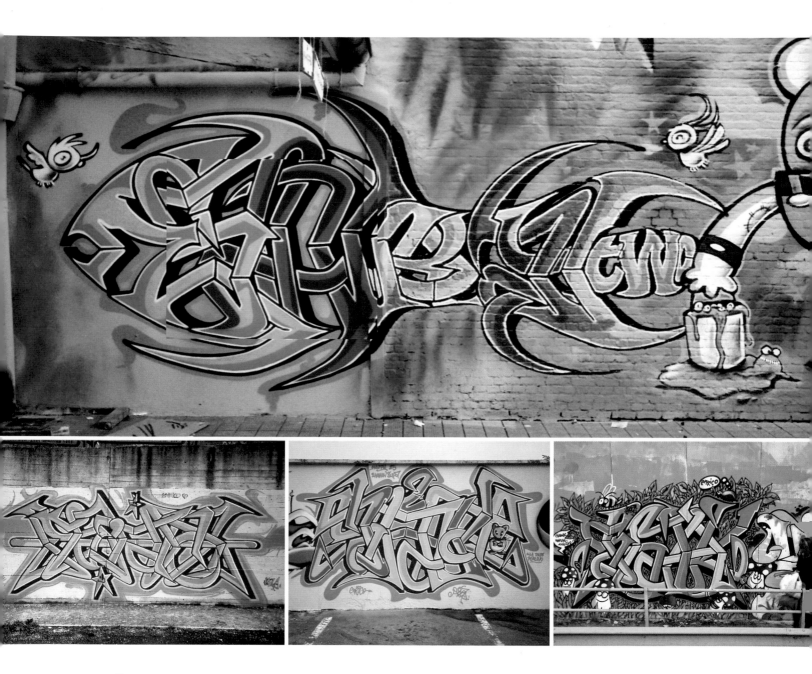

Supa B2

Supa B2, from Mestre in Italy, got into graffiti when she was a teenager after seeing pieces by old-school artists like Sat and Slog175 in her home town. Her own pieces are influenced by the New York wildstyle, but she tries to find her own individual slant: 'Right now I'm trying to paint a piece as if it were two pieces in one. One day I was sketching a piece on transparent paper just for fun, and I was amazed by the effect I got by placing it over a sketch of the same piece. The two sketches didn't match perfectly, and the piece looked kind of "doubled". So, that led me to create these "double wildstyles". First I concentrated on "Supa", with two styles of "S" interwoven, and in their turn looped with two styles of "U", and so on. It was such a mess! Then I started writing two different words in the same technique: for example, my two tags, or my name interwoven with my boyfriend's…so the first letter is a mixture of an "S" and a "J". You get the idea!'

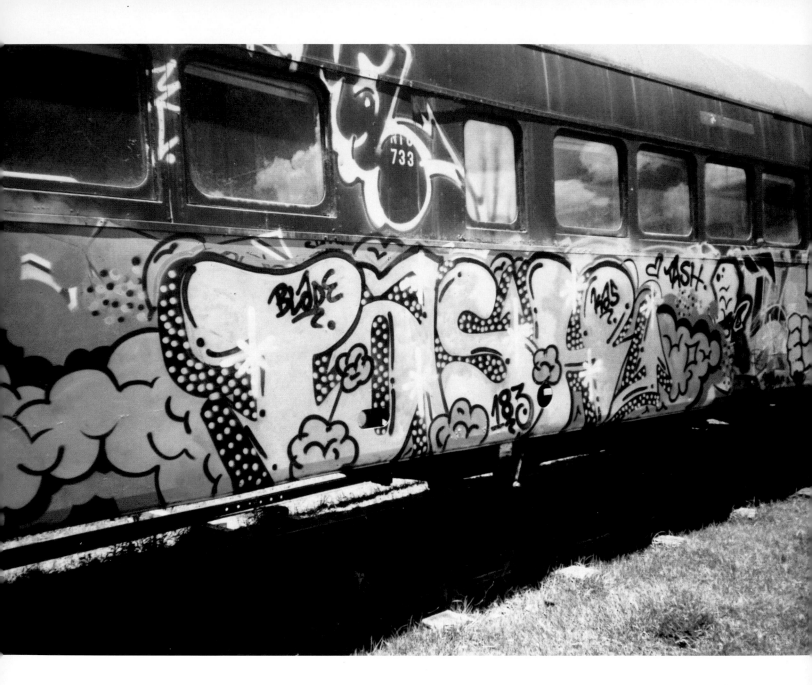

Tash

Tash was born in a small Aboriginal town called Whyalla, but now lives in Queensland. She is one of Australia's longest-standing female writers, a well-known media personality, rapper and old-school hip-hop fanatic. She bombed for the first time in 1990 but didn't do her first real piece until 1994.

'Anarchy, love of hip-hop and graffiti, old-school aesthetics and militant post-feminism' all feature in her pieces, she says. 'There are some advantages and some disadvantages [to being a woman], but that's true for everyone, no matter who you are. Being a female writer I get in fewer fights, less sex, less hassle from the cops, ugly nails, more fame, stalkers, more paid work, I'm judged more on my looks, who I date, who I paint with….'

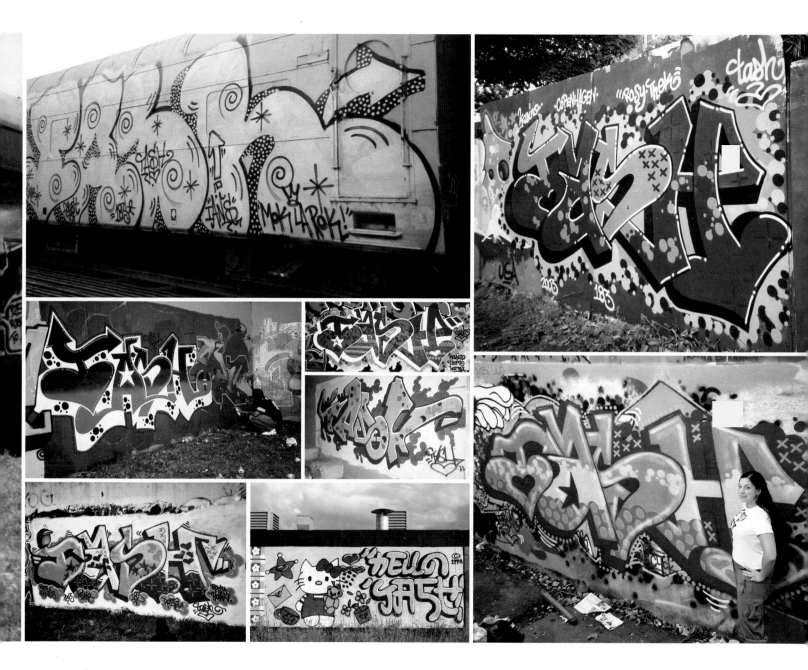

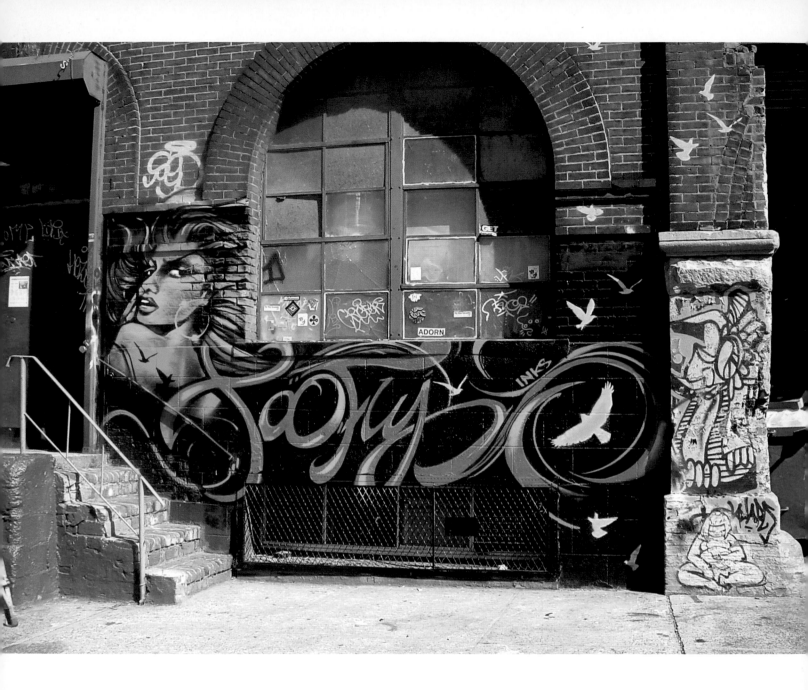

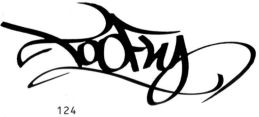

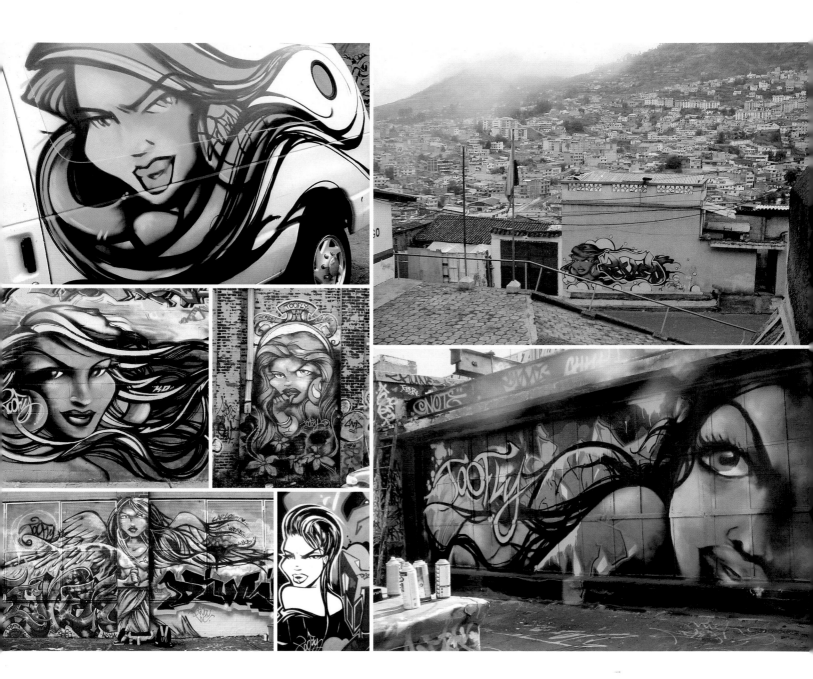

Toofly

Ecuadorean-born Toofly is a well-rounded artist and graphic designer, and works in the fashion industry. 'I portray anything and everything female,' she says. 'My work exudes it so much – to the point that it will take other things to change it. Why? Well, because it's a voice I need to express. There is a limited amount of imagery of dope "Spanish fly girl" superhero-type characters that resonate with young people of colour. When I was growing up I only saw "white characters" in comics, cartoons and toys. What I am creating is a voice, a message of our existence, our style and our own kind of look.'

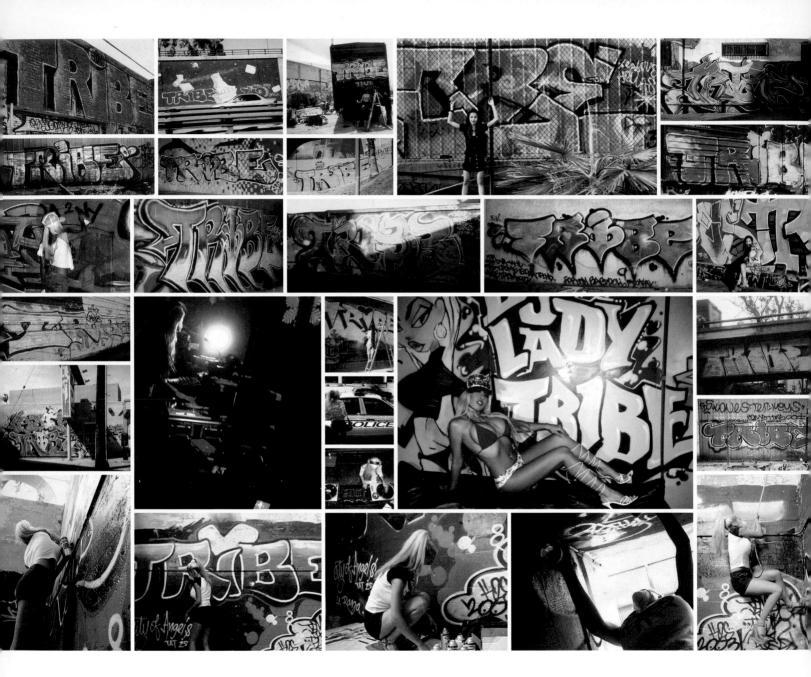

Tribe

Tribe has done pieces all over Los Angeles, but has also made a name for herself as a model and DJ. She turned to turntables when, after ten years of illegal bombing, the cops finally caught up with her and put her under house arrest for six months. Now she's also known worldwide as DJ Lady Tribe.

'I was expressing how down I was for the art and that I can be the uppest graffiti writer regardless of my gender,' she explains. 'I loved to get fresh spots that no one had ever hit – the ones you can see off the freeway, high as hell. I loved getting billboards when other people paid thousands to promote their shit. I was promoting myself for free, but it looked tight and clean and readable. That's how I became a legend of the art! You can't become respected unless you've bombed! I went to jail for this and risked my life. I've been in and out of jail my whole life.'

126

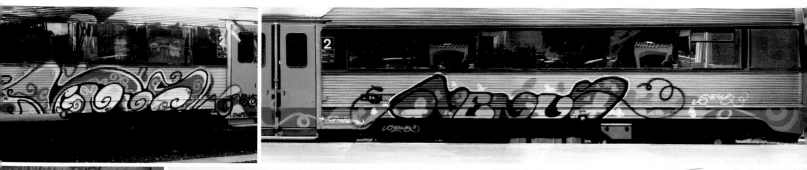

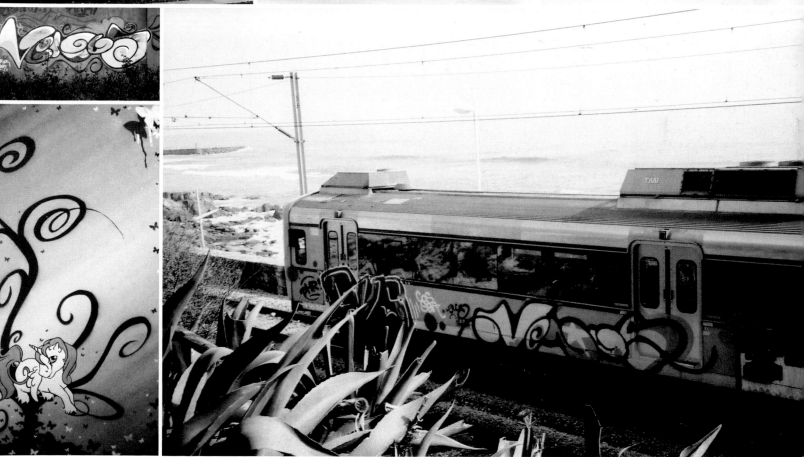

Venus

Venus did her first pieces in 2000 in Lisbon, where she still lives. 'My aim isn't to show female aspects in my work,' she says. 'All I do is paint how I want to, and the way my hand drives the lines.'

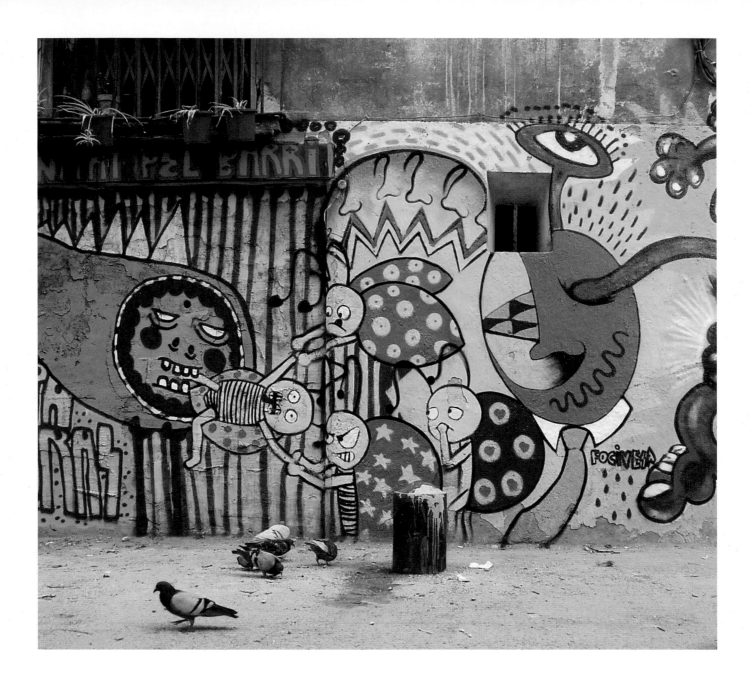

128

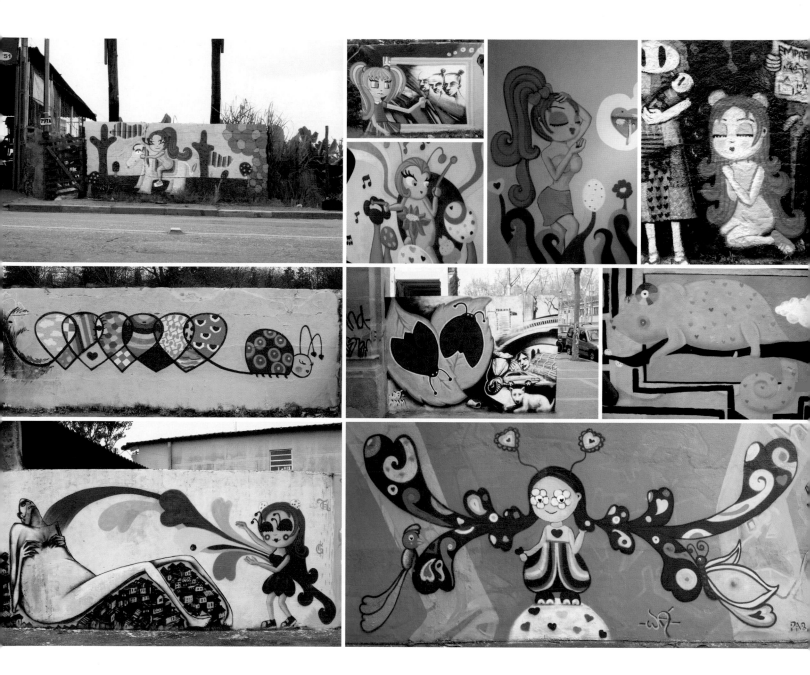

Waleska

Sometimes known as WA, Waleska is a São Paulo-born artist but now lives in London with her husband Adam Neate. She got into graffiti at an early age through her brother Tinho, who has been active since 1986 and went on to found the Terceiro Mundo graffiti school in the late 1990s. In early 2004 Waleska started her own project entitled *Spreading the Love and Positive Energies to the World*, where she uses her art to convey this message.

Waleska uses all sorts of materials in her artwork, including the spraycan, paper, cardboard and canvas, and her style has changed quite considerably over the years: 'I first started painting traditional letterforms using wildstyles as my main influence, but after a while I started experimenting with different characters and enjoyed being able to express my feelings in different situations. I still like to write traditional-style letters occasionally though and sometimes incorporate letters into my pictures.'

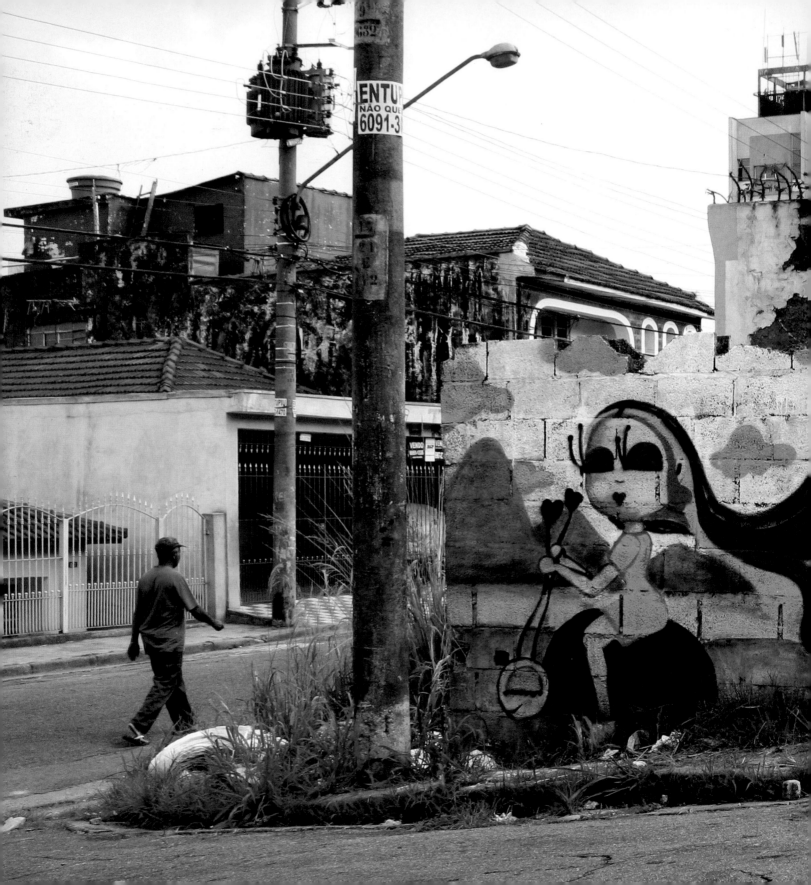

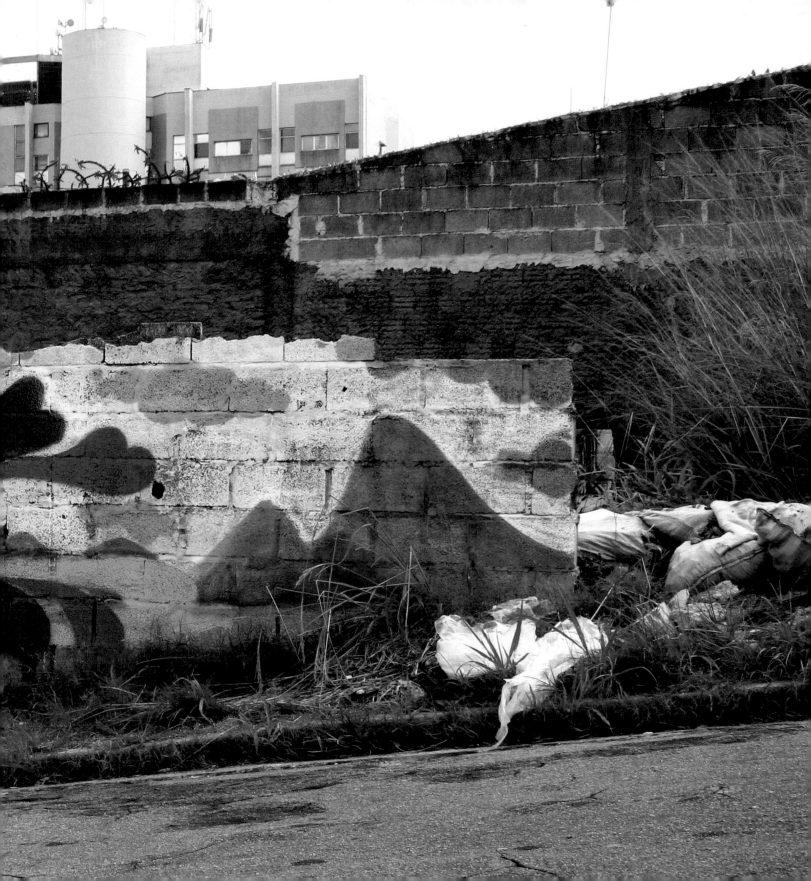

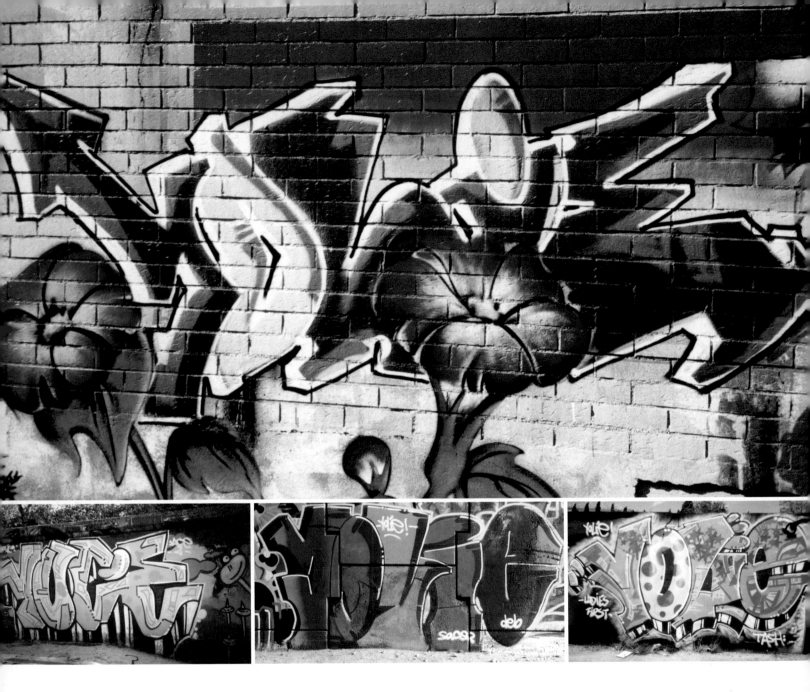

Yolie

Yolie is from Madrid and painted her first piece in her teens, influenced heavily by rap. Until 1994 her graffiti was sporadic as cans were expensive and the ones she nicked didn't last long. Fellow artists Sace2, Eddie, Joke and Lama also helped and inspired her. 'At the beginning male writers didn't consider girls as serious writers,' she says, 'but that has changed. Now I think we all get the same respect.'

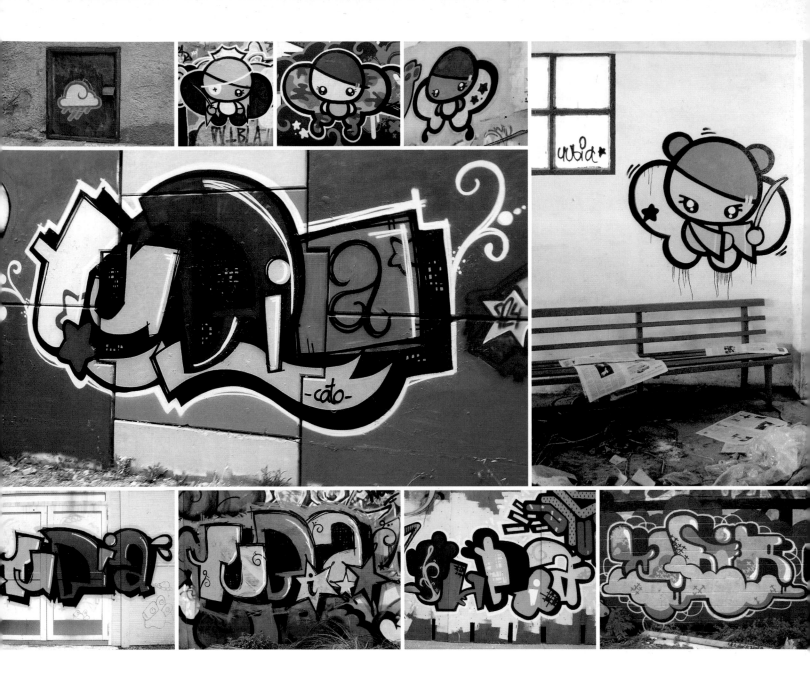

Yubia

Yubia comes from Bilbao and is relatively new to the scene. Most of the time she works illegally, but she has also done numerous surfaces for schools and shops. Graffiti helps her to experience life, shake off frustrations and grow as a person.

'The truth is that there are not many girls dedicated to painting graffiti seriously over here [in Spain],' she says. 'Some girls start painting because it's fashionable, but you know when girls and boys are doing it for that reason or really taking it seriously. And those that start 'cause it's trendy don't usually last too long.'

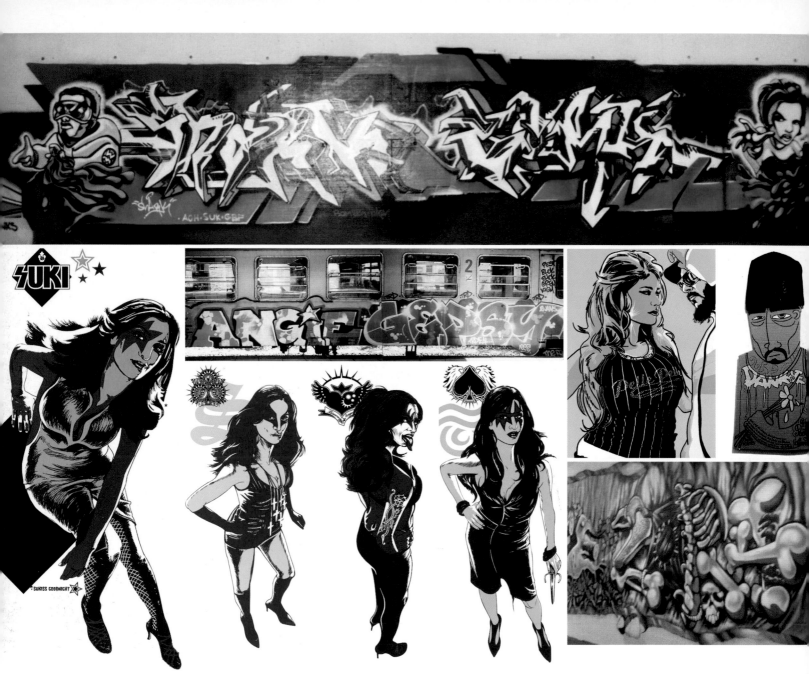

Zora

Swiss-born graffiti artist Zora has been active since 1989 but has also carved herself a successful career in graphic design and motion graphics. She says: 'I like peace, harmony and order, and I have always been more of a character- than a style-painter. If I want to express something, it starts off with a task, a question that I pose myself, and I begin to look for the answer. At best it's like "the path is the goal". The solution should end up emerging as a harmonious, well-proportioned and perfectly executed picture. That is my personal criteria. It's a bit like maths, only I'm not counting with numbers but with pictures. For me art is a mix of an interesting, progressive question and perfect technical execution. This stimulates creativity and fascinates me. I also see the same thing among other artists. It's as if someone has taken away my mental work and served it on a silver tray. It's extremely interesting and inspiring to see other solutions to the same question.'

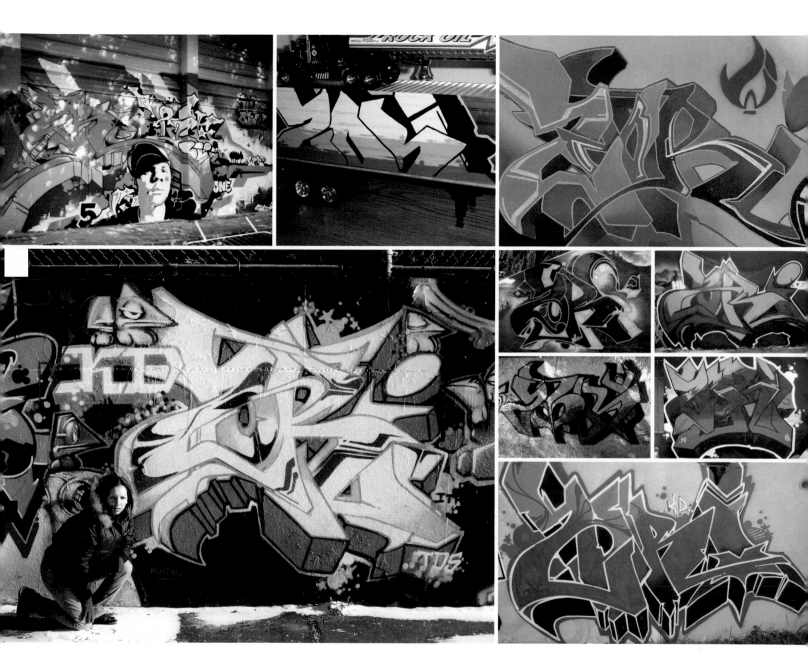

Zori4

'When I sketch, paint or do letters I want to project the feelings I have inside,' explains Puerto Rican graffiti artist Zori4. 'This fire, the red lava that I feel, the intensity, but also the gentleness and intuition of the woman I am – that we can be rude, soft, intelligent, brilliant, talented, dynamic, creative, full of power and will, and that we are strong. My pieces *are* me. Since I started writing I've experienced a lot of wonderful things, thanks to people who have given me support, love and understanding. This is not an easy career when you're on the reverse of the coin, on the other side of the mirror or perspective…when you do things that you're not supposed to, not because they're wrong, but just because people say so. You have to be strong, determined and reach your goal. I tell other female writers to be careful, to respect themselves, to fight and break rules without violating the ethic that exists between writers.'

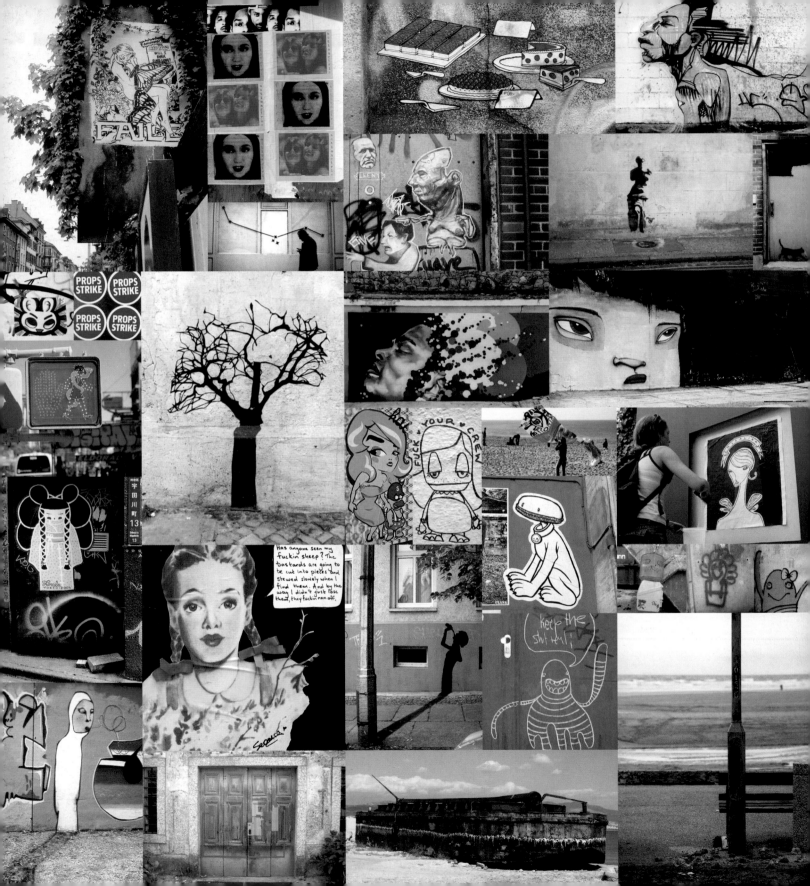

∞+ ∞+ (aka Laurie/The Laboratory of Living Arts) spray-painted her first stencils in Toulouse at the age of fourteen but she didn't do her first real pieces until 1988–89, when she moved to Dublin and painted critical texts and sentences on the street. When she settled in Barcelona, in 2000, she did her first colourful pieces. Through her work, ∞+ fights against cultural manipulation and 'dumbing down', which she claims are foisted upon us daily in the media and advertising.

'If we think about the place of the artist in our society,' she says, 'we have first to define what we see as art. If we need art to represent, encourage, inspire us, to express our feeling good or bad about a situation, it's pointless looking to the galleries, as they generally carry as much social conscience as a key-ring. What we are left with are the streets, the walls, where the militants leave their painted words during marches, when governments choose to ignore their democratic rights of freedom of speech, showing that the cities are not just big shopping malls, or touristy money-making facilities, but places of life and energy.

'It's a lie to say that without graffiti the streets would be "clean". Every street is stained grey with car fumes, every brand is advertising on giant billboards all over our landscapes, every multi-national has incrusted its logo in every part of our lives, credit card stickers on shop windows outnumber our stickers. Banks, cash machines, billboards, fake naked women with no name, men with machine guns on the front of cinemas or on video-game shelves, politicians' grinning lies in our faces, cameras intruding into our right to privacy 24/7. This is what truly has become of our streets.'

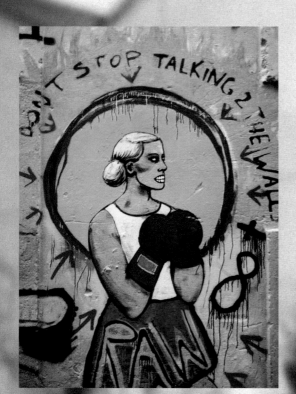

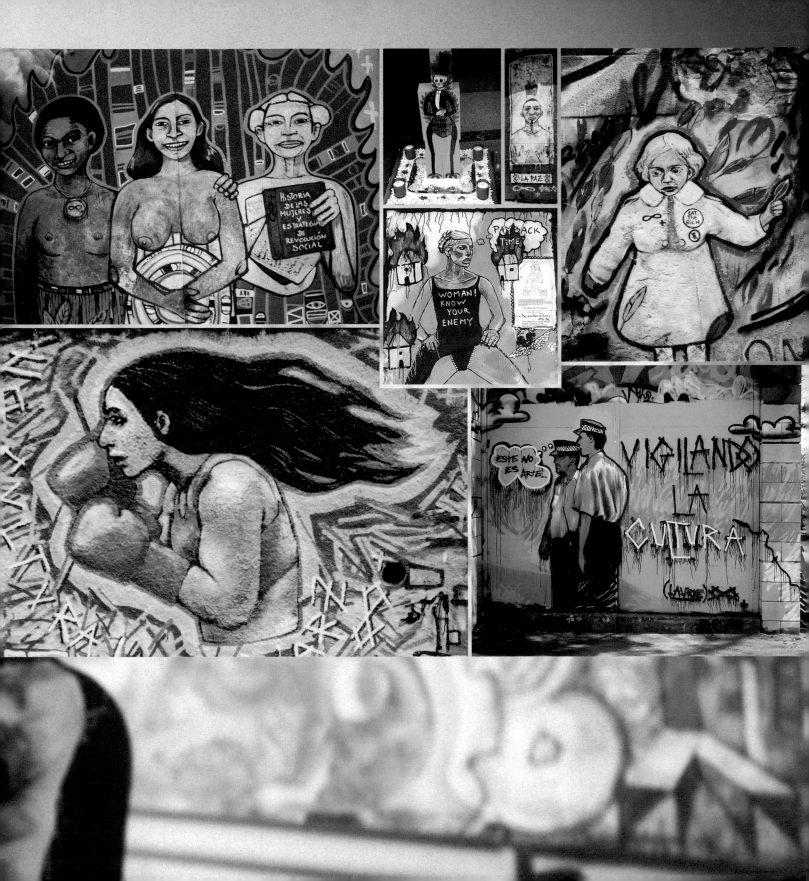

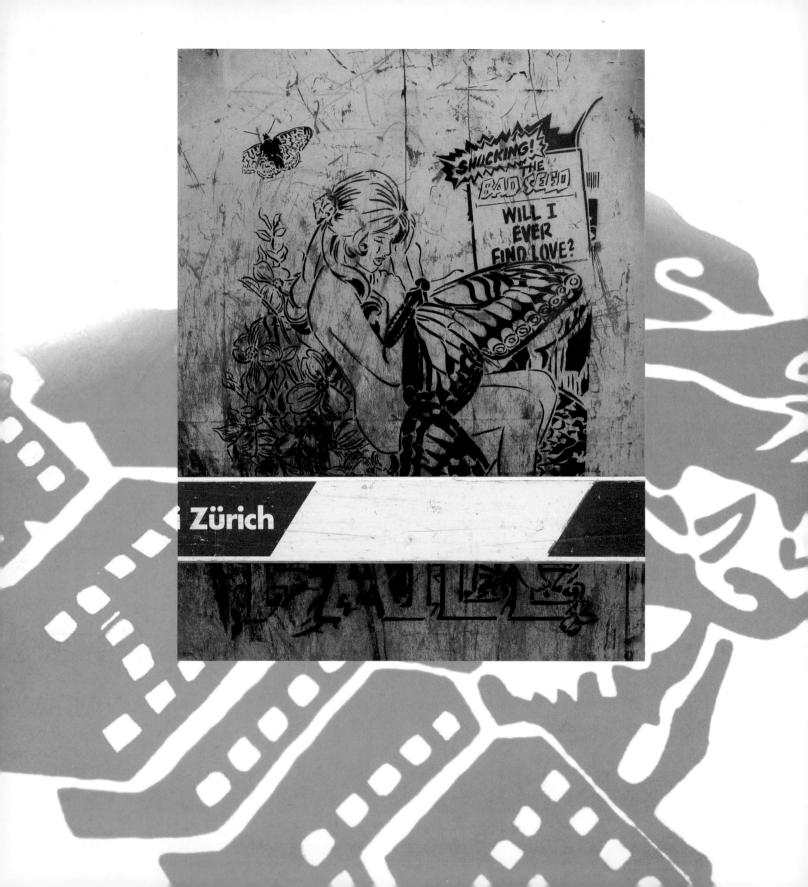

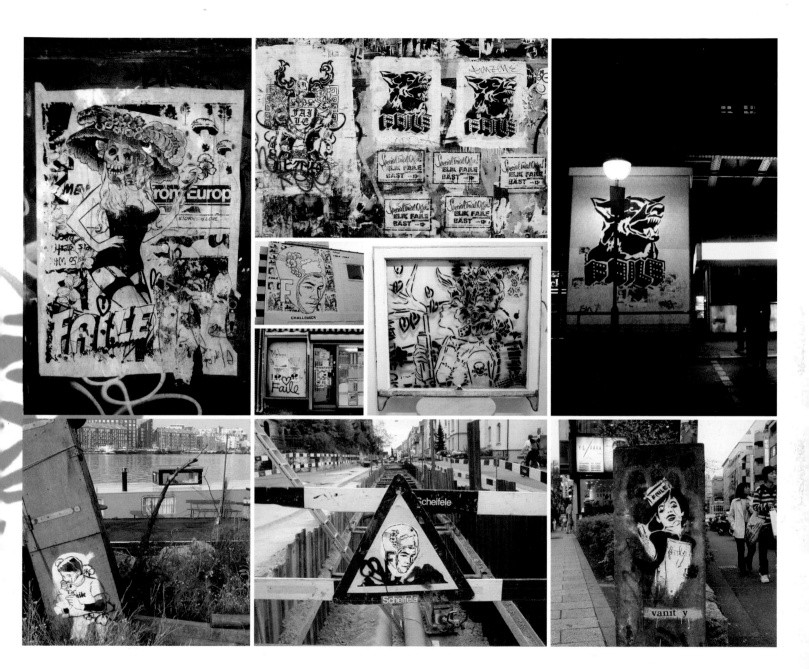

Aiko

Aiko (aka Faile) was born in Tokyo and belongs to the renowned NYC Faile crew, which has been active for many years. 'Some graffiti and street artists have a serious concept and/or a political message,' she says. 'Of course my art has a message too, but street art is more about having FUN, travelling with friends, finding spots and bombing.'

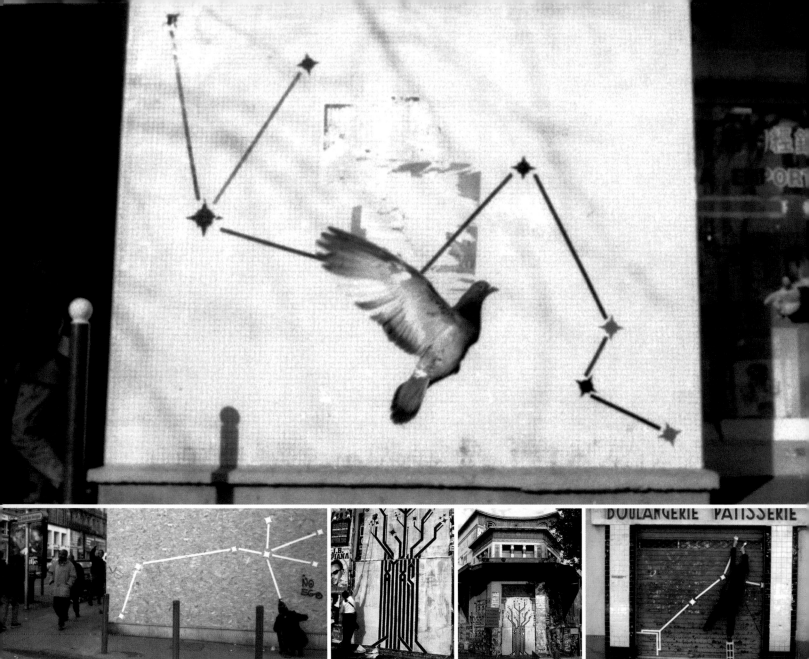

Aleteia

In ancient Greek, *aleteia* means 'truth' – a virtue that definitely inspires the Breton-born artist. Viewing herself as an urban artist, Aleteia uses her pieces as a means of confrontation, hoping to reach people in the street, in her neighbourhood and even further afield, to start up a dialogue and escape from her own small world.

'I have started to make a constellation in the street in the hope of getting a universal message across, and to offer people something to reflect on as they go about their daily lives. The night stars come from childhood and the old tradition of storytelling to express the hopes and fears of mankind. I hope it's a medium for reflection, meditation and invention. As Heraclitus said, "When there is no sun, we can see the evening stars."'

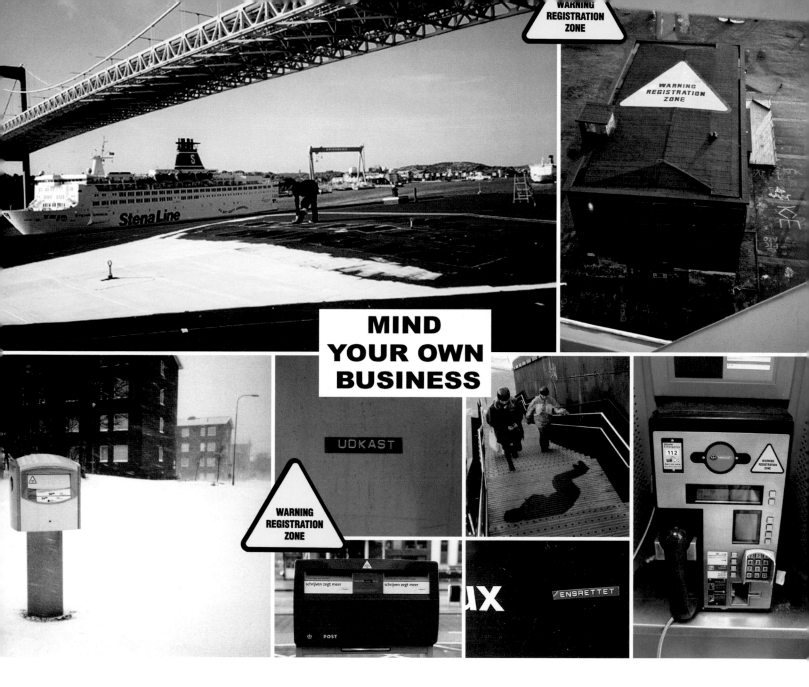

MIND YOUR OWN BUSINESS

BRING OUT THE GARBAGE

BRING OUT THE GARBAGE is a Norwegian and Danish collaboration, working on different, often politically motivated projects. One of their most intensive projects is *Warning Registration Zone* – yellow, triangular stickers were plastered everywhere to draw attention to the daily surveillance and control of the State and repressive institutions: 'Soon we'll be living in a world where there are no secrets, no unexplored corners and – worst of all – no rights or freedom to speak, think, walk or do anything without being watched and investigated. Today we know about spy systems, information networks and other database registration systems such as Europol. If you walk on the pavement, use public transport, send a letter, use your computer, go to the library, travel, shop, talk on the phone, work for the "wrong" company, then you're always in the zone of registration. *Warning Registration Zone* aims to make the registration and surveillance visible and a part of people's consciousness.'

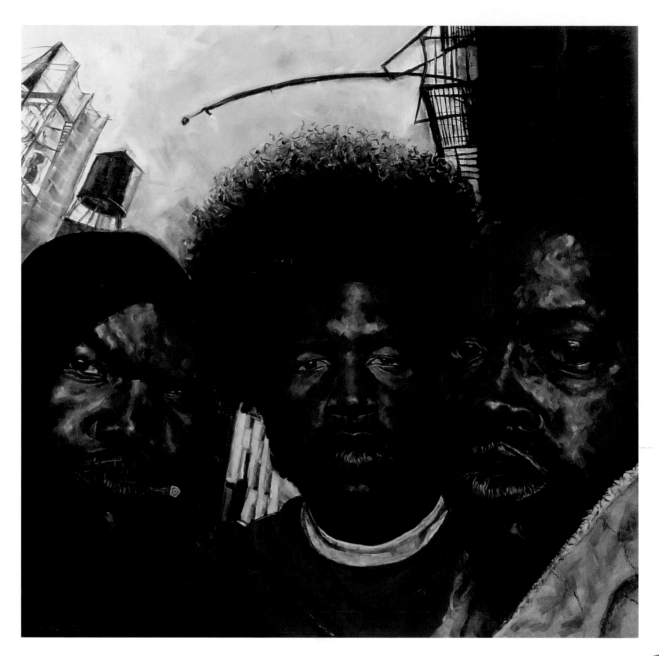

Cade

Cade (aka Nika Sarabi), originally from Toronto, now lives in New York. She started off doing pieces and was amazed by the array of shapes and surfaces used by artists. Later she moved on to painting canvases and portraits of people in her neighbourhood or the public eye, but she was searching for something more.

'Often people create hype around a chick just because she's a novelty,' she says. 'So some female writers ride on that and have no real substance. Respect should be based on merit, regardless of gender. The fact that I'm a chick is just a coincidence; I didn't point to a twat and say "I want that"!

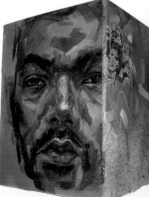

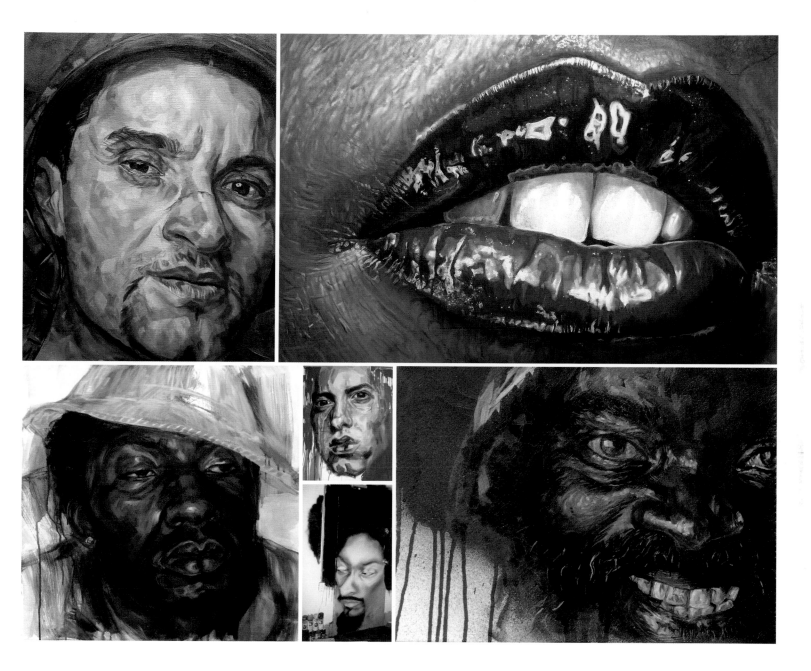

'I'm an urban artist, not a writer. I love and worship everything in the city. Cities have an abundance of personalities who are forced to integrate and deal with each other every day. Cities are fully fabricated and organized by us. What does the city tell us about ourselves and one another? How is it that people from completely unique backgrounds can come together and follow the same general rules to function as this mass in our own creation? These are questions I work out every day by making what I make.

'My goal right now is to bring graffiti into the foreground of the world of fine arts. Art history defines graffiti as Keith Haring and Jean-Michel Basquiat, and we all know that's not exactly true. I'm trying desperately to make art aficionados realize otherwise, and bring forth the faces that once lurked in the shadows of the night.'

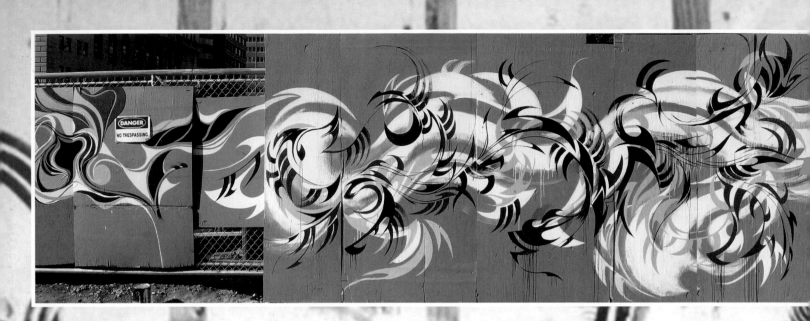

Che Jen

Che Jen is a painter from NYC, USA.

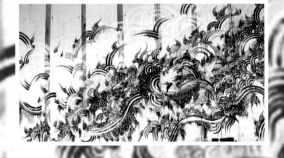

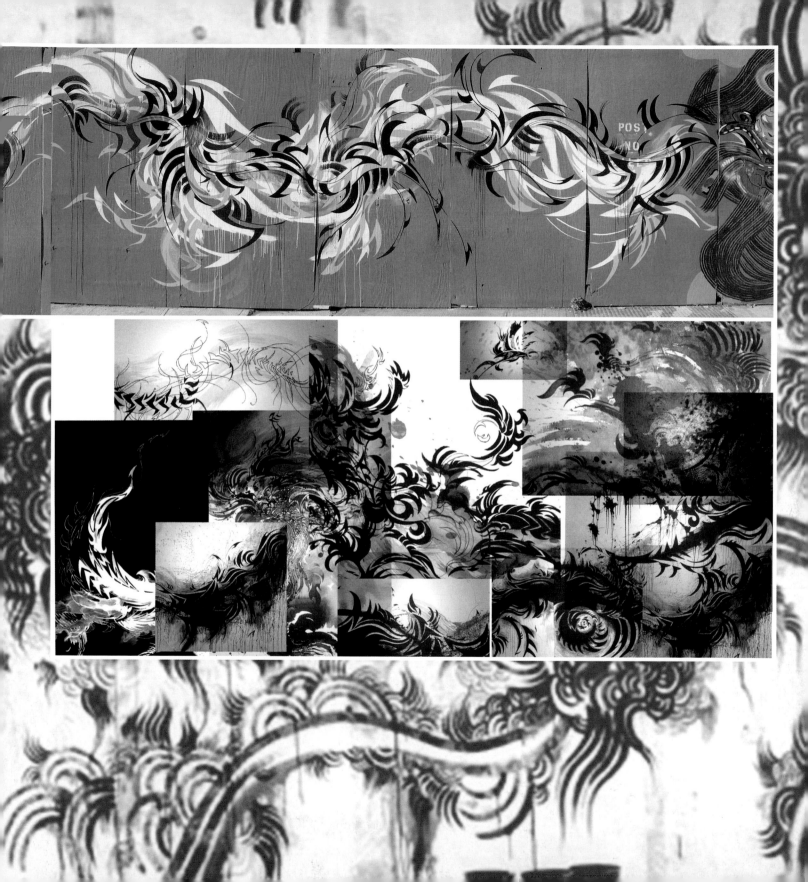

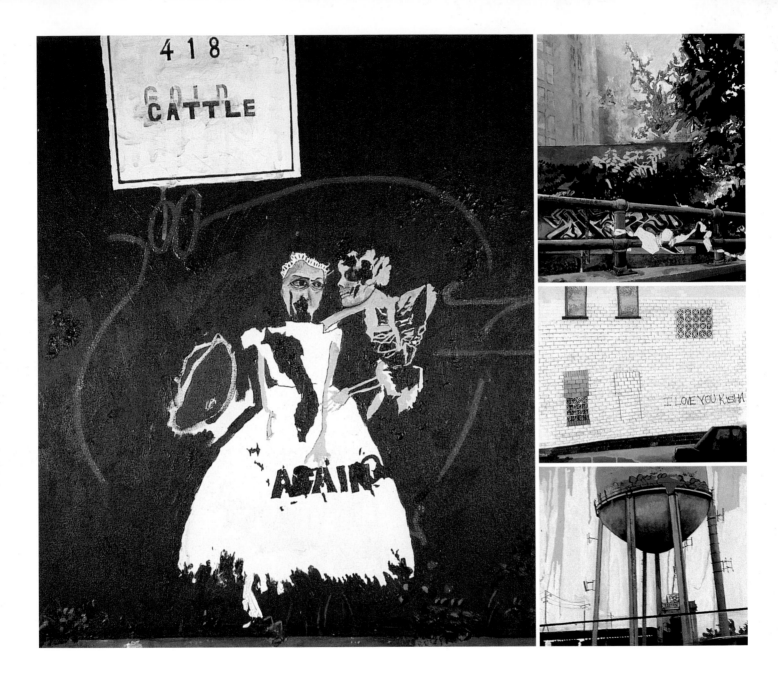

Constance Brady

Constance Brady (aka Cattle) is an artist living and working in Brooklyn, New York. Inspired as a teenager by her father's 'Free Ireland' tag in the artist's home town of Wilmington, Delaware, Brady explores non-traditional notions of beauty in architecture. Her works on canvas document the agitative dialogue written on the walls of New York City. Brady is attracted to the poorly matched colour swatches with which building owners choose to cover graffiti (only for it to be bombed over again), thus creating an effective public conversation. 'I attempt to pronounce these subtle disruptions in the fabric of our culture,' she says, 'not design theatrical gestures that replicate the machinery of the spectacle.'

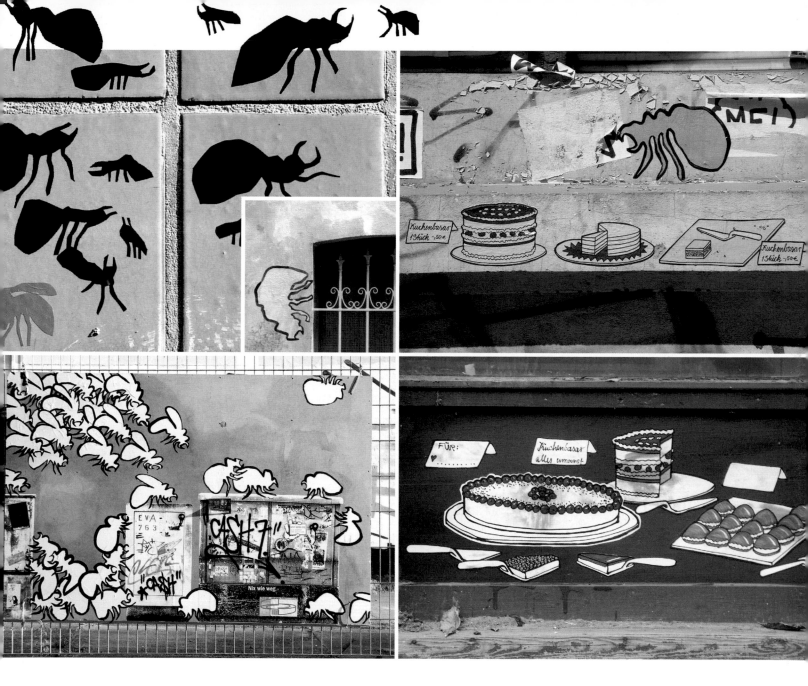

Dani

'At some point I discovered posters and stickers for myself,' says German artist Dani, who got into graffiti in *c*.1998 after piecing a legal wall with a friend and his crew. 'I could prepare everything at home and put my work up in specially selected spots. In hindsight, that's what reignited my passion for illegal actions at night because I didn't find sticking up posters as aggressive as bombing, although it did enable me to focus my attention on specific themes. Street art is still illegal, of course, because you put up your work wherever you choose. But the advantage of graffiti lies in the fact that, when you're caught, it's much easier to get rid of a sticker or a poster than a spray-painted piece. With street art I also like the idea that the pictures weather and gradually disappear, as if they'd never existed. Nowadays I create images using both techniques. For me graffiti and street art have merged into one – a vehicle through which I am able to realize my ideas and creativity.'

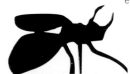

Den

Den got into graffiti in 1995. The artist, who comes from Bilbao, paints realistic portraits on walls, façades and canvases. Through her pieces, she tries to express what she sees in the faces of others.

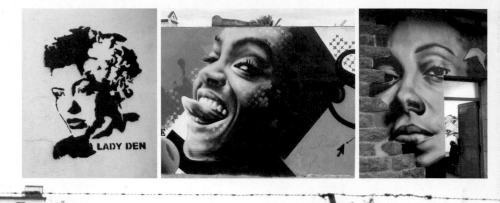

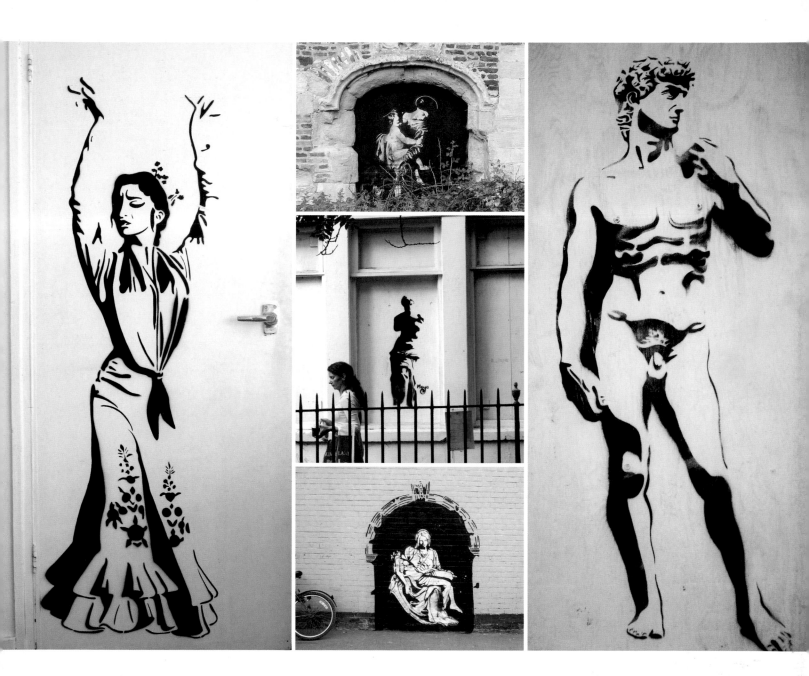

*In the depths of night
like a spider
I paint my intricate web of Maya.
Fragile images briefly weeping
from fissured walls.
In the sobriety of morning
as I brush intricate cobwebs
from my bike
some c**t obliterates my image
tears and all.*

Maya Deren

Maya Deren

This English stencil artist from Cambridge named her daughter Maya, after the 1940s avant-garde filmmaker Maya Deren. She hasn't been active for all that long, and unfortunately her (often life-size) stencils tend to get buffed by the authorities very quickly. Inspired by classical portraits, she dreams that graffiti will be taken seriously, that the city will provide legal walls to enrich the landscape, and that she will subtly convey her own attitude to people through her stencils and stimulate an intellectual change.

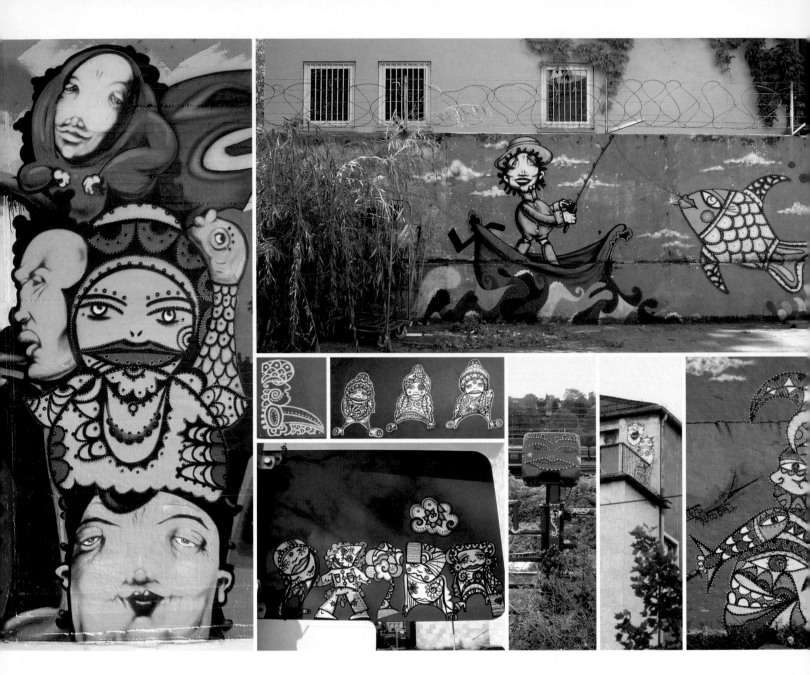

Donna

'The aim of art is freedom,' says German artist Donna. 'Freedom from the often pressing constraints of duty, from the one-dimensional illusion of order fabricated by self-appointed management, and from the omnipresent current of daily life. Artistic expression thus seeks innovative ways of life and the reinvention of being through the limitless power of imagination. The town should be reclaimed. It's poisoned by the day-to-day grasp of modern-day, all-encompassing capitalism. People have been dumbed down and their differences wiped out – they have become passive consumers through advertisements and TV as well as the way in which life itself has been made uniform. In place of the usual order of everyday life, a creative chaos has arisen, from which a new truth can emerge, and finally a change to something positive, as Theodor Adorno noted in 1957 when he said, "The task of art today is to bring chaos into order."'

152

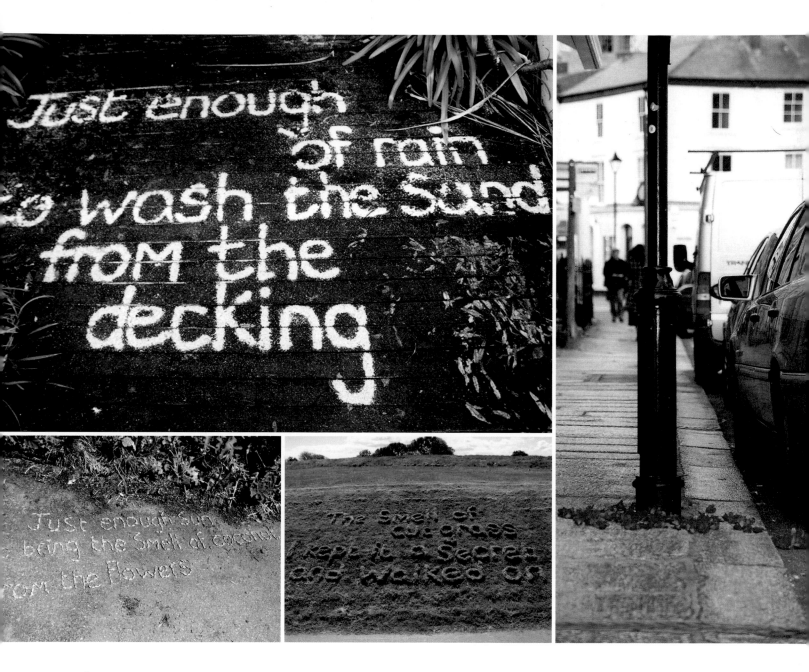

Becky Drayson

English artist Becky Drayson, from Cornwall, is active in a number of different fields and brings a lot of creativity to the streets. Her materials include poems, haiku, photographs and projected animations. Shadow projections form another project, as she explains: 'The idea behind the projections was to re-enchant public spaces through the communication of visual haiku. The project explored the use of illusions by creating hyper-realistic shadows cast by unseen objects in order to draw attention to the small gestures observed by nature which often get overlooked, such as a tree gently swaying in the wind or a bird in flight. Things that can help evoke a feeling of enchantment.'

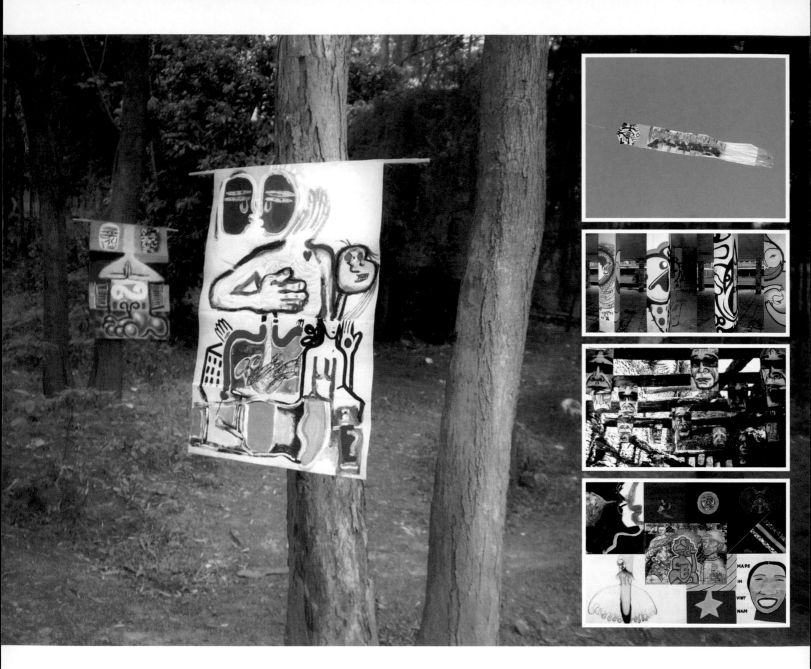

Rienke Enghardt (Hope Box)

Rienke Enghardt comes from The Hague, the City of Peace and Justice,
and did her first murals in the early '80s. Since 1991 she has created
and initiated mobile art-projects and has organized various art events
in twenty-six countries worldwide. *Hope Box* is the collective noun for this
and includes her most recent projects *Kites of Life* and *Piece for Peace,*
which also gave her the opportunity to get back to her roots. All the art
coming from the *Hope Box* is collective.

154

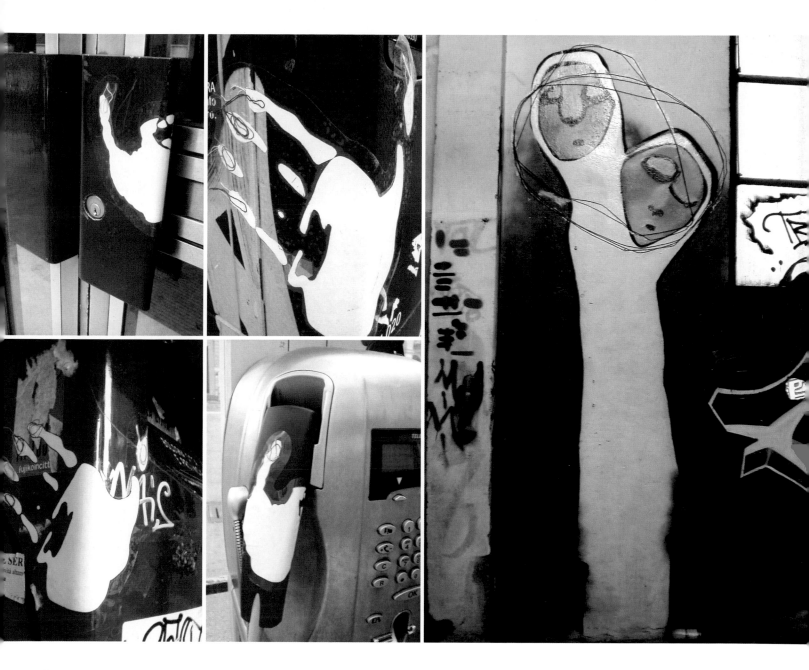

Fairy

Born in Turku, Finland, Fairy now lives in Bologna, Italy. She has been involved with art her whole life, and was painting on canvases until a few years ago, when some spray artists she was friends with encouraged her to try her hand at spray-painting. 'I immediately fell in love with the scene and started to paint more pieces, bomb and do stickers and stencils. I found a new, mind-blowing world, being able to leave a mark wherever and almost whenever I wanted, rather than just in my room, like before.'

Along with her spray-painted pieces she has tried out various techniques and has her own way of injecting some female content into her work: 'These days I'm really into wool, because I find it a bit warmer and more concrete than the usual graffiti materials. Traditionally wool is a material strongly associated with women, so it's cool to use it in this male-dominated scene – and up till now I think I'm the only one to use it.'

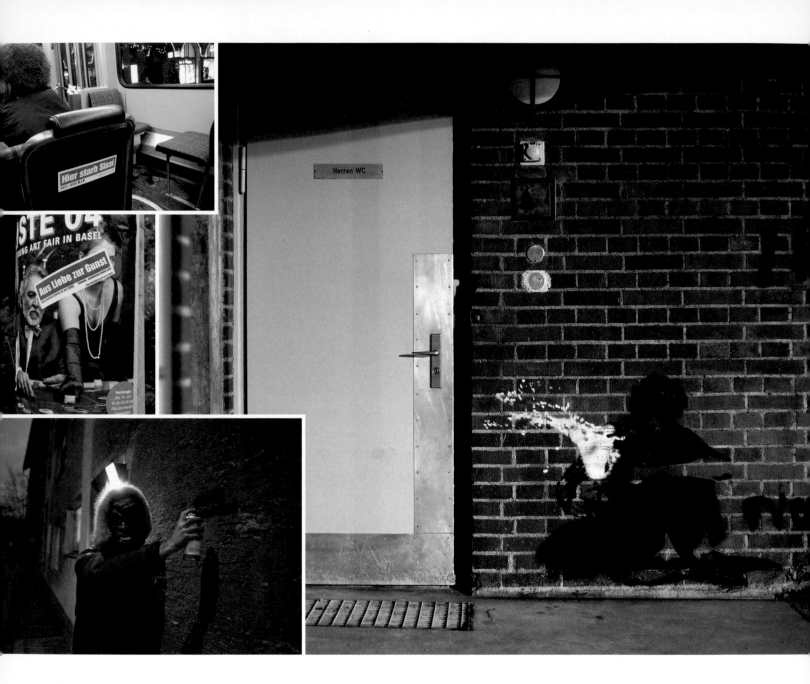

Friendly Vandalism

Friendly Vandalism was founded by two Swiss women in 2001. For their first project, *600 cars for sale,* they plastered 'For Sale' stickers on cars around their town in an attempt to encourage the owners to consider alternative means of transport. Other projects included a series of stickers with poetical, political and Dadaist messages, pasted in noticeable places for the ultimate impact.

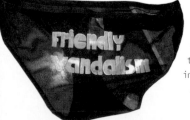

In 2004 one member went on to realize various enterprises of her own – such as the Tagman stickers, showing staged photos of a male spray artist with the words 'I love Tagman': 'People automatically assumed that whoever did the stickers must be the guy in the pictures. On the one hand I think the fact that I never even considered that Tagman could be a woman is sad and fucked up. On the other, representing myself has never been my main intention. I concluded that people probably don't give a fuck about the gender of a certain artist, so why should I?' In 2005 they were invited to take part in 'Unrest!', a forty-eight-hour-non-stop event in Zurich, Switzerland.

up your ass since 2001

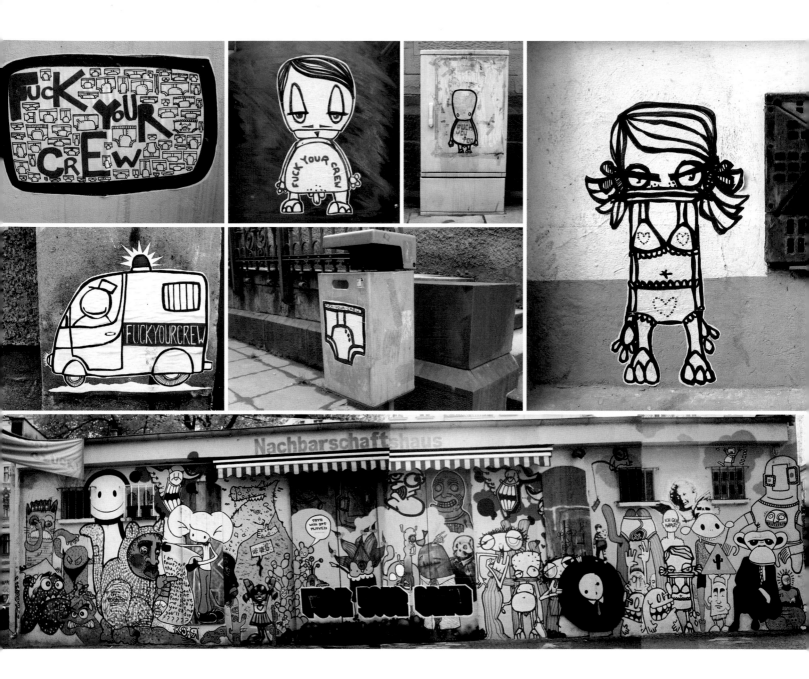

FUCK YOUR CREW

The female member of FUCK YOUR CREW, who shall remain anonymous, often includes underpants and individual figures in her pieces: 'I spent a lot of time sitting home alone trying to handle boredom, when self-adhesive foil came my way and became my new friend. One night a warm summer breeze lured us outdoors and that was when the first underpants hit the streets of Berlin. One year later two friends came along for another street game. I fell in love with paste and paper. FUCK YOUR CREW went out to play. Every now and then we go to the playground with other friends to have some fun....'

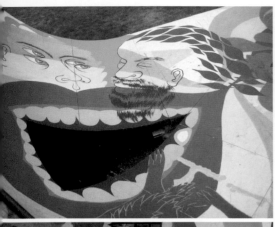

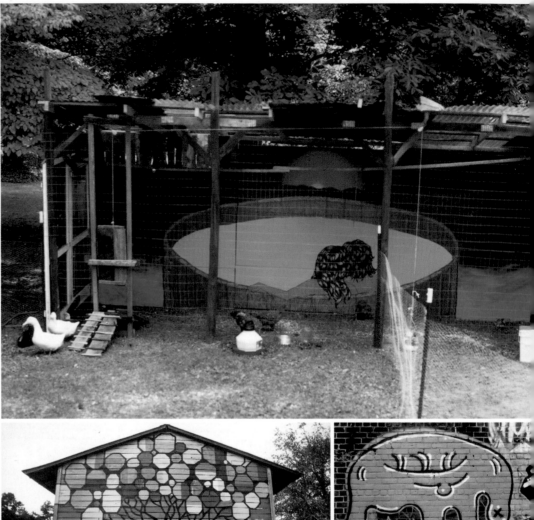

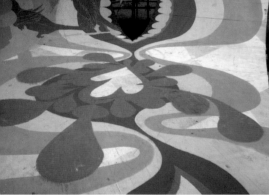

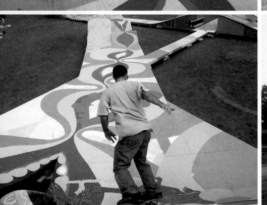

Maya Hayuk

New York-based Maya ('illusion' in Sanskrit) Hayuk was born in Baltimore and has lived in Toronto, Boston and San Francisco. Her work is varied and not restricted to the street, and her private and public projects draw on a spectrum of emotions.

She says: 'Hopefully I am giving gifts of joy and arousal, both erotic and liberating, in the work I show publicly. Oftentimes it is the response to songs, dreams, stories or jokes which put me in this meditative state. I use big brushes and rollers on walls with water-based paints. For smaller work, I have a favourite Japanese brush pen and a bag full of gouaches which I've been using on coffee-stained paper or small scraps of wood.'

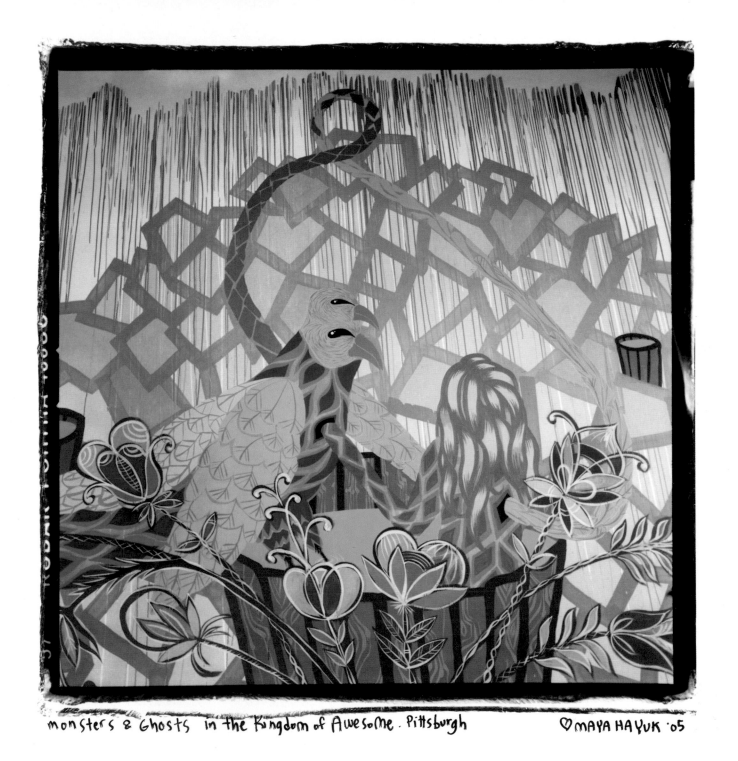

monsters & Ghosts in the Kingdom of Awesome. Pittsburgh   ♡MAYA HAYUK '05

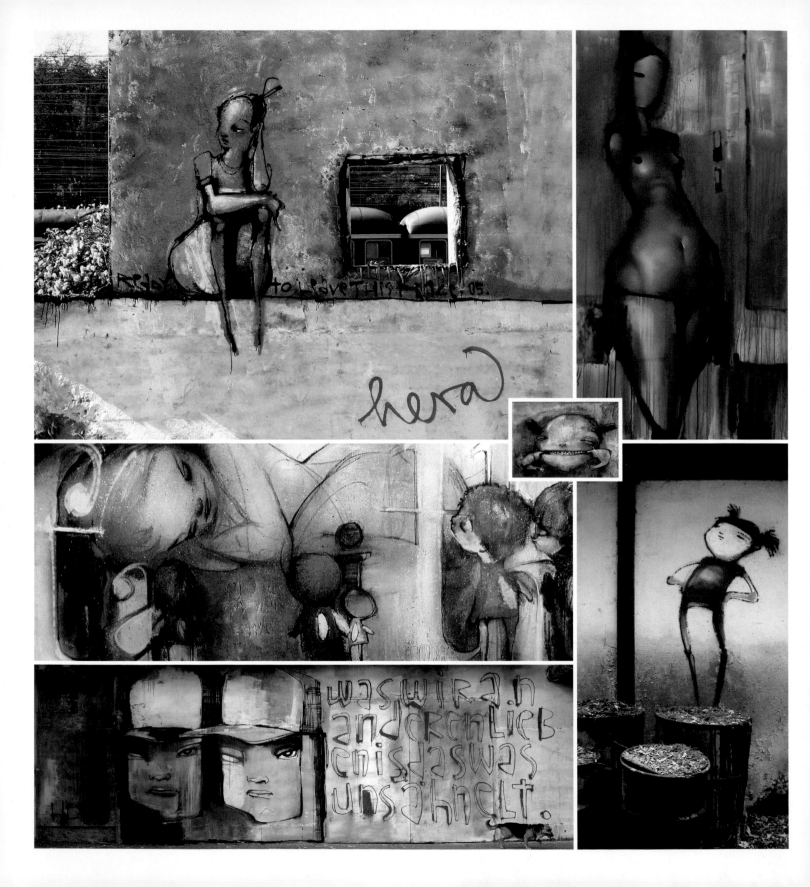

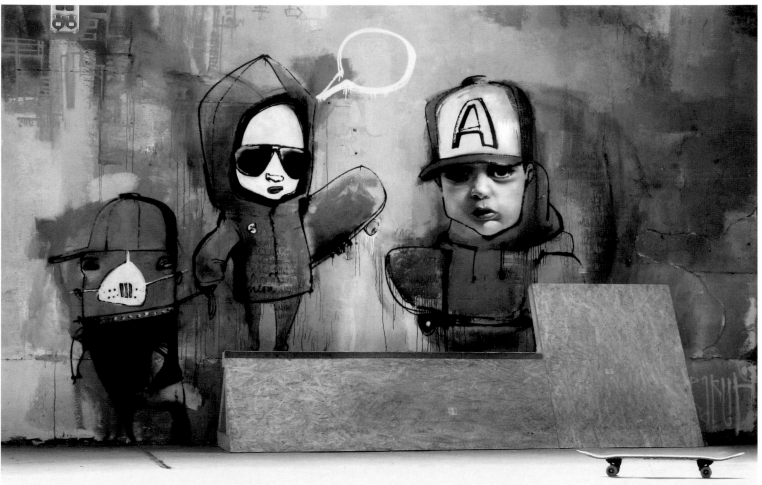

Hera

'I like Greek mythology because its gods have quite beautiful defects despite their divine status,' explains Hera. 'Hera, the highest-ranking goddess in Olympus, was taken for a ride by Zeus and then became jealous and violent – I can see something of myself in that too!'

When she was just thirteen, Hera drew letters in her diary, but she didn't do her first piece until seven years later – on the slaughterhouse premises in Wiesbaden.

'I knew enough female characters, painted by men, which were meant to look sexy…a truly monotonous world of images. In my pieces I show the other side of being a woman. So sometimes they really are sexy, but most of the time they are just beautiful mummies pushing their shopping trolleys, with small breasts and chunky thighs. That's important 'cause one day a little skaterboy asked me why in the world I had painted a pregnant woman and told me in all seriousness that there was nothing more disgusting than pregnancy!'

161

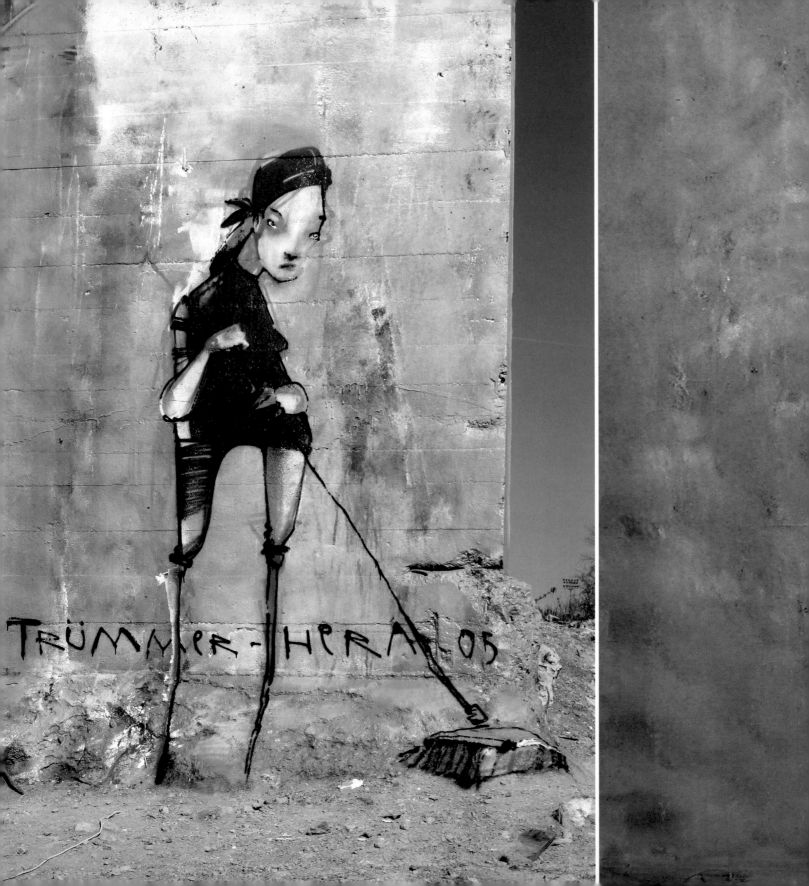

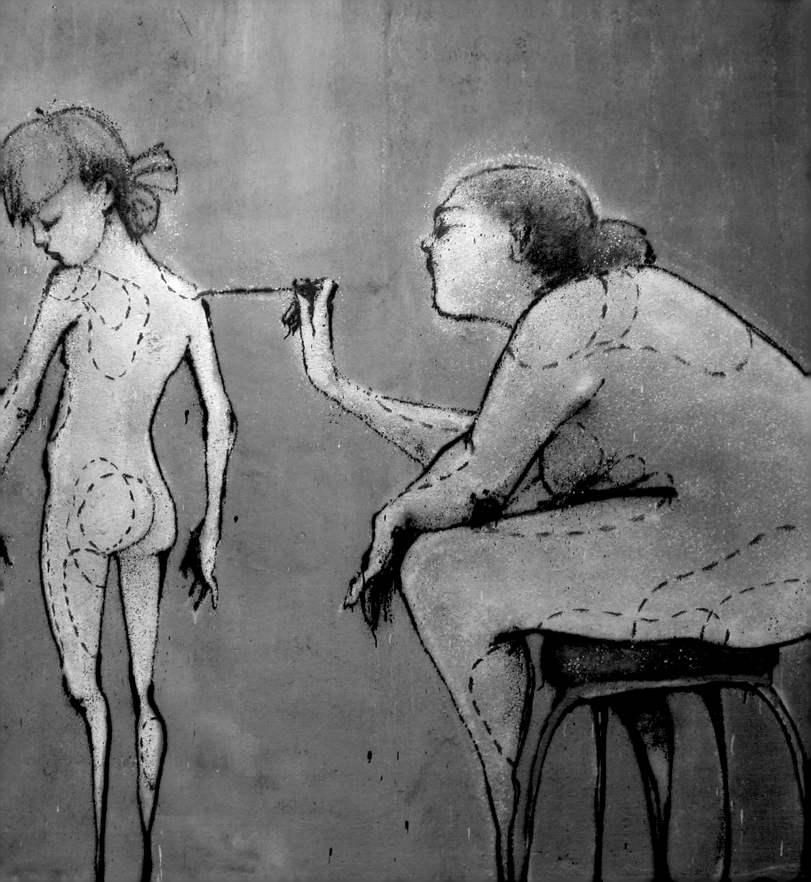

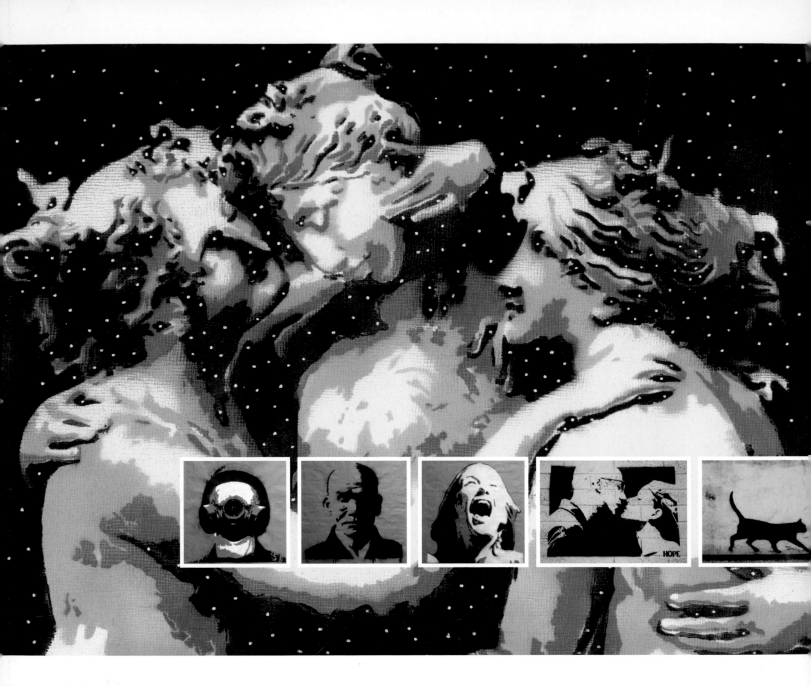

Hope

Hope comes from Montreal and got into stencil graffiti in the late 1990s through a friend. In her pieces she aims to represent themes that give her hope.

'I love painting alone in train yards late at night,' she explains, 'in dark alleys and remote places. I like the quiet, the peace of those empty spaces. There's something meditative about it, and it helps to keep me somewhat sane. I've been painting on canvas more and more, but I don't consider that graffiti – it's just semantics, really. Even if I've painted a certain stencil all over the city, when I put it on a canvas, I no longer call it graffiti. It's not worse or better, just something different.'

164

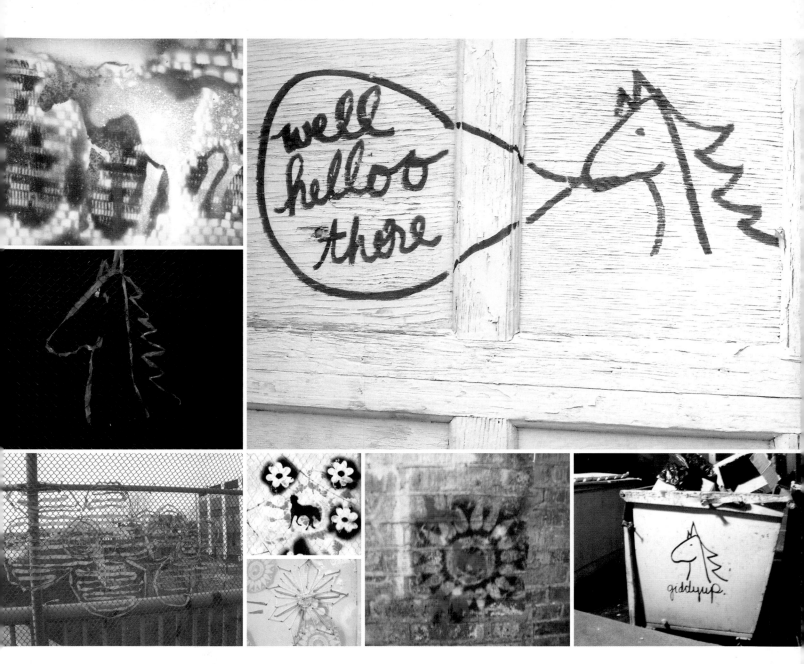

Horsie

Born in 1964 in Pittsburgh, Horsie lived in Germany for a few years but has since returned to her native city. She got into street art in 2003 after spending too long on her own in her studio and becoming bored of the whole gallery scene. She uses long, colourful materials and ropes, which she works into fences, or tries out new techniques.

'I want to express my experience and hopefully communicate with other people. With my street art I also want to work on my relationship with my city and the spaces in it. Get intimate with it…. What occurs to me right now is how the Situationists talked about "spontaneous acts of authenticity" as a way to create a new society, of HUMAN BEINGS, not a bunch of zombies bogged down by the drudgery of life, mired in meaningless obligations. In other words, trying to bust out and do something joyous and meaningful and free.'

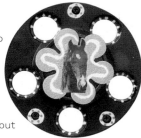

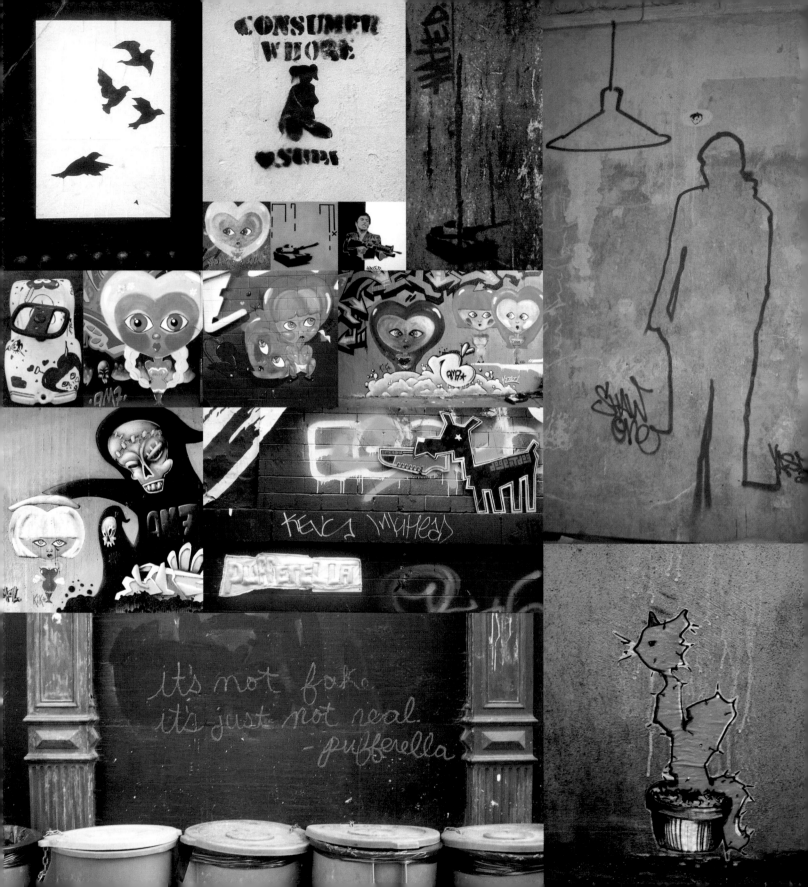

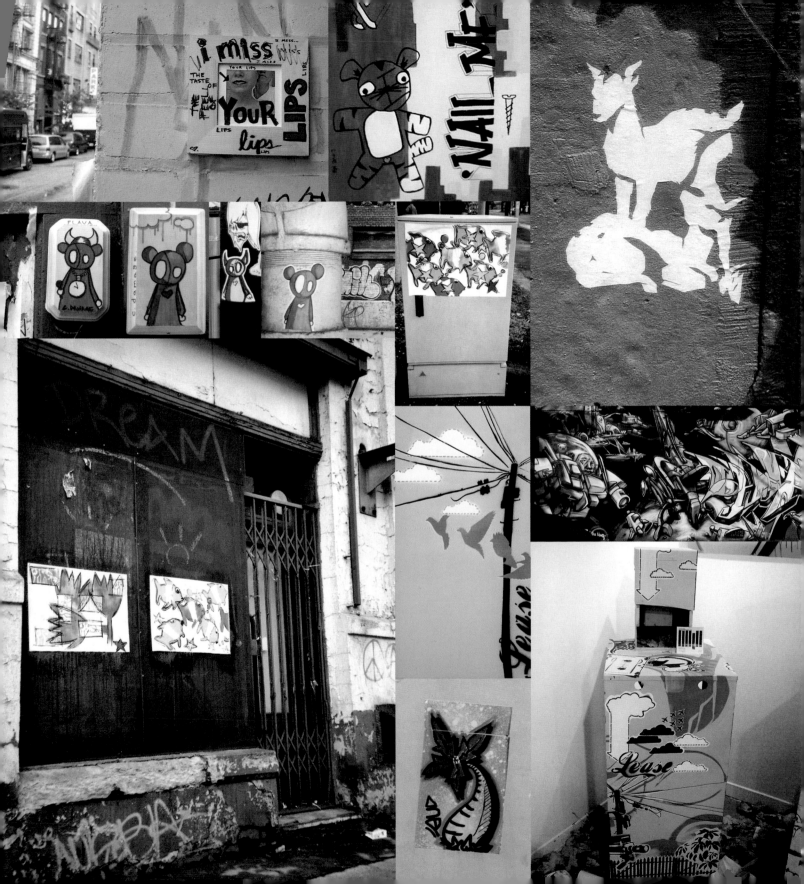

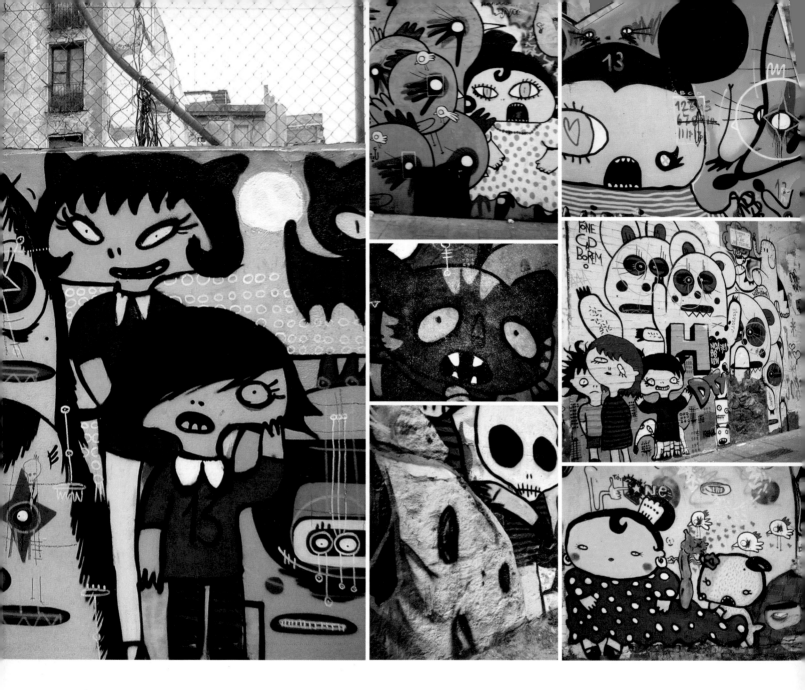

Irena

Irena is a Spanish street artist and was born in Girona. When she moved to Barcelona in 2002, she was impressed by the street art all over the city and immediately started to do creative works of her own.

'With my art I don't want to express anything concrete,' she says, 'but I think art explains all the unexplained things. I like to be aggressive with my work, 'cause in your normal life you must be patient with a lot of things and art is a way to freedom and truth.'

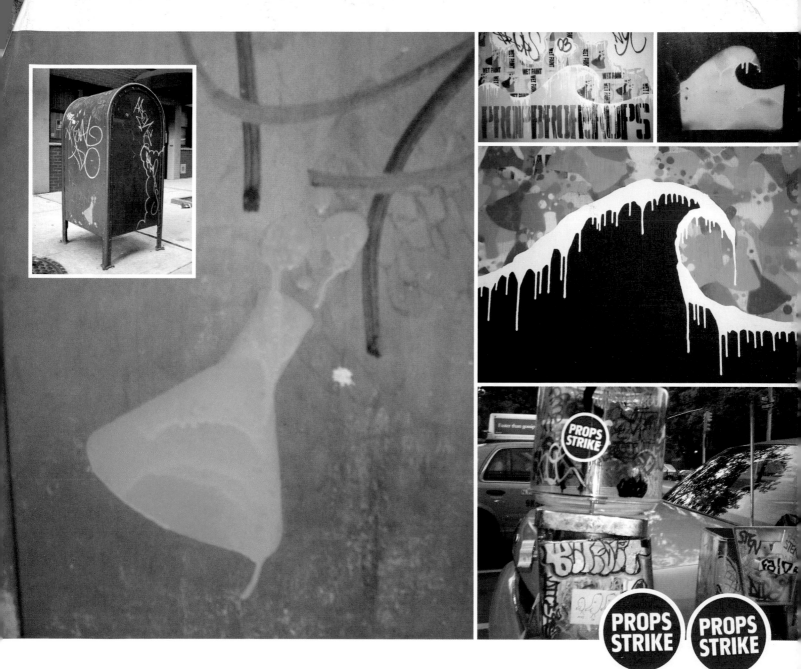

Jen Props

Jen Props grew up in Long Island. She got her first impression of graffiti and street art when she went to New York with her parents and saw Keith Haring's mural *Crack is Wack*. Later she came across the work of Jean-Michel Basquiat, which really inspired her. She started off stencilling everywhere, particularly on the old New York fire alarms.

'I like the fact that I can control the perception of self by blurring the lines of imagery via colour and texture, while evoking emotion...too much is judged on appearance alone. I strive to awaken the senses and destroy the gender assumptions of "female art", to just have "great art".'

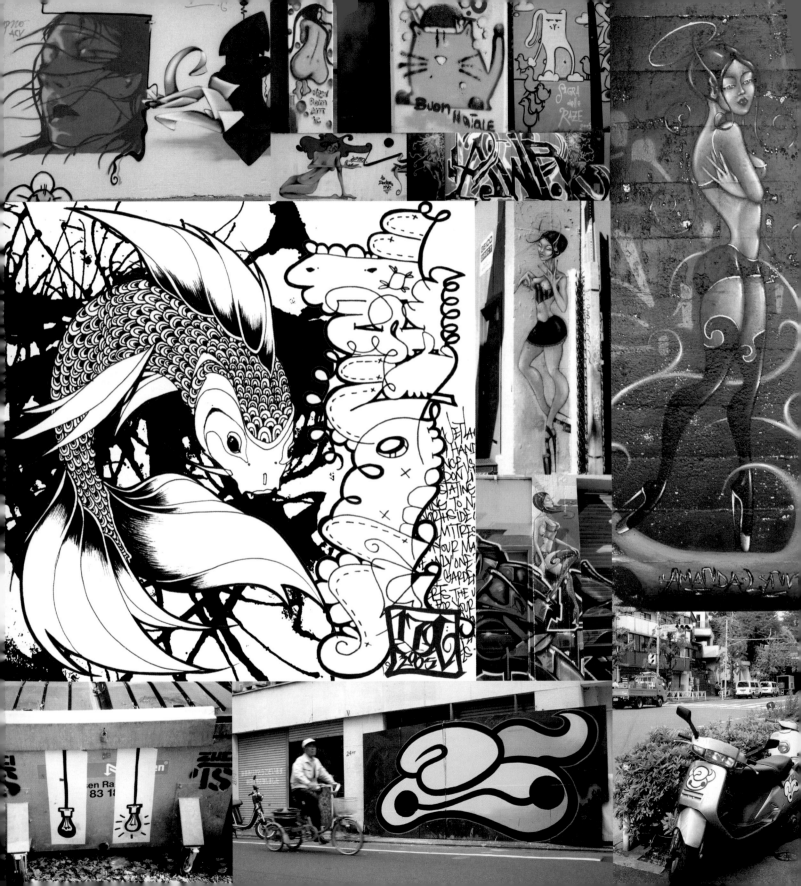

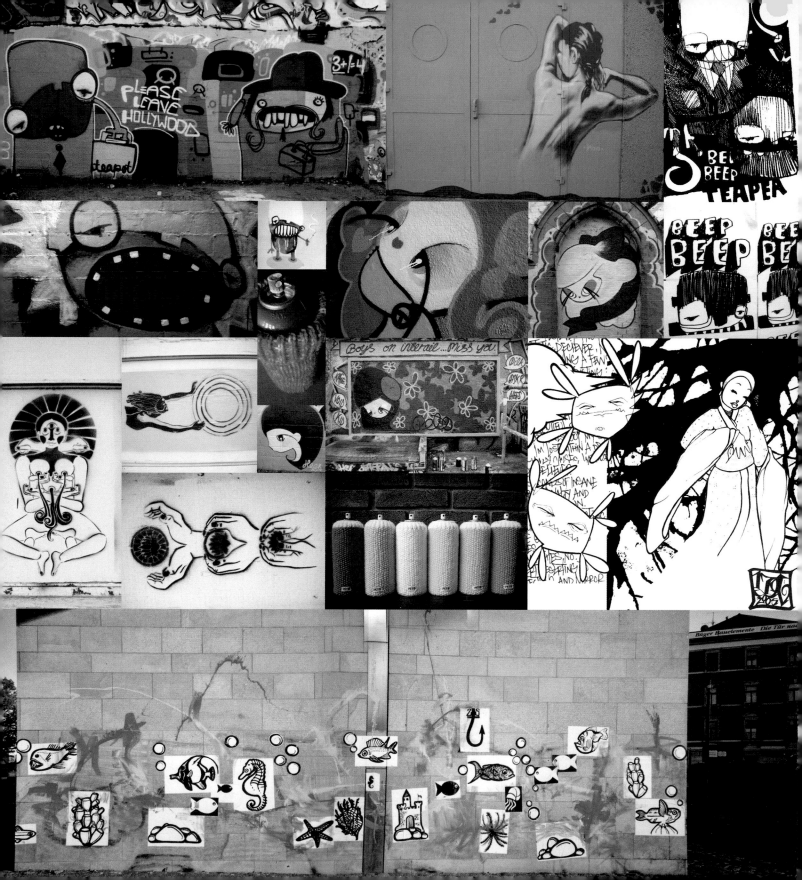

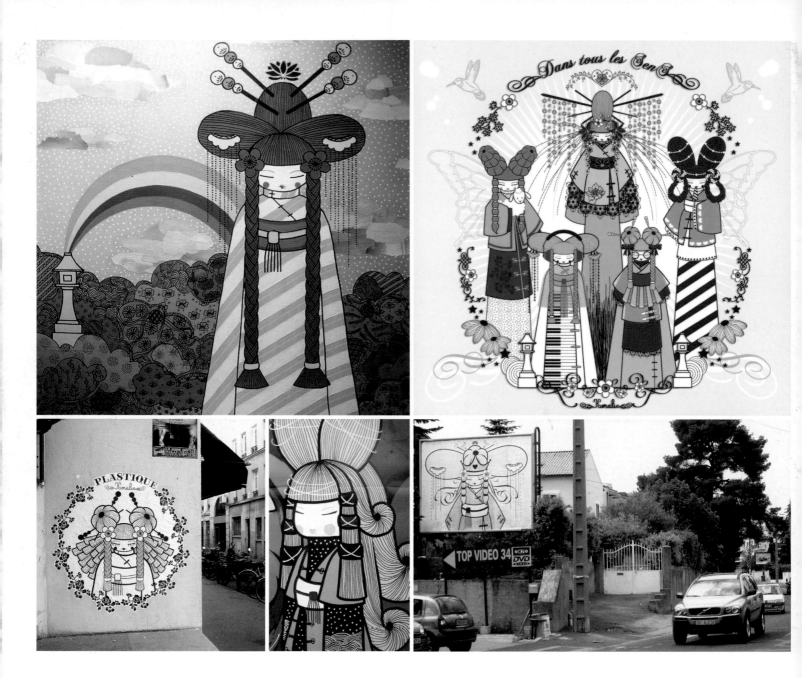

Koralie

French-born Koralie, from Montpellier, used to focus on painting canvases but was motivated to broaden her artistic arena by Fafi and Lus. Like them, she mostly uses a brush and acrylic paint with a little spray-paint on her pieces, paints posters by hand or uses graphic design techniques. She also runs a shop, Plastique Graffiktee, with her friend SupaKitch, and travels around the world.

'I try to please myself, to put in colours that are in my head and my heart,' she explains. 'It's a quest for aestheticism in the juxtaposition of traditional and contemporary Japan, but most of all it's about painting in the street.'

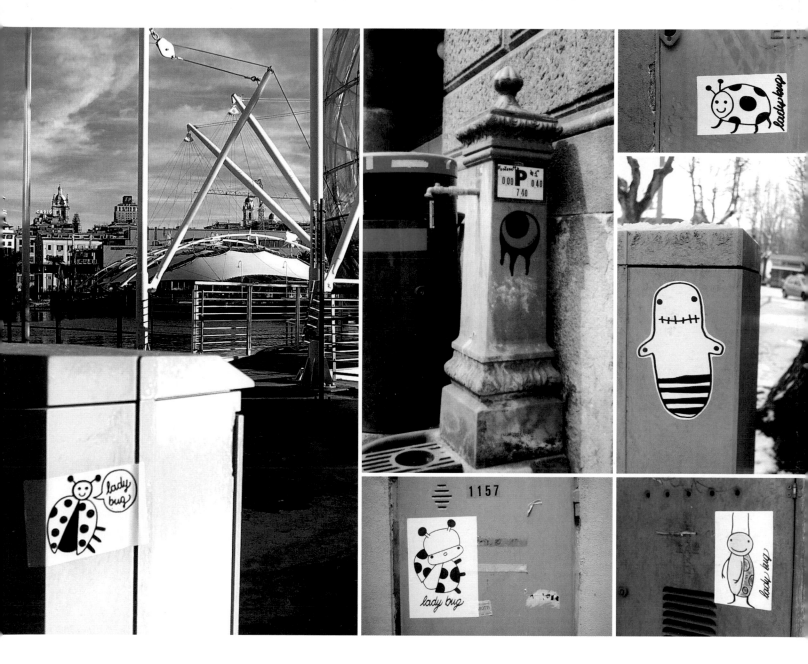

Lady Bug

Italy's Lady Bug started off spray-painting with the tag Bee but switched to her present name after working on a project with 108, taking her inspiration from a similar game to Pac-Man. Through her stickers of insects and beetles, executed with marker pens, acrylic paint or crayons, she'd like to bring some life to the grey monotony of towns.

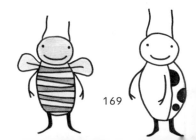

169

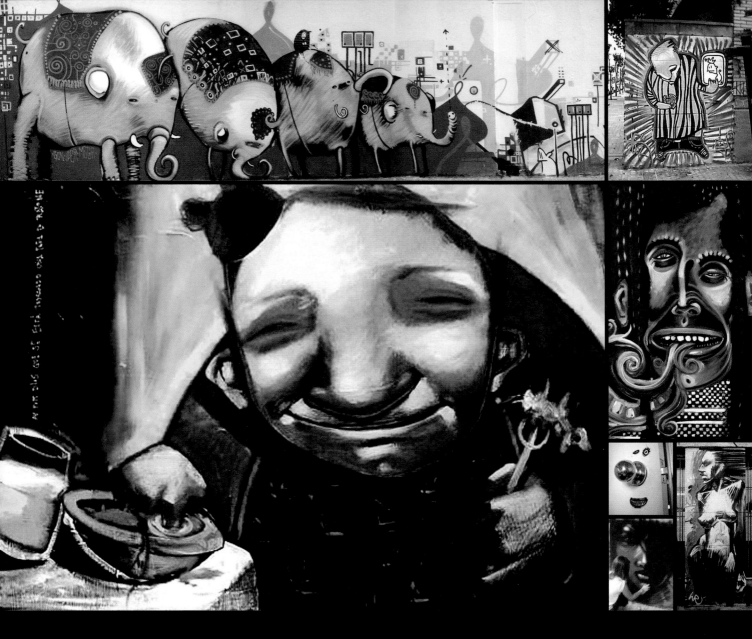

Lahe

Lahe, from Seville, used to paint on canvas. She was fascinated by the huge, spray-painted pieces around the city but didn't have anyone to go out spray-painting with — until she met Fafa, while she was studying art. In 2001 Lahe did her first pieces. Initially she used the tag Heldt but changed it because it's difficult to pronounce in Spanish.

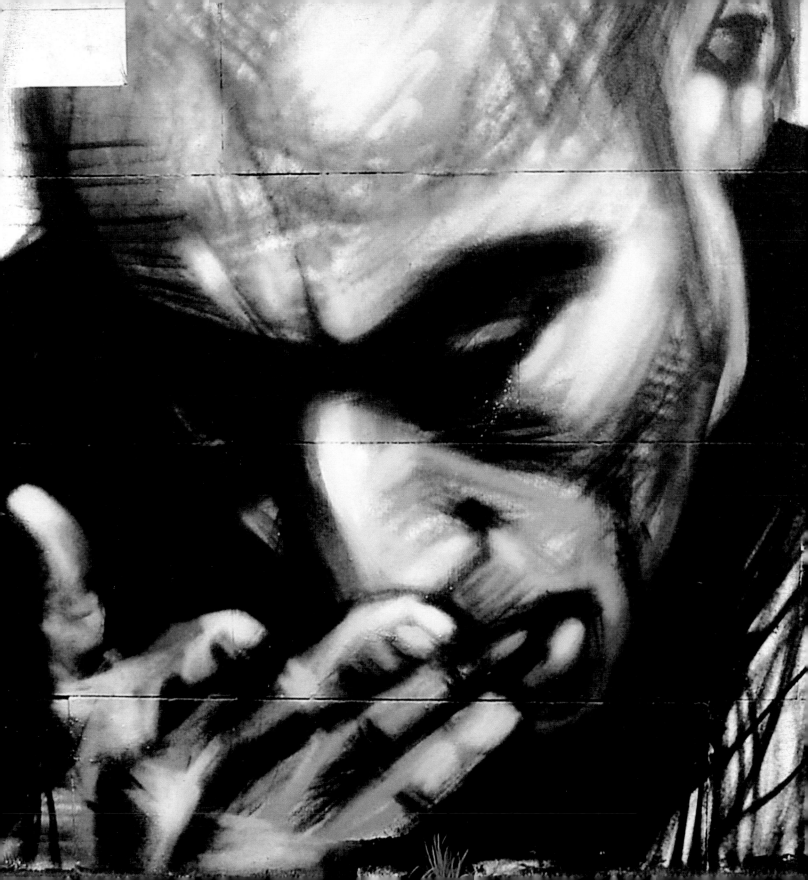

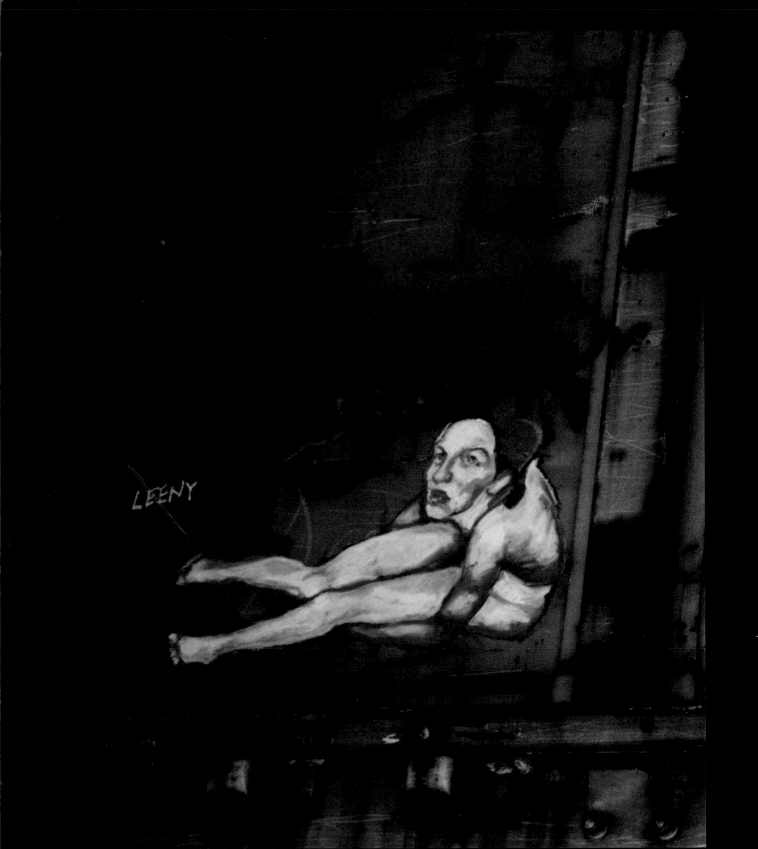

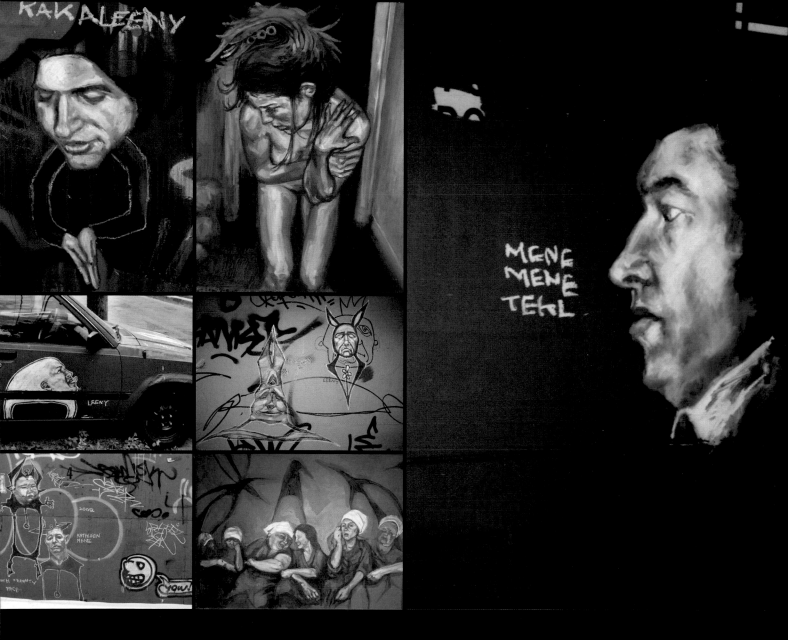

Leeny

Montreal's Leeny has been drawing and painting since she was little and says she likes to portray 'humans, animals, spirits, our relationship to nature and to the past, personalities, archetypes, primitiveness, imagination, icons and artefacts'. 'I only really got into graffiti when I started using oilbars,' she explains. 'I found they enabled me to paint the way I like – a cross between painting and drawing. I'd rather work within a space than try to dominate it, so they suit my purposes very well.'

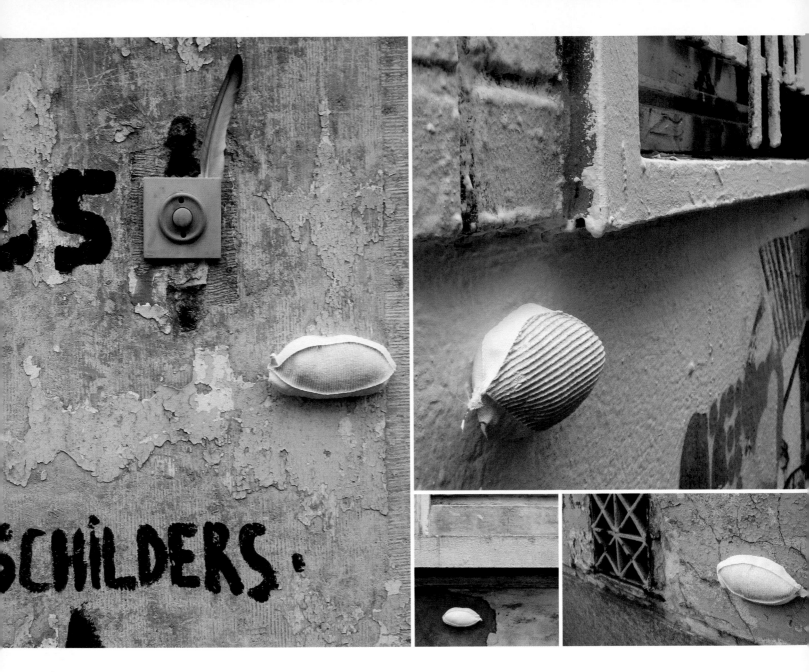

Louise

Louise and Eugene are a couple from Antwerp who got into street art in 2003 after the extreme right (Vlaams Blok) got into power in Belgium. Using posters and stencils to get their message across, they wanted to make people aware of the considerable harm they believe has been inflicted by the voting public through this result.

'I started experimenting with textiles during my final year at the Sint-Lucas College of Arts in Antwerp,' says Louise. 'I studied ceramics and spent my last year doing research, both on material and on shape. I wanted to find a way to create shapes in a very personal, yet playful and spontaneous way. That's how I started knitting stuff and made plaster models of it.

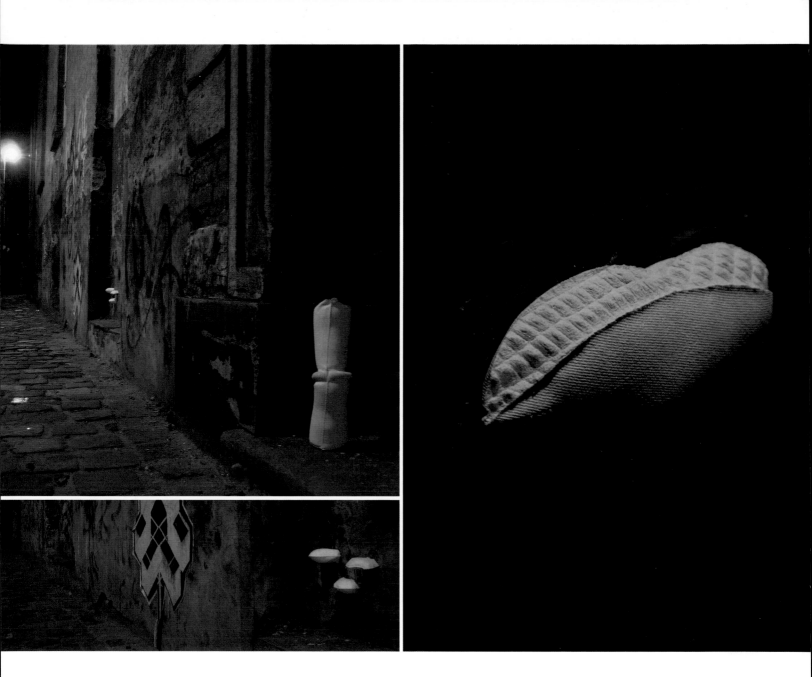

'When Eugene and I came into contact with street art, I suddenly realized that street art doesn't always have to be two-dimensional. And the little Louise creatures found their way to the streets.... My world is filled with naivety, in a lonely kind of way. My little creatures play hide and seek, but mostly end up never being found. My only goal is to offer a short, intimate moment to the happy few who notice a little Louise creature in the hustle of the city.'

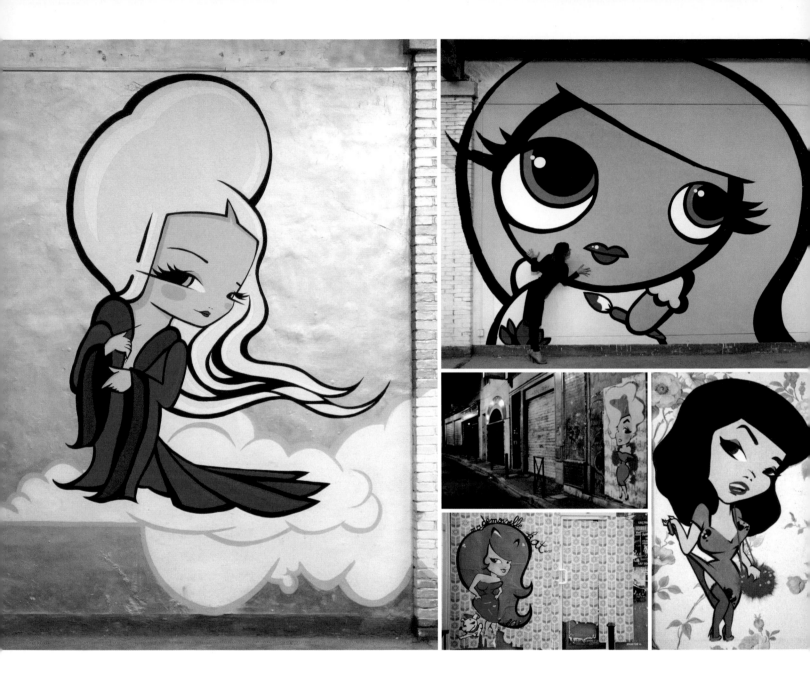

Mademoiselle Kat

Mademoiselle Kat started out in the early 1990s, at around the same time as Miss Van and Fafi, and was one of Toulouse's first female spray artists. She works on her pieces with a brush and acrylic paint, but also makes posters. 'The major theme running through my work is female identity, or more precisely my own feminine identity,' she says. 'All over the world different women have images of themselves, which have prompted me to find my own image, my own feminine identity. I like to use poetry to show my femininity, my humour, my brittleness.'

Mademoiselle Kat's characters look like they come from comics and cartoons but she uses real-life 'superwomen' such as Marilyn Monroe, Bettie Page or Debbie Harry as inspiration to express women's different facets. Following a trip to China, Asian femininity has become a focal point of her art, affording her 'a very sweet view of humanity', she says. 'I put my characters on stage on the city walls, like a composition on a canvas. Even my art can be subjective. I want it to be popular and understood by everyone, and I want to give off positive vibes and show freedom of expression.'

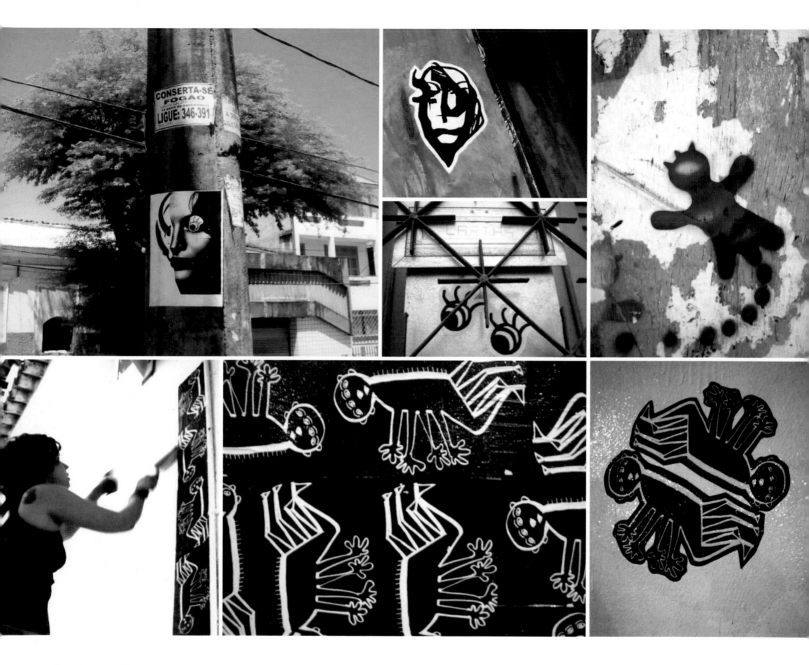

Andrea May

'I found street art through the Internet and research,' says Andrea May, 'and by keeping in touch with some urban artists from other states who encouraged me to start. I did some stickers and posters and glued them on my street. Afterwards I applied for an exhibition and was selected. It encouraged me to start doing my own projects.'

Andrea May comes from Salvador, Brazil, and started her street art in the early 2000s. She works mainly with paper but is also into graphic design. She experiments a lot, using different themes and techniques to reflect her feelings and view of the world.

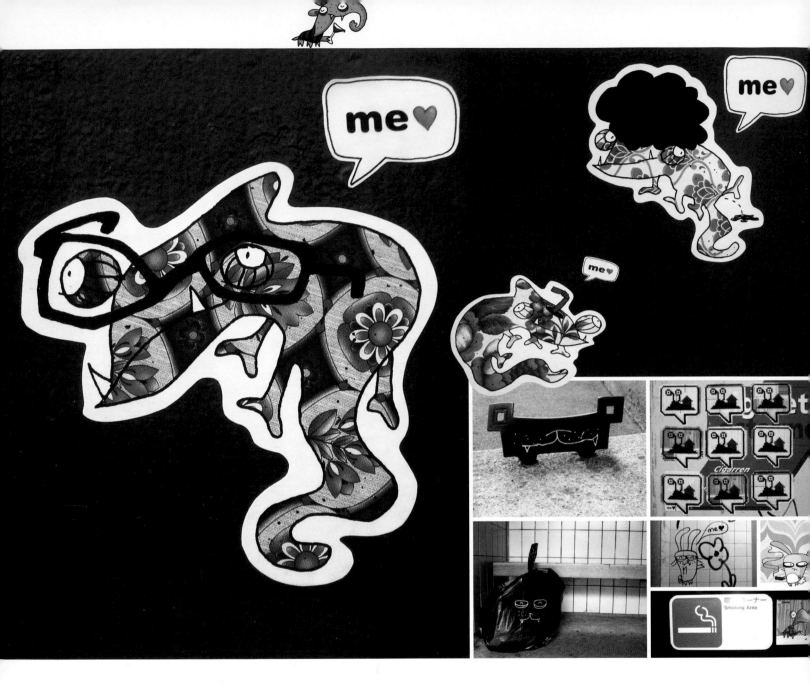

me love

Munich-based me love hopes to convey her passion for life through her images. 'I always take my sketchbook everywhere, so that I can capture the things and situations around me,' she says. 'Then I either scan it and colour it in on the computer straight away, or copy it and colour it by hand – in which case it's scanned once more, collaged on the computer and printed out. I'd prefer to draw all my stickers completely by hand if I had the time…it makes them more personal, something special and unique. I like variety, originality, spontaneity, hand-drawn work and collaborations. I want to broaden my horizons, beautify, make my art accessible, not plaster the same logo over and over again.'

Melina

New Yorker Melina has been active since 2001 and is known for her creative and political art, including her 'Freedom of Expression' posters and her 'Bikini Lady' tag, which targets the American obsession with beauty. 'The female characters in the advertising culture are from a male perspective,' she says. 'I want to make female characters from my feminine point of view.'

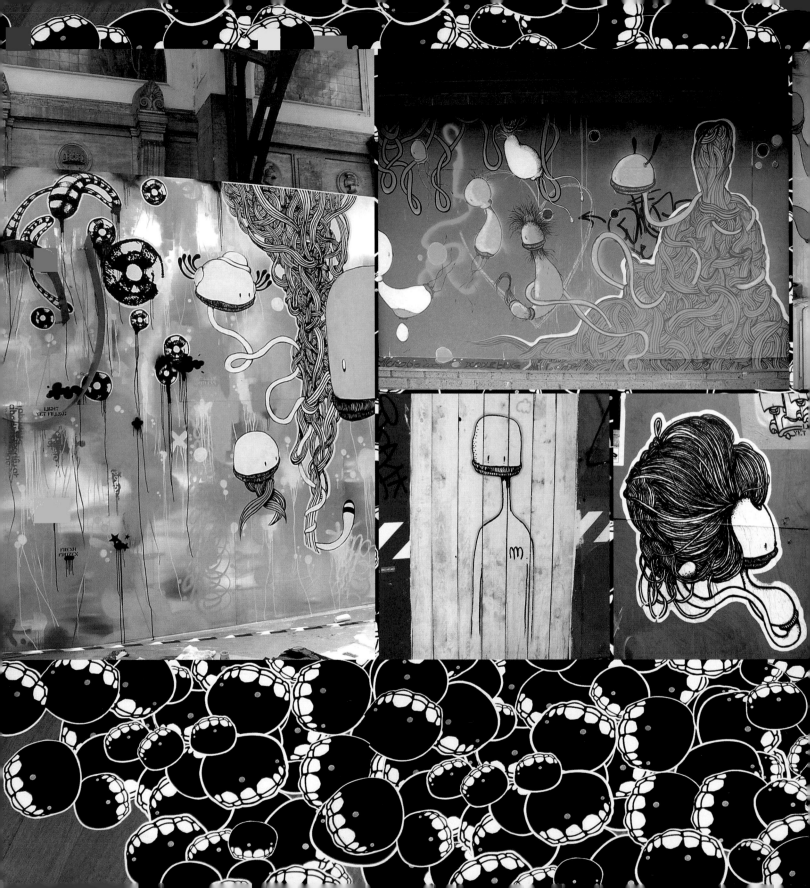

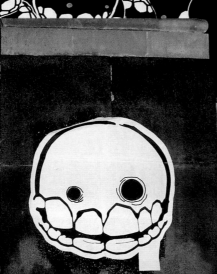

Microbo

Microbo is part of the modern street art movement and, together with her husband Bo130, is very active not only in Milan but also worldwide. She generally works with microbe-like figures that have come from her own personal cosmos, as she herself explains: 'By definition, microbes are invisible without the aid of a microscope, and a microbe is any living organism that spends its life at a size too tiny to be seen with the naked eye. Most of the diversity of life on earth is represented by microbes. Every time you walk on the ground you step on billions of microbes. It is estimated that we know fewer than 1% of the microbial species on earth. Microbes are the tiniest creatures on earth. Yet despite their small size, they have a huge impact on us and on our environment. Many years of evolution have created a stunning diversity of microbes. Understanding the richness of this awesome and mind-blowing microbial world puts our lives into perspective and gives us new respect for other beings. Don't do to others what you don't want done to you...peace, love, share and evolve.'

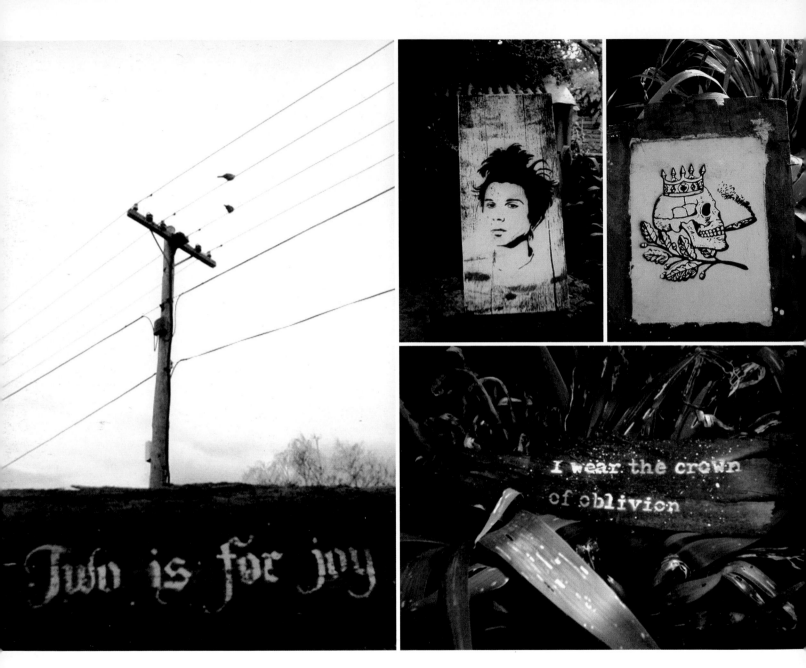

Misako

'I'm part Japanese, and my heritage means a lot to me so
I chose to use the name "Misako", after my grandmother,'
says stencil artist Misako. 'I love working with a Japanese
name.' She likes to stencil colourful portraits of friends
and musicians and plain lettering, and she also launched
Overspray Magazine with other spray artists.

182

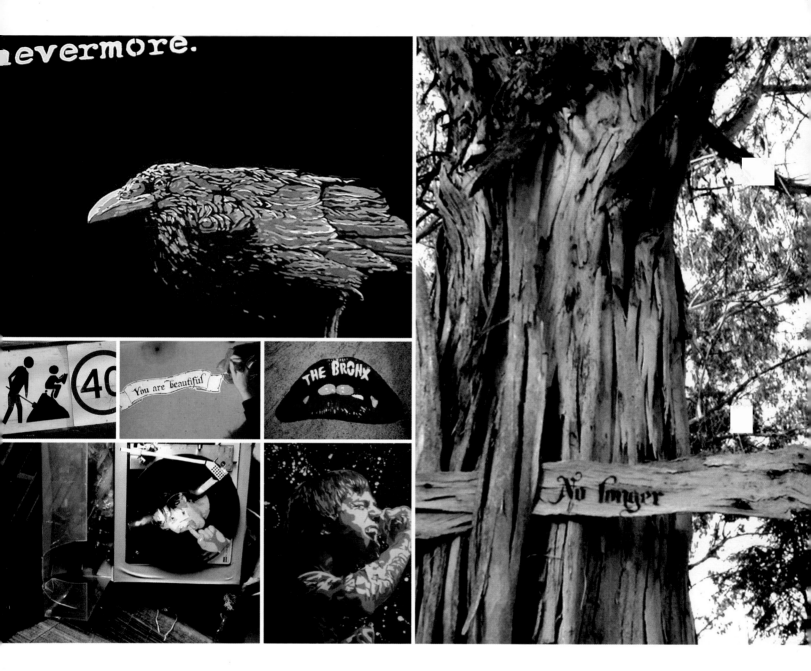

'I want to express beauty,' she explains. 'When I put my work up on the streets, I usually choose a run-down, sad-looking area to paint around, so I can brighten it up and feel that I have made a difference. I want as many people as possible to see my work, and I want it to affect them, and put a smile on their face, or make them wonder about the piece of work. I love it all.

'Get out there with your art and paint. Let everyone see your work, and have a go at seeing how easy it is to brighten up an area with your own artwork or a collaboration with other artists. There is a lot of competition out there among street artists, so it's important to be passionate about what you do. Stay strong and you'll get far, I promise.'

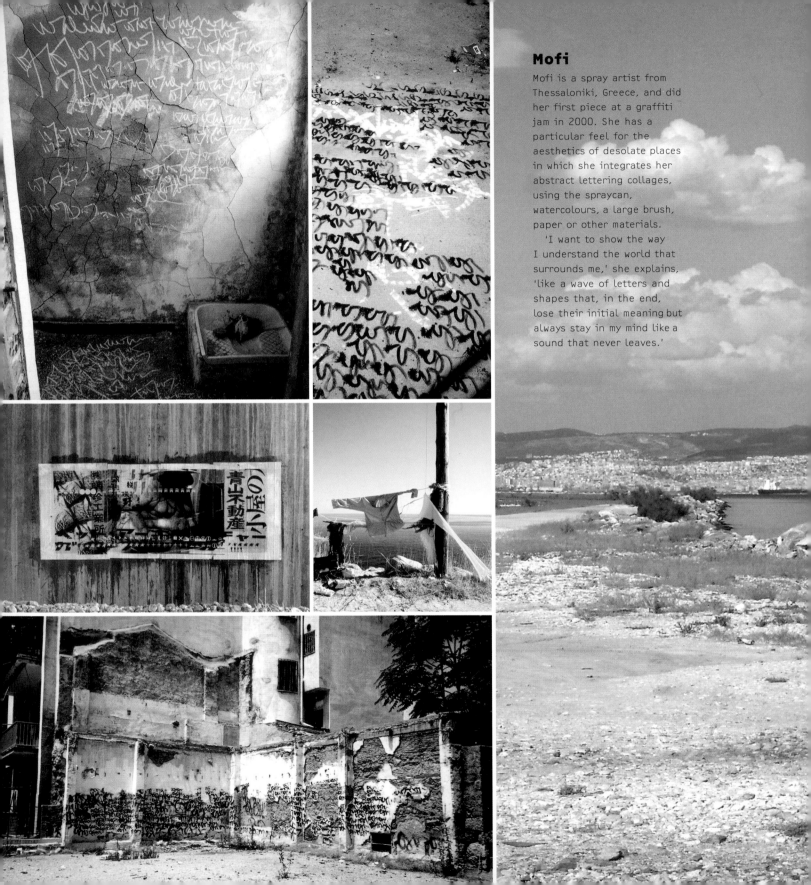

Mofi

Mofi is a spray artist from Thessaloniki, Greece, and did her first piece at a graffiti jam in 2000. She has a particular feel for the aesthetics of desolate places in which she integrates her abstract lettering collages, using the spraycan, watercolours, a large brush, paper or other materials.

'I want to show the way I understand the world that surrounds me,' she explains, 'like a wave of letters and shapes that, in the end, lose their initial meaning but always stay in my mind like a sound that never leaves.'

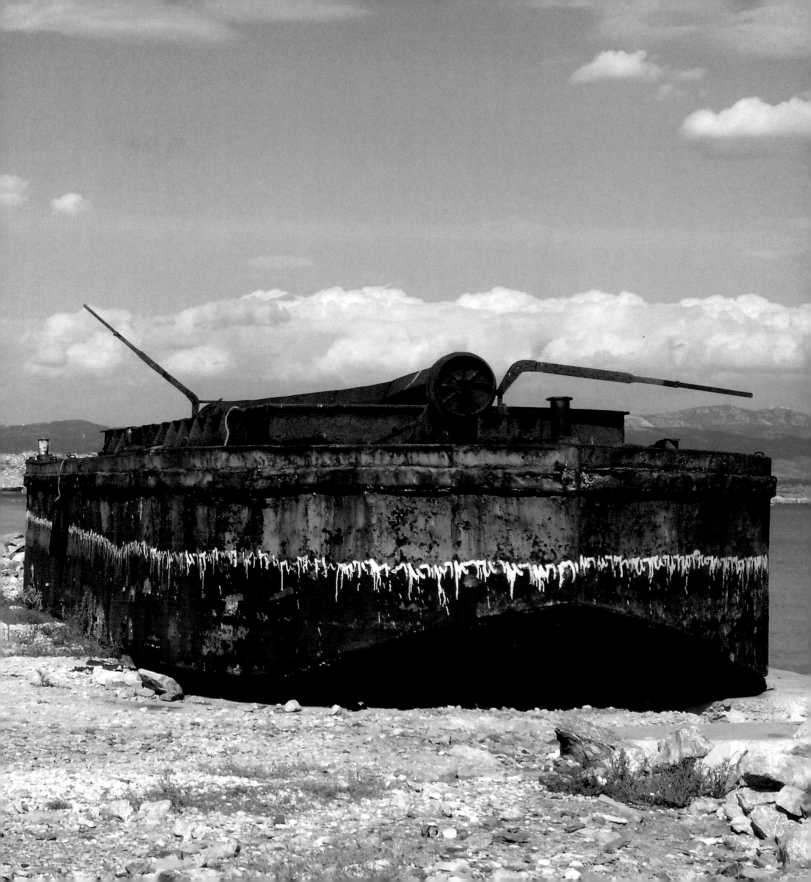

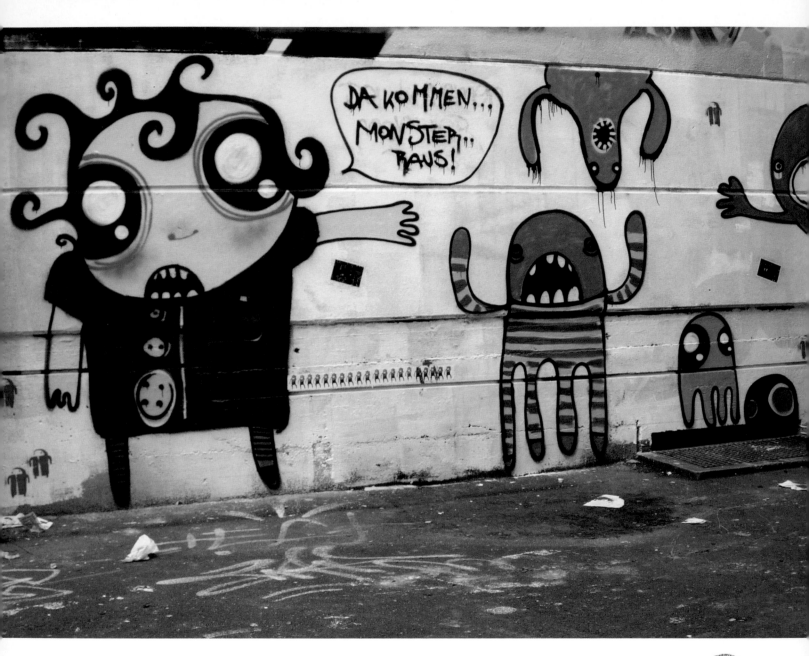

mymonsters

186

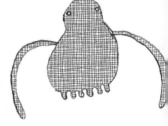

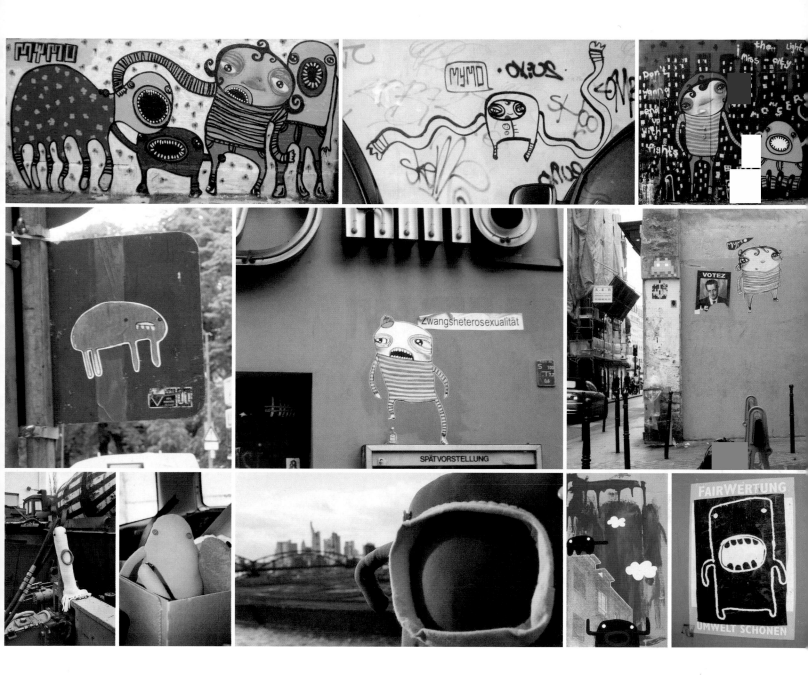

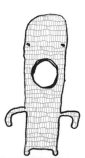

The woman behind MyMonsters was already painting potato men at the tender age of three. She didn't turn to the spraycan and the wider world of graffiti until she was fourteen, but they have dominated her life ever since. Her monsters pop up in all sorts of shapes and sizes, and she uses a whole range of techniques, although she tends to focus on cardboard or cloth.

'MyMonsters stand for themselves,' she says. 'They have feelings. They are friendly, happy, sad, bizarre, absurd, funny, ill, likeable, and have a good sense of humour.'

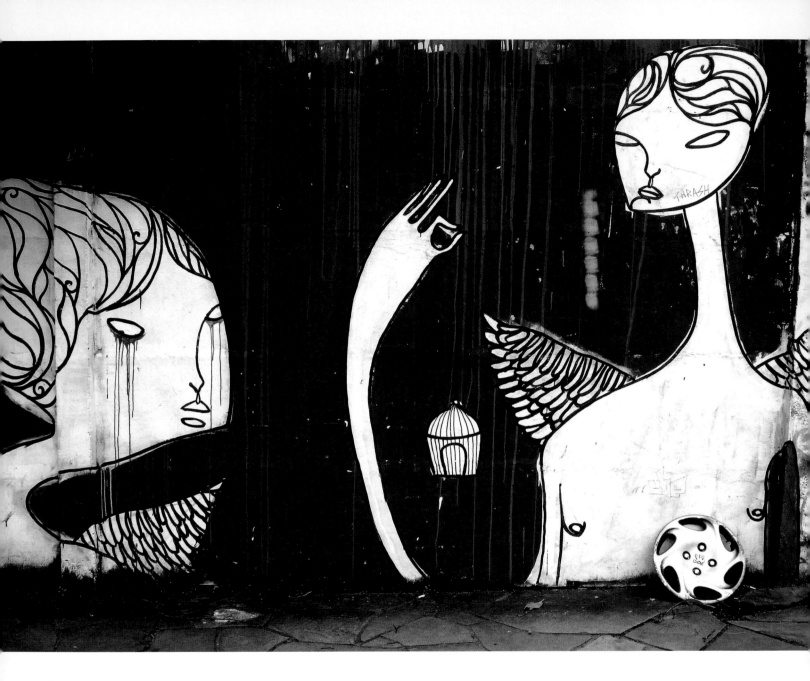

Nina M.

Graffiti has spread from Brazil's metropolises to towns such as Porto Alegre, Rio Grande do Sul, where Nina M. grew up. 'My drawings contain worlds and imaginary beings that I have created especially to inhabit the city,' she says. 'I love doing pictures. My beings are very particular. I think this has something to do with the way I see humans. The duality of the Nadine sisters, the Siamese sisters, the anthropophagous love and visceral desire of the cannibals, the melancholy of the Cry-Blood women, the mystery and symbolism in magic, or the wings all of us want to have. These are all elements with which I compose a symbolic picture of our existence and feelings. These characters cause strangeness, maybe scare us or even make us laugh. I think this is very close to our freaky, chaotic and sentimental nature.'

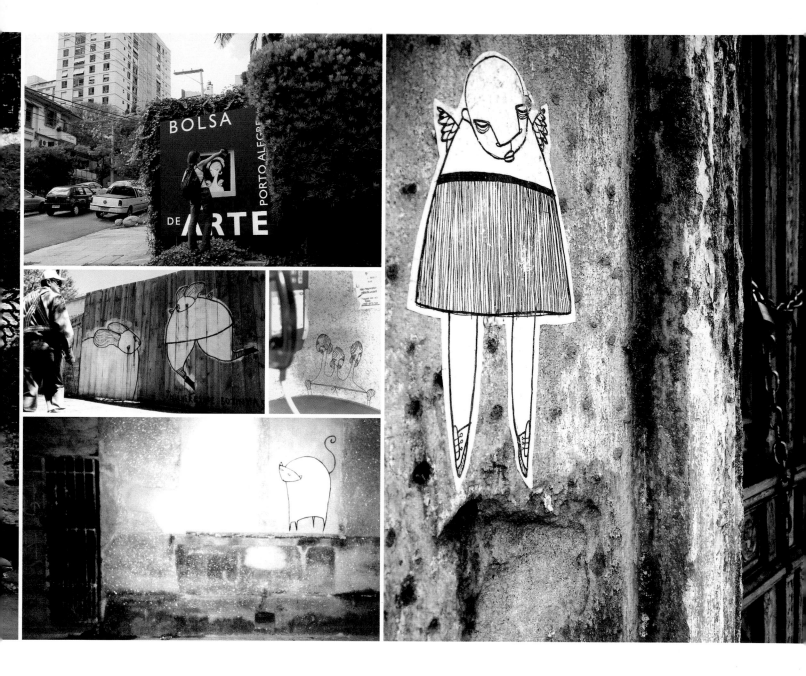

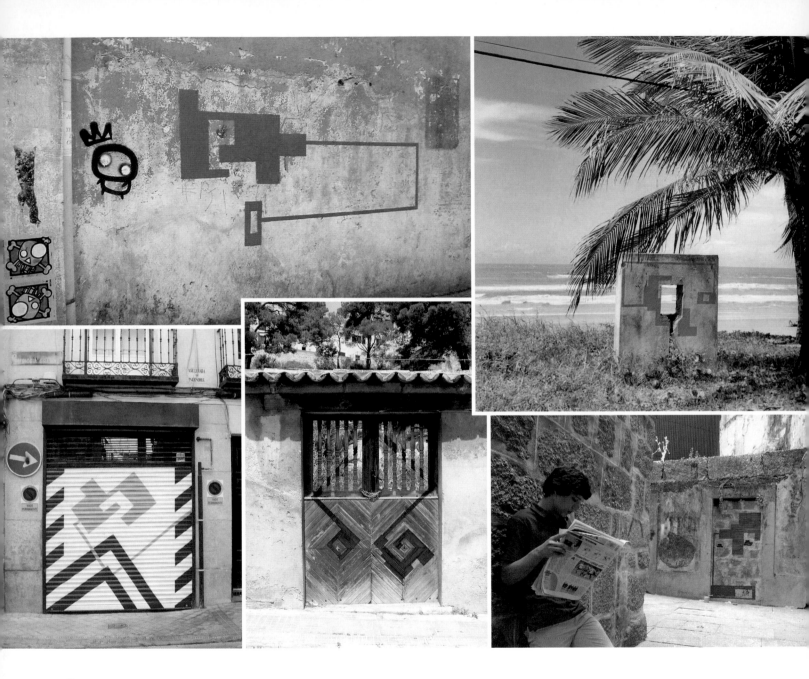

Nuria

Nuria goes out with El Tono and, when it comes to abstract forms, these two are unbeatable. Nuria achieves her free interpretation of a key using a brush, with which she integrates her art into the urban architecture and structure of façades and surfaces. Rather than seeing herself as a graffiti artist, Nuria prefers to look at the universal meaning behind her work, which is generally illegal.

'I never got into loads of trouble,' she explains, 'maybe because I am a girl and I try to explain what I am doing and also flutter my eyelashes as if to say "What do you mean?" This is not vandalism, it's art!'

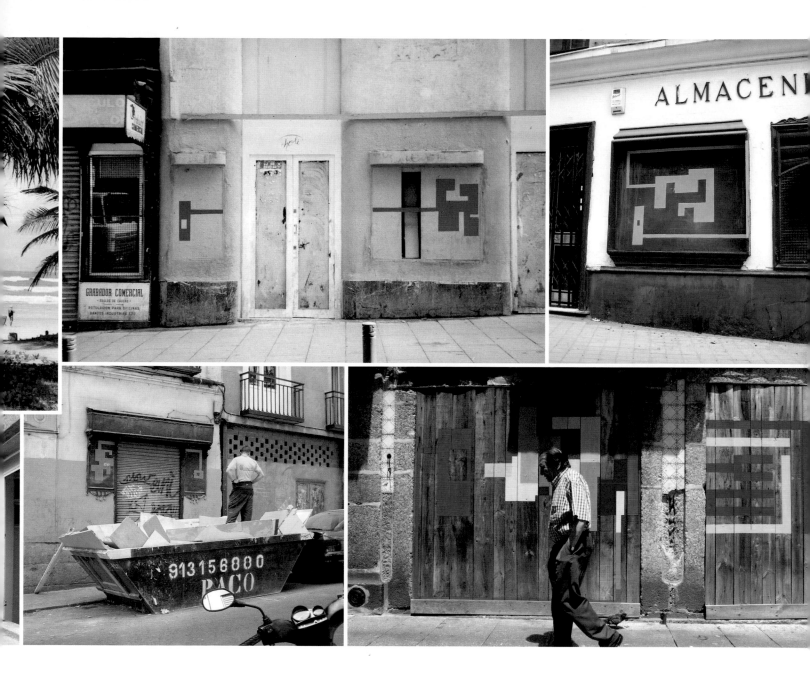

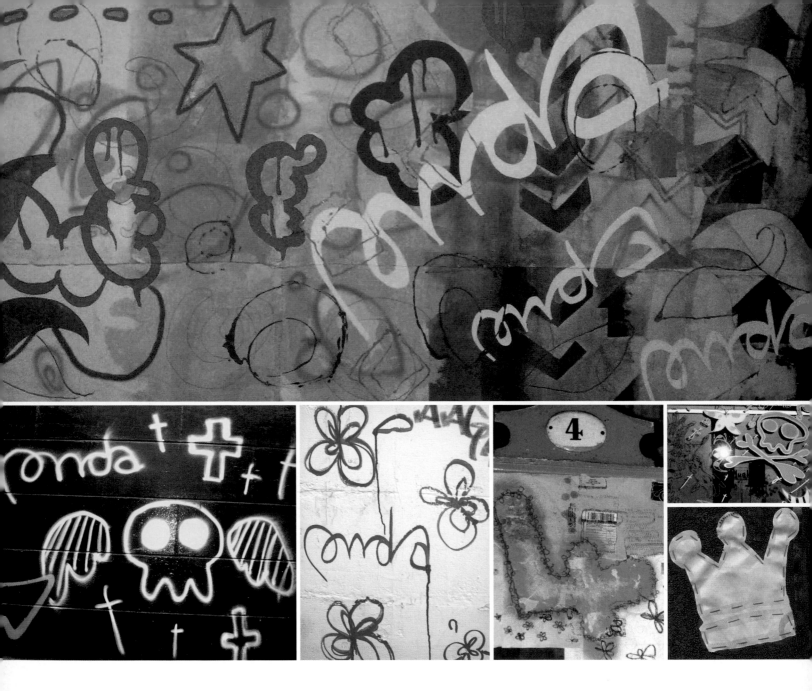

Panda

Panda comes from Guiseley, near Leeds, but now lives in Manchester. She was always fascinated by graffiti but didn't venture into the scene until 2002.

'I definitely work better with fabric,' she says. 'I love screen-printing and really enjoyed creating graffiti-inspired prints. I also used industrial machines to add big chunky stitches. I've tried using spray, which is a lot harder to do. I'd like to be able to do big pieces in spray but it would take a lot of time and practice.'

Pian, from Caracas, Venezuela, has been active since 2003 and uses her art to convey issues close to her heart: 'As some people say, you're ALWAYS communicating even when you think you're not. At first, through my posters, I was trying to raise awareness of social issues, 'cause here in Venezuela, and maybe in many other places in the world too, it has become more and more dangerous and violent over the past few years. The phrase *la Lucha por la locha,* which appeared in my posters, means something like "the struggle for money" because that's really the tough thing here. That's why there's a girl with a gun in one hand and a doll in the other, because sometimes people learn to be violent to survive. That was to start off with, and now I'm trying to give the environment a touch of delicacy, with one girl balancing, another relaxing in a ballet pose, for instance. That's pretty much what I'm about right now, bringing some light and cosy scenes of little girls and ballerinas in contrast to the madness of my home city.

'Apolonia from Femalehiphop.net wrote about my work and I think it's really very apt: "Pian's task on the streets is clear. She likes to bring a little light and cosy feelings to those who forget about [such things] in the harsh concrete jungle of Caracas. Her signature stencils are *las niñas* ('the little girls') – they float, swing and dance delicately on billboards, traffic signs and walls in the most unexpected places of the city, although she prefers spots where [there's] a lot of traffic. The contrast made by these gracious creatures, in a city where street art is tough as nails, leaves the viewer with a smile and the feeling of a love regained for the valley of madness and chaos that is Caracas."'

Pian

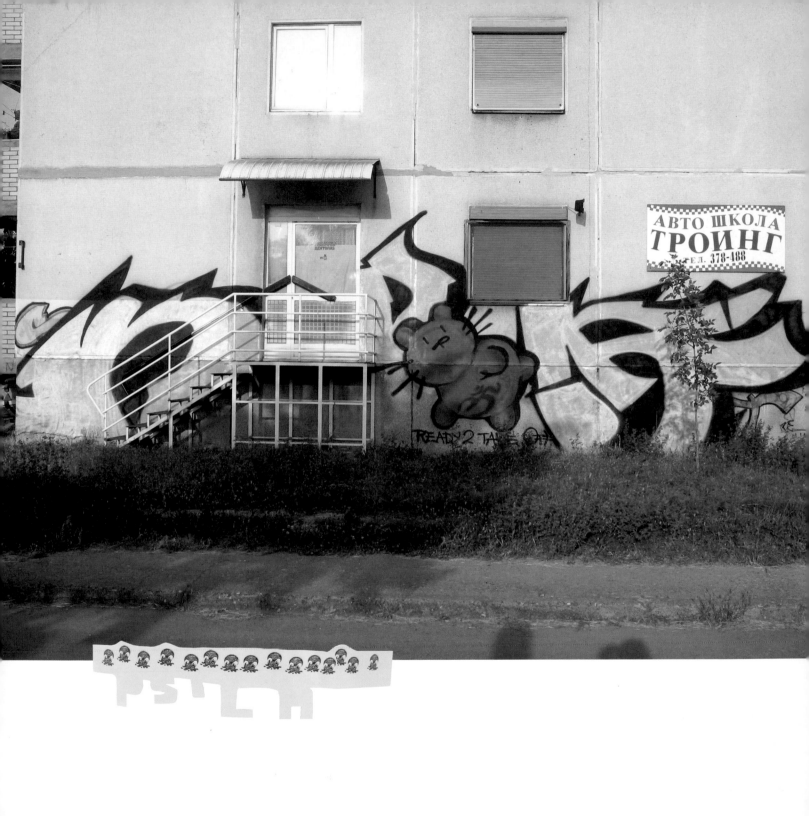

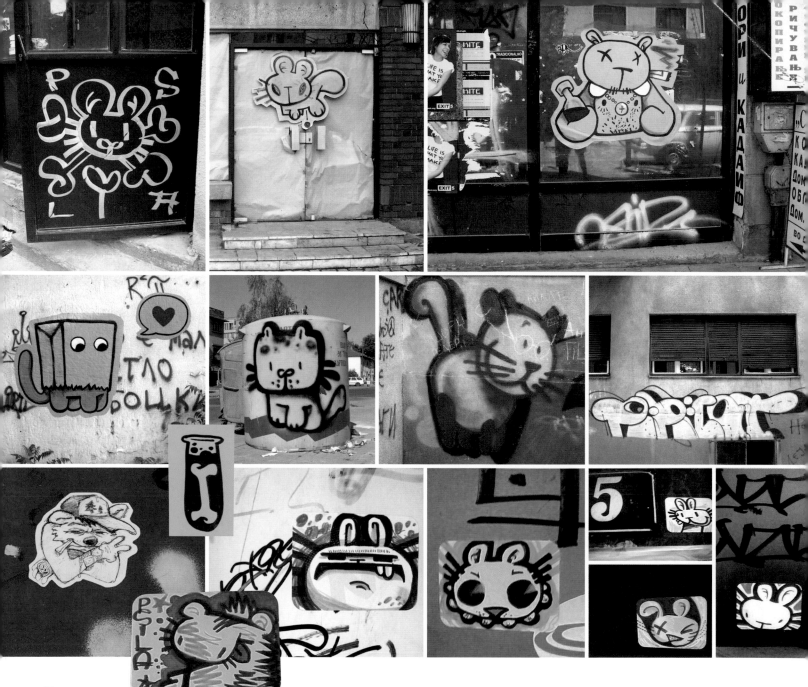

Psila

To date, Psila has been the only serious female spray artist to emerge from Skopje. 'Sila' translates as 'strength', but Macedonian artist Psila prefers to give her name several different meanings. Through her pieces and posters, she tries to animate her grey, monotonous town with colour and a sense of fun.

She did her first piece in the mid-1990s, a memory that has remained with her: 'I still remember the experience of sharing a nice shade of metallic blue with my neighbourhood. It just had to happen. The surroundings were very sterile and dull, especially for a kid.'

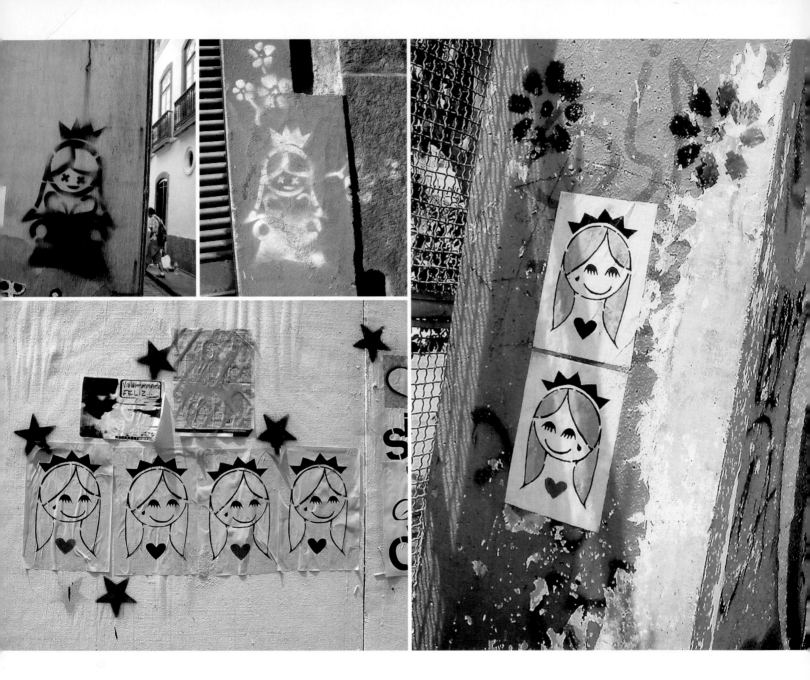

Popdesign

Rio de Janeiro's Popdesign is a relative newcomer to the scene, working primarily with stencils and stickers. 'My work is influenced by popular culture, Brazilian funk, pop music, football and all cute and happy characters,' she says. 'My stencil *Fama de Putona* ("the whore's fame") comes from a famous funk singer called Tati Quebra-Barraco and I use her image like a yell of female protest – against all the crap that guys think, because in most Latin American countries guys are very sexist and they think that, if you're too open-minded, you're a bit of a bitch (or *putona* in Portuguese). I'm just an ordinary girl who works and has a simple and monogamous life with my dear boyfriend and future husband.'

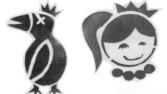

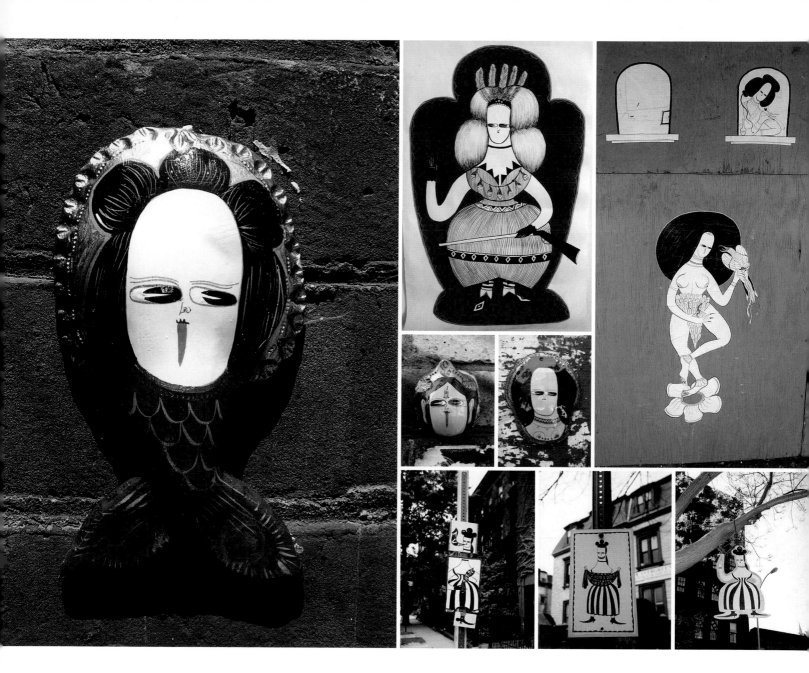

RB827

RB827 was born in Milwaukee and got into graffiti in high school. 'I think my initial impulse to do street art still stands,' she says. 'I feel like art shouldn't be a contained thing, that it has an ability to have a place in many different parts of society. I feel that is the overarching reason I do street work. As far as my own agenda, so to speak, I think it's my attempt at instilling a space with mystery, to share a secret with a passer-by. Though my work may be personal on many levels, I try to work with imagery that has a certain familiarity to it. My goal is to create a dialogue rather than to try to create a specific reaction.'

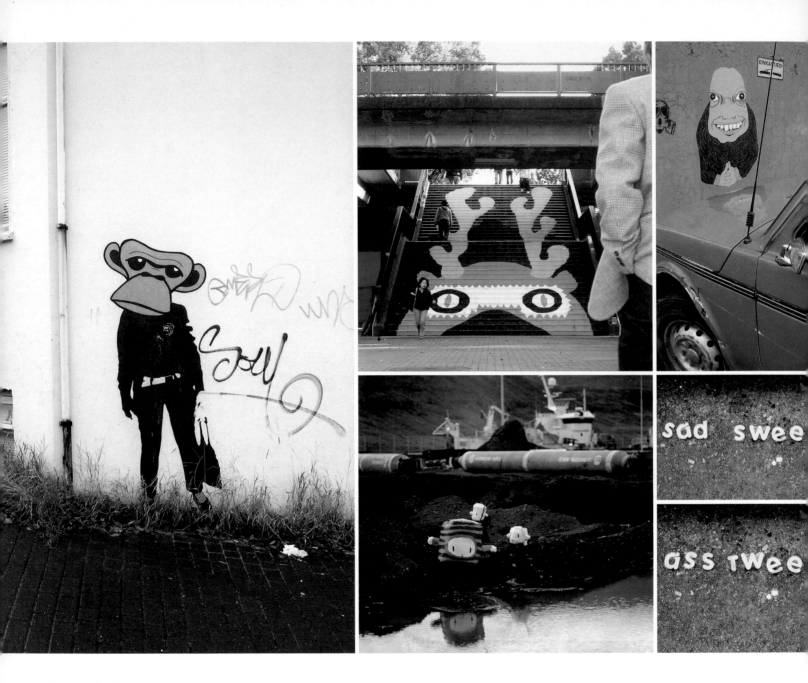

Miss Riel

Miss Riel was born in Copenhagen, brought up in Iceland and now lives in Berlin, where she was inspired to create on the streets: 'I began doing street art after I moved to Berlin to study at the Kunsthochschule Berlin-Weissensee, in 2001. First I tried out some stencils but I found it a bit of a hassle running around with cut-outs that were still wet and sticky. Then I got to know the big fat markers and I've had massive fun with them when freely styling my character-tags on walls. But the challenge lies in using all kinds of methods and materials that fit the spot you are changing.'

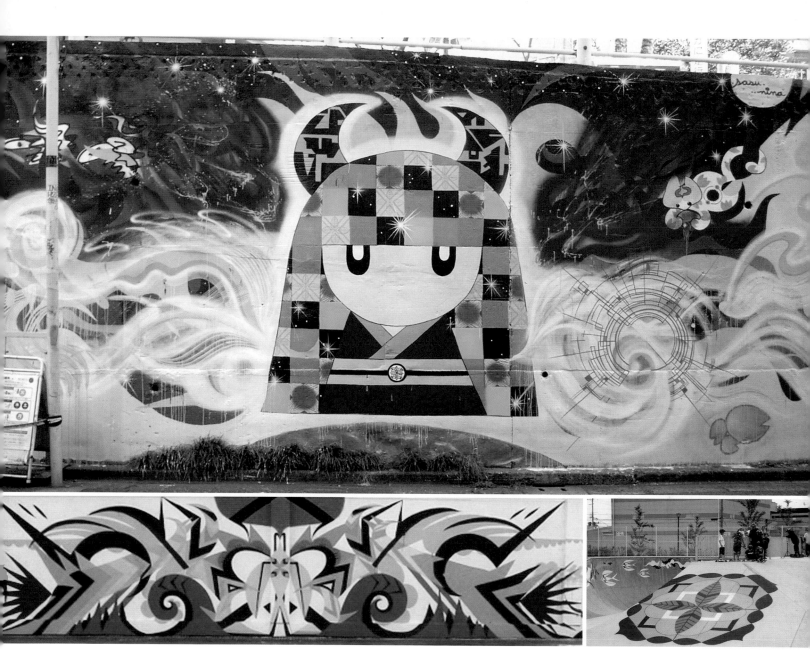

Sasu

Born in Tokyo in 1974, Sasu is inspired by daily life and takes any steps necessary for true artistic expression. Her work celebrates gentle and sometimes intense things and the power and joy of life itself. Generally her pictures are abstract or linked to natural elements, often reminiscent of a mandala or prism, and they occasionally feature characters. Check out hitotzuki.com to see Sasu's work for *HITOTZUKI,* which she created with her partner Kami.

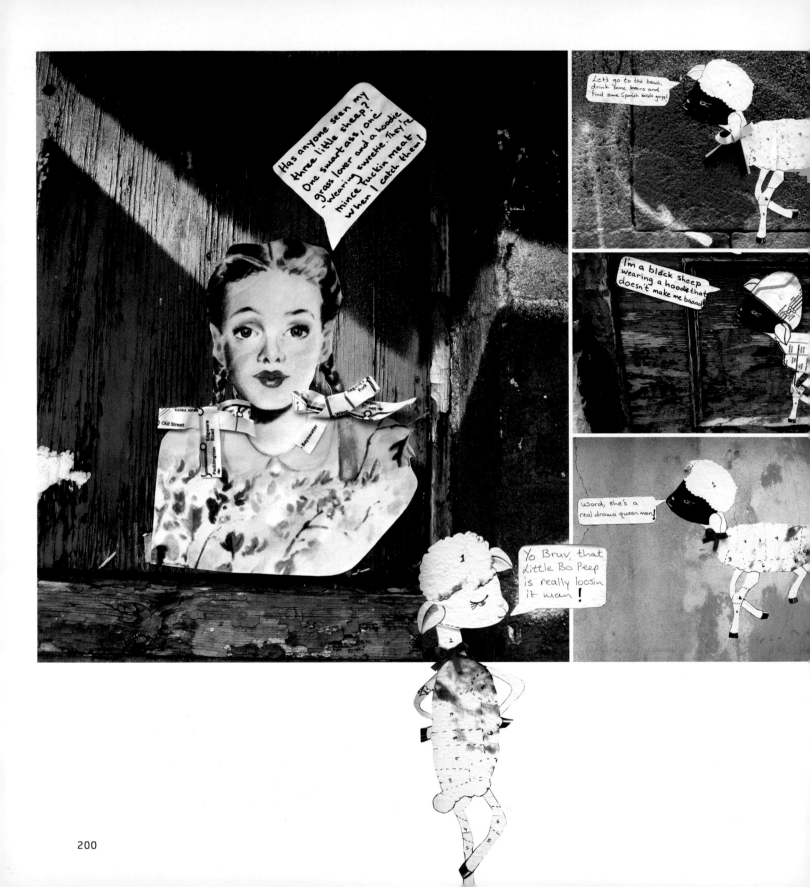

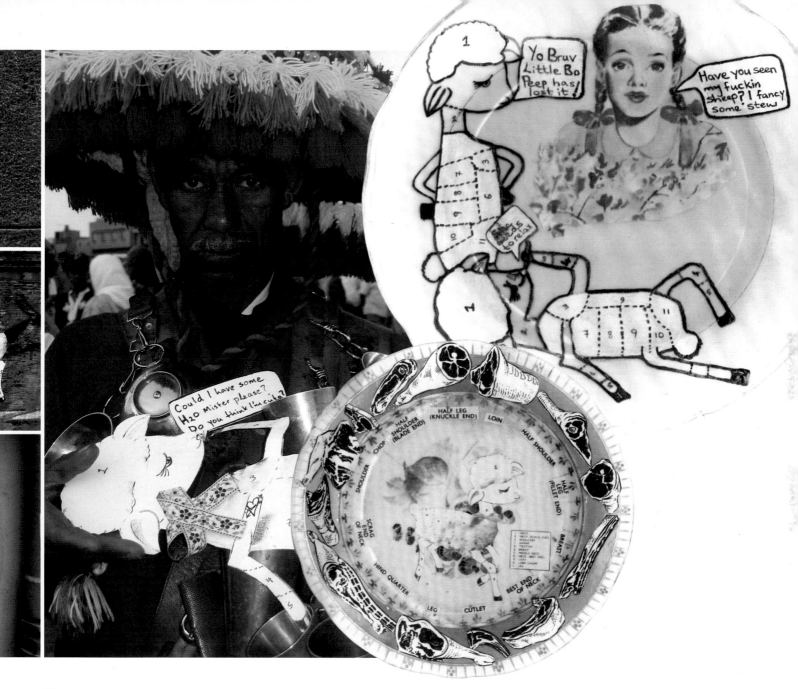

Seomra

This Dublin-based artist does a lot of work with her partner Asbestos, who first sparked her interest in street art. Inspired by D*Face and the Finders Keepers crew, and other artists like The London Police, Galo and Mysterious Al, she continues her constant globe-trotting with their vision in mind. 'All these guys are legends,' she says.

Seomra takes her name from the Irish word for 'room' and she is particularly well known for her talking sheep, which she takes with her on her travels. This has led her into some strange situations – in Marrakesh, for example: 'When I arrived in Morocco, I realized that the only street artists there were children who used chalk. I was nearly arrested twice but a few dirham later and I'd paid the cops off and got a police escort around the city to throw up my stuff. It's really corrupt there and everyone and everything seems to have a price. A police escort for paste-ups is ten dirham.'

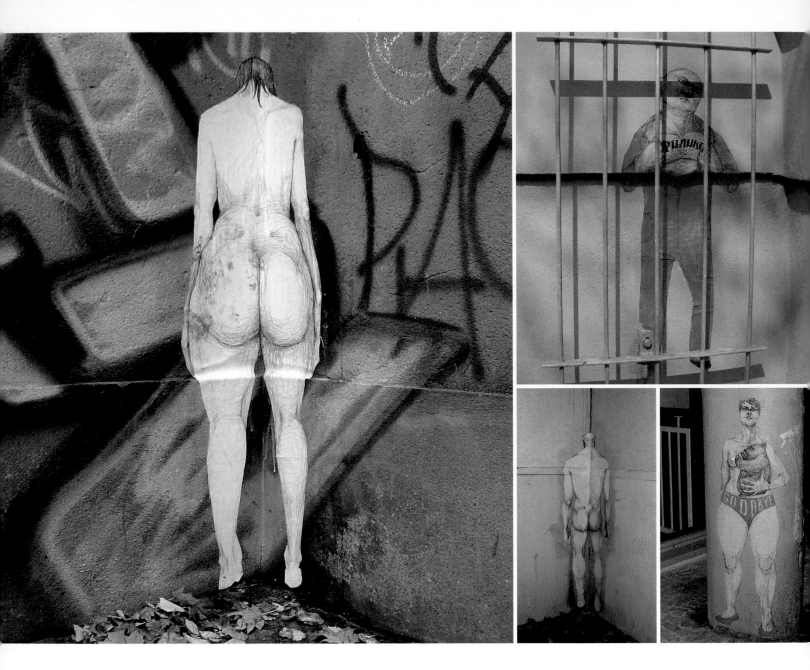

Solovei

'When I began doing street art, it was less a claim to public space than an attempt to place my work in the middle of people (which worked both ways: now my art is in the middle of people and now people are in the middle of art),' Solovei explains. 'It was necessary for the art I make not to fall into the bottomless pit of art made before me or in the shallow pit of an appreciative elite. Art lives when it is perceived, and this was my hope. I did not want to compete with the omnipresent demand of advertising and thought that, by placing no name on my work, I secured it with the selfless purity of a gift. It is in this purity that beauty is possible, though whether the purity itself is possible is my current doubt. I am in this book, after all, which proves that my work is not an entirely selfless pursuit. But let's say it is possible. Let's say that the work is entirely

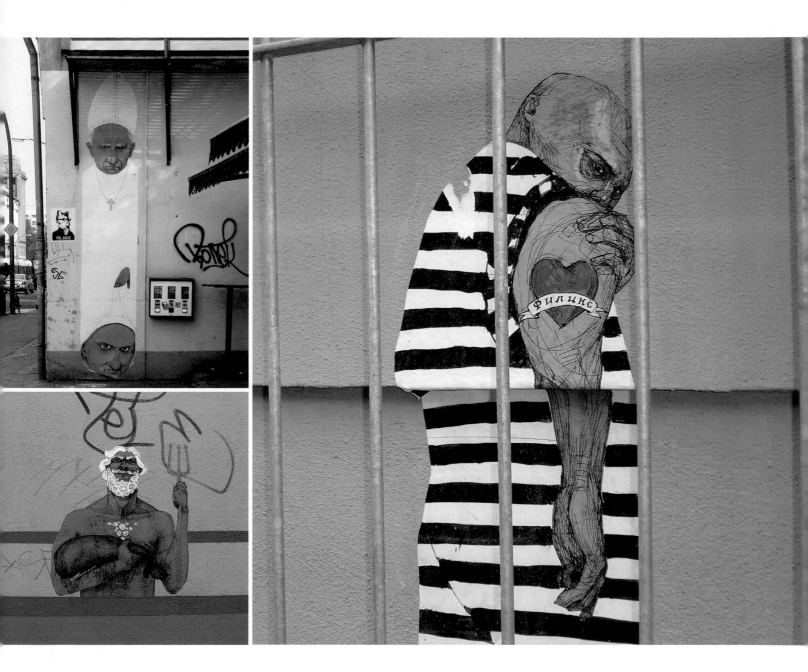

a gift, and many gifts worthy of the public are placed accordingly. I wonder then if this pit is also bottomless, whether these worthy gifts are at all distinguishable to the eyes of the passers-by, tired from the constant flow of images and information. This is what I am thinking right now, precisely because the phenomenon of street art and graffiti is increasing. But I love the action of tattooing a body that doesn't just belong to me, to use the external parts of a city to reveal an internal, singular voice. And I love these voices for manifesting themselves despite and in spite of obvious difficulties.'

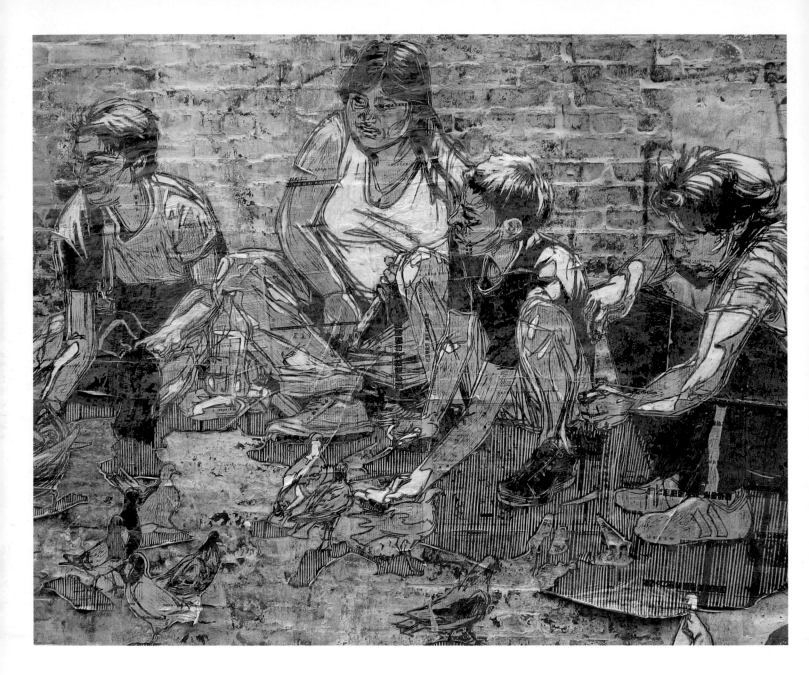

Swoon

'I want to express my love for the overflowing vitality of the city in a way that makes the city even more overflowing and vital,' says Swoon, one of the best-known poster artists. 'More and more, I am thinking about people, about real life as I see it in the faces of all these millions of lives walking around. Lately I have wanted to give all of my attention to reflecting our humanness, our fragility and strength, back out at us from our city walls in a way that makes all of these fake images screaming at us from billboards seem irrelevant and cruel, which is what they are. I feel like if I can show people images from our own lives that are beautiful and real, and not asking for anything in particular (no pressure to be anything or buy anything), then what I am doing can function like a tiny gift pasted onto our everyday existence. If it is at all possible, I want to make a small moment of refuge in human connection out of paper stuck to a wall.'

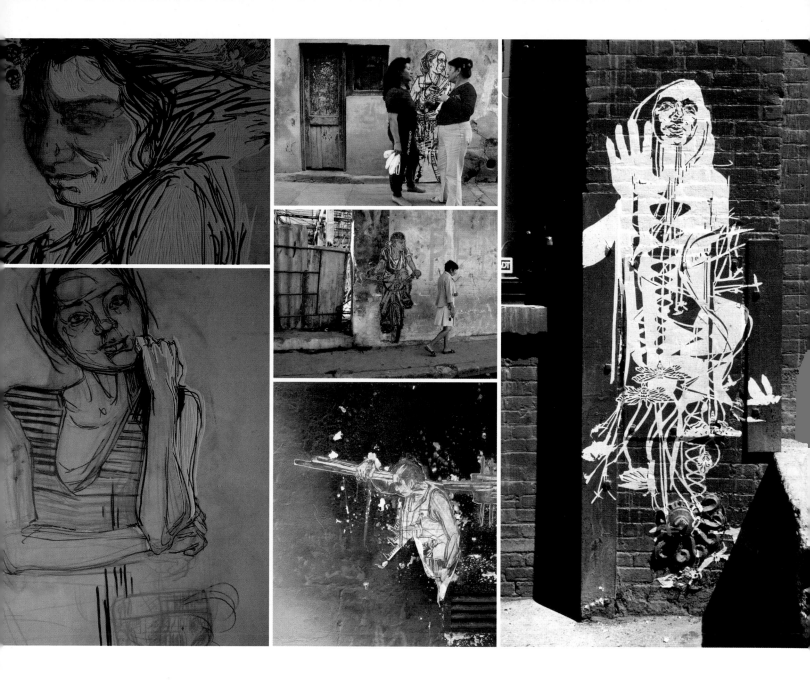

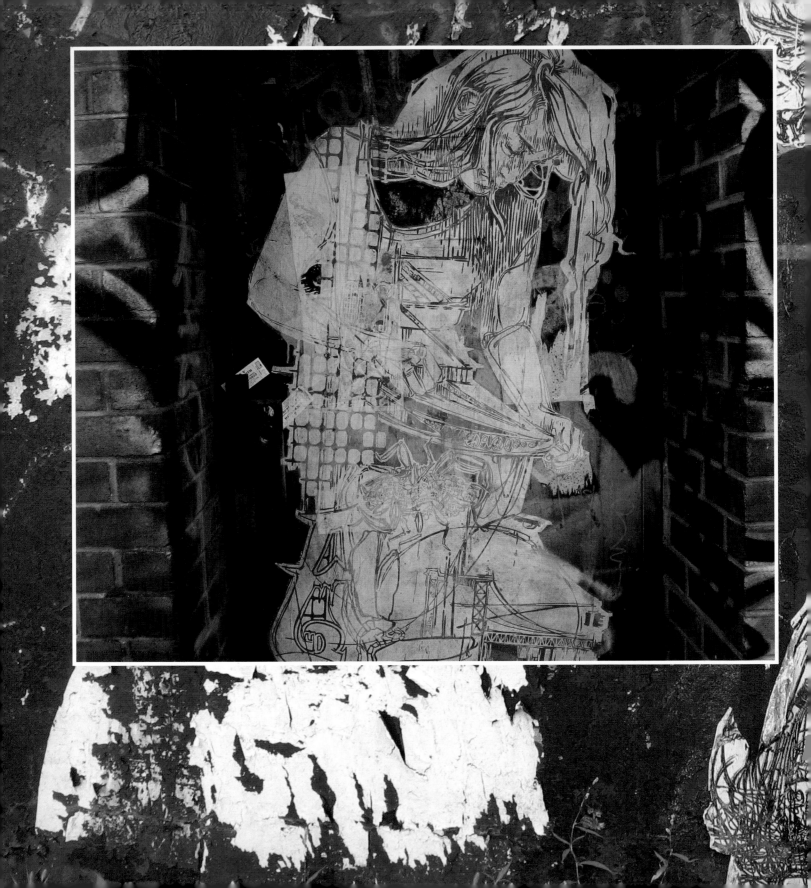

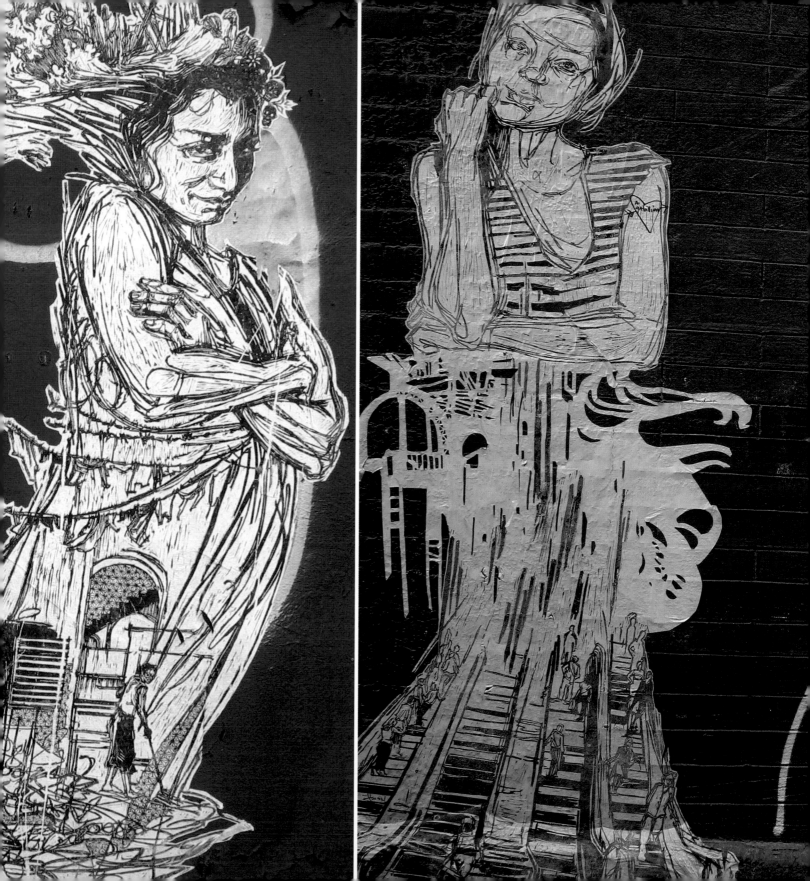

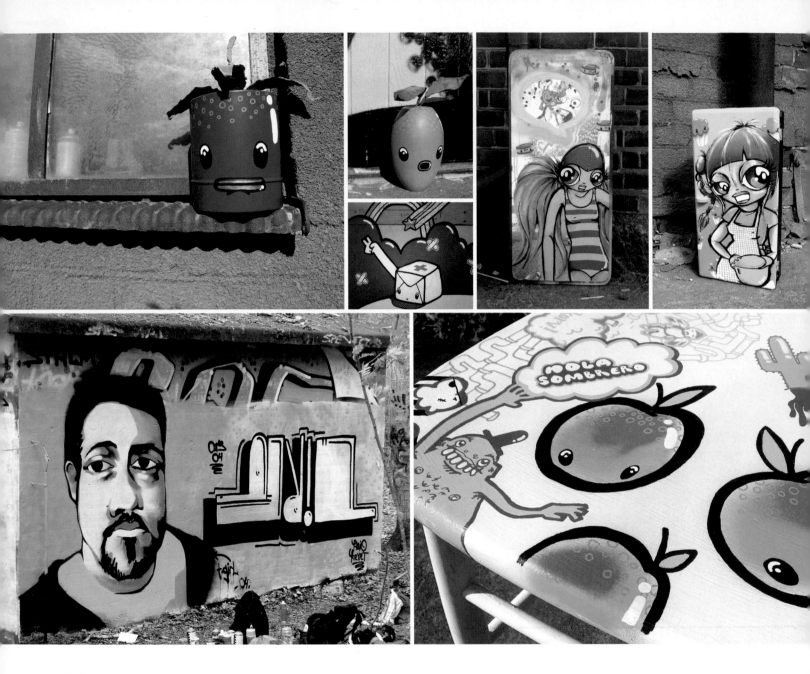

T-Girl

T-Girl was born in Varberg, Sweden, and has been active with her figures since 2000. Generally she has been keeping it legal in order to spend more time on her pieces, but she also seeks out the odd illegal spot to share her art.

'Graffiti had inspired me for a long time,' she says, 'and as I've always been playing around with colours, drawing, painting on everything that got in my way, graffiti felt like a new way of expressing myself. None of my friends were into graffiti, but I got in touch with two guys in my town who were.'

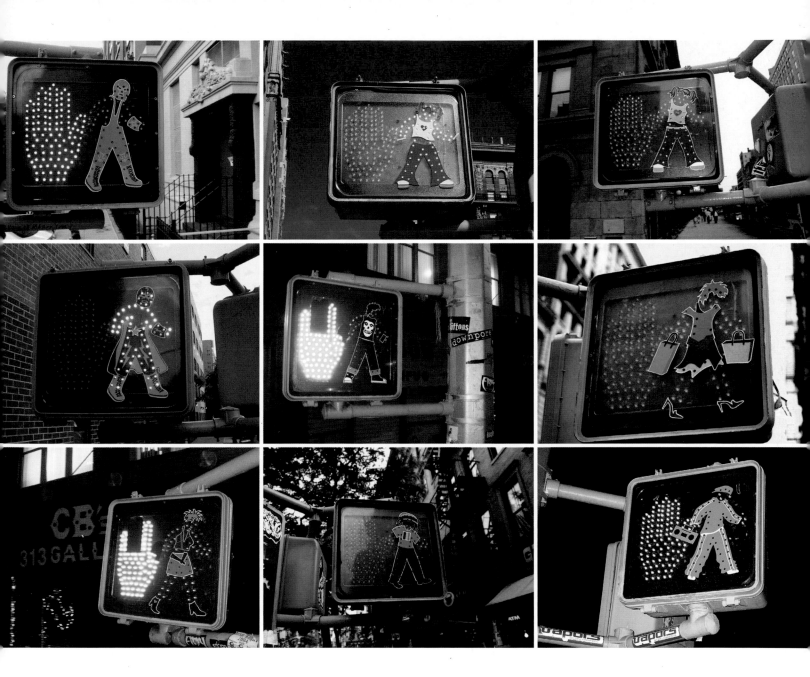

Thundercut

This New Yorker has carved herself a rather unusual niche in street art. Every day we come across images of naked men (and/or women!) at the traffic lights, without even thinking about it — in the UK the red man forbids us to cross the road and the green man gives us the go-ahead, while for New Yorkers it's a red hand for 'stop' and a white figure for 'go'. Thundercut makes clothes out of adhesive vinyl for these anonymous men and women and gives them each a bespoke item to wear, sometimes adapting the outfit to match the surroundings. The punks at CBGB in Manhattan are a good example. Her other projects involve woodwork and seahorses.

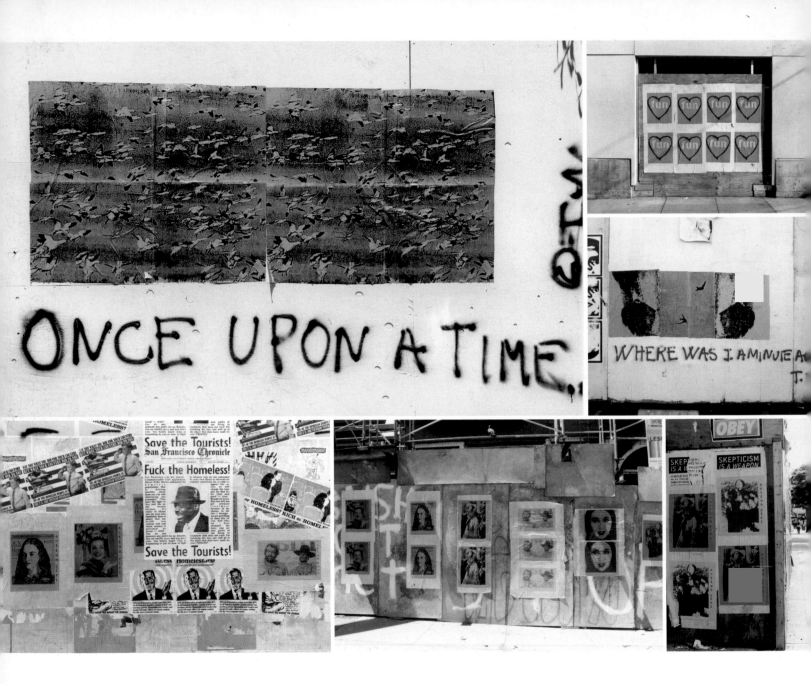

T.W.

Brazilian-born T.W. lives in San Francisco and is known for her silk-prints, to which she often adds spray-painted text. 'My name T.W. has two meanings,' she explains. 'It refers to all the thirsty walls that existed in the cities – thirsty for some art – but it's also short for "Third World", where I came from originally.'

   T.W.'s street art has socio-political content and offers the onlooker a certain sense of escapism from this hectic world through fantasy and dream: 'Using the urban landscape as your canvas to put your art or ideas out there in the streets for the world to see is a fun way to break the visual routine of everyday life. It's a way to brighten up the clustered city spaces and surprise the passer-by with an unexpected message. It's a direct and fresh way to put your word out there.'

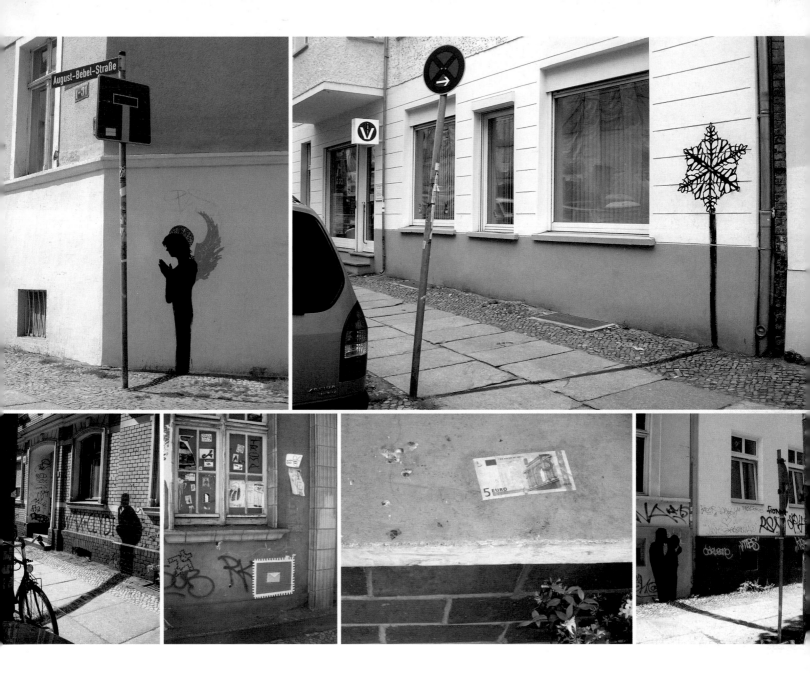

Various

German artist Various says: 'I don't sign my work with a name, and I'm not interested in adhering to a certain style – that's why I call myself "Various". I'm from Berlin, studying visual communications, and I slipped into "street art", urban activism, public art – whatever you want to call it – in 2003. A friend from New York (Solovei) introduced me to the pleasure of using the streets for my inventive skills. It's been like discovering what I've always been looking for – suddenly my eyes were opened to the city space and all its possibilities. With my pieces of banknotes and envelopes, for example, active communication with my surroundings is in the foreground. With my shadows, on the other hand, it's all about visual confusion or games.'

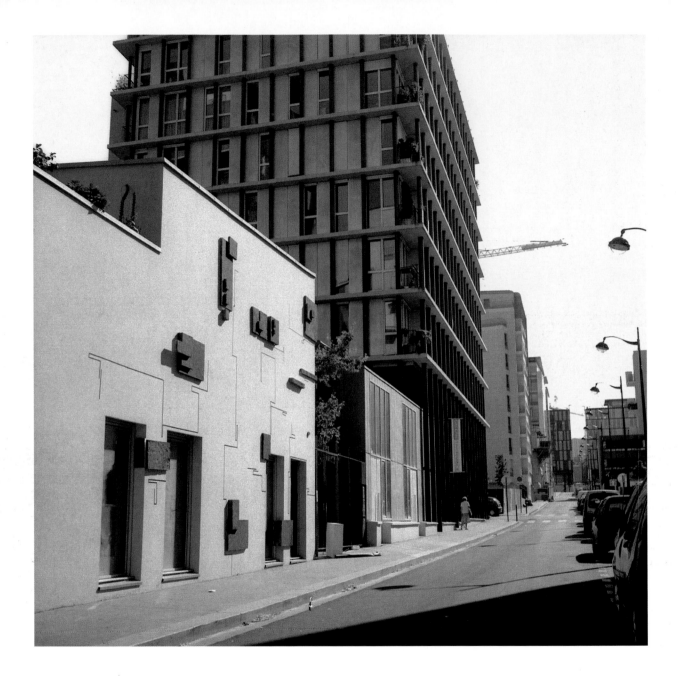

YZ

Parisian artist YZ has been active since 2000 but has been painting on canvas for years and also works on video art. She often focuses on projects with strong messages, as she explains: 'Each project I work on has a meaning. It has to say something. *Open your eyes* started in Paris in 2003 with Missill, at the beginning of the Iraq war. A giant's face, painted on the tombstone-like electricity boxes of fifty or so Paris streets. The selected locations were crossroads, stations, intersections, which symbolize the web of communities, exchanges and sharing between cultures. Painted on the network of electricity boxes (which are supposed to bring us light), these faces, in turn, constitute a giant face superposed over the map of the city. What I'm interested in is making people think about what they see in the

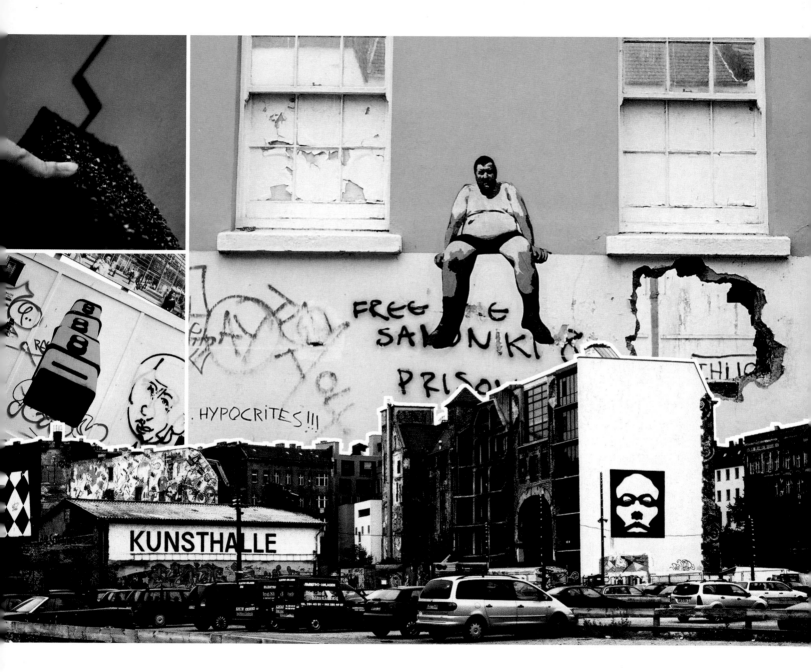

city. How it interferes in their urban living. *We are getting fat* is a series of fat characters. I just wanted to humanize characters that people could relate to and make people think about how we consume. How we can get very fat because of overeating, or because of too much TV, brand belief, services, cars etc. *Push* is a visual project which is meant to initiate the idea of pushing, activating something, turning on a device. The general idea is that if "we" or I don't turn on the device, nobody will do it for me – meaning that nothing will happen in my life if I don't take care of it myself. Lately I've been working with volumes on walls, using sculpture. It enables me to be even closer to the city and the architecture. *Irruption* offers a reflection on the city and the link between integration and circulation that exists in the original elements and innovative elements. An installation questioning the dimension of our heritage in contemporary space.'

213

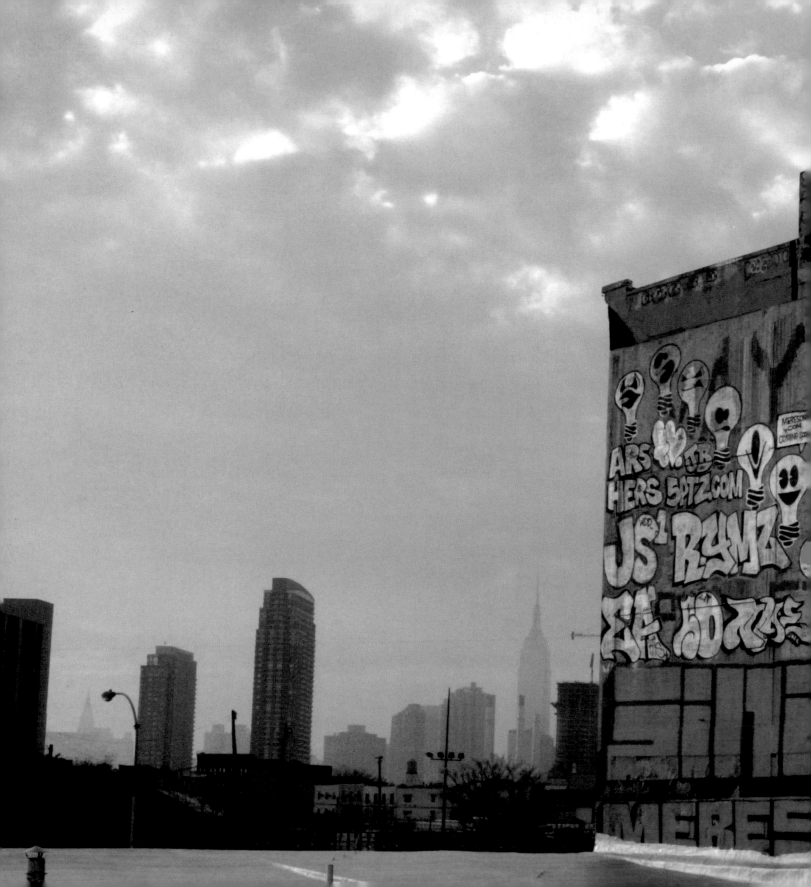

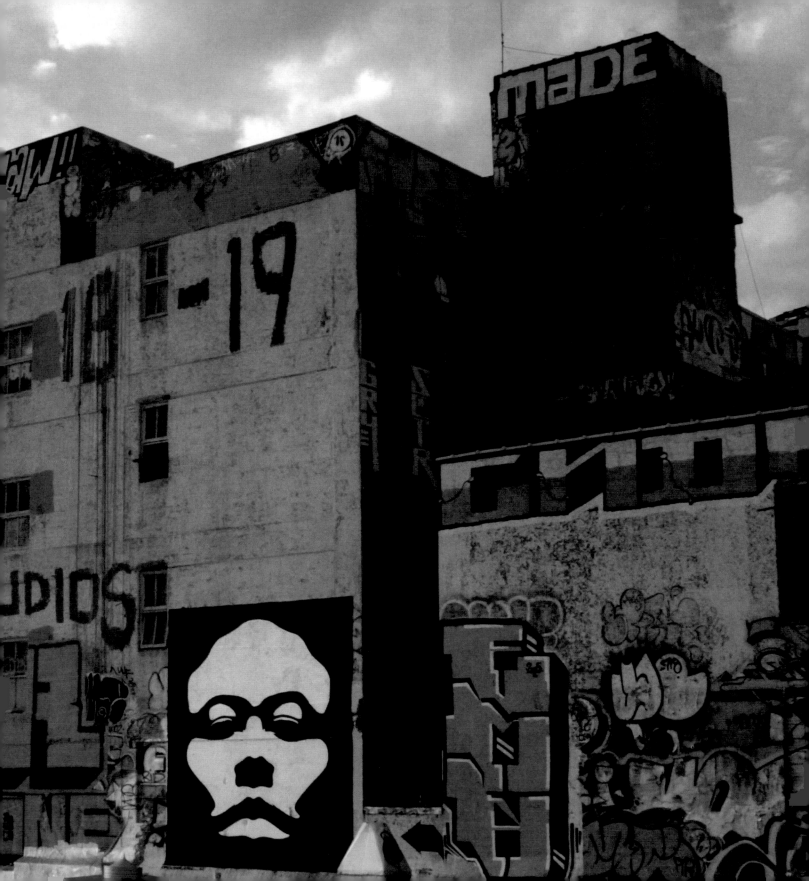

Collage Maps

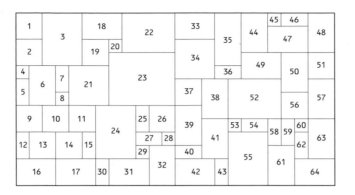

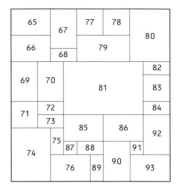

Portraits, pages 2–4

1 ACB, 2 YZ, 3 Blue, 4 Peste, 5 Z (Coletivo TPM), 6 Lady Pink, 7 Chour, 8 Dune, 9 Plume, 10 Indie, 11 Tribe, 12 Karma, 13 AFC Crew, 14 Luna, 15 Shiro, 16 Friendly Vandalism, 17 BRING OUT THE GARBAGE, 18 Erotica67, 19 EMA, 20 Chez, 21 Girl23, 22 Fafi, 23 Claw, 24 Cant4, 25 Musa, 26 Ice Cream Specials (Dusan, Djordje, Jovan, Sale, Angel and Rienke Enghardt), 27 Jana Joana, 28 Femme9, 29 Muck, 30 Deninja, 31 Casie, 32 Andrea May, 33 Gloe, 34 Donna, 35 Aleteia, 36 Omri, 37 Nina, 38 Koralie, 39 Lus, 40 Suez, 41 EGR, 42 Bule, 43 Jozki, 44 Redy, 45 Becky Drayson, 46 Venus, 47 Katherine Dessert, 48 Poise, 49 Klor, 50 Chour, 51 Nuria, 52 me love, 53 Toofly, 54 Fern, 55 Mademoiselle Kat, 56 Lahe, 57 Psila, 58 Slice, 59 Prima Donna (Coletivo TPM), 60 Aiko, 61 Laia, 62 Kika, 63 Binx151, 64 Meek, 65 Thundercut, 66 Tash, 67 Dona, 68 ∞+, 69 Yubia, 70 Chour, 71 Siloette, 72 Jana Joana, 73 Stef, 74 Hera, 75 Malicia, 76 Chock, 77 Queen Andrea, 78 Microbo, 79 Akit, 80 Aiko, 81 EGR, 82 Peto, 83 MyMonsters, 84 Luna, 85 Fever (Lady K) & Zori4, 86 Miss Van, 87 Kif, 88 Smirk, 89 Omri, 90 Mofi, 91 Teapot, 92 Miss Lili, 93 Fafi

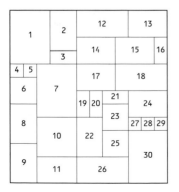

Graffiti, page 18

1 Are2, 2 De Professionella Konstgangstrarna, 3 EGR, 4 Tash, 5 Femme9, 6 Toofly, 7 Malicia, 8 Chock, 9 Casie, 10 Muck, 11 Akit, 12 Siloette, 13 Lady Pink, 14 Fever (Lady K), 15 Jana Joana, 16 Peste, 17 Jana Joana, 18 Miss Van, 19 Miss Lili, 20 Waleska, 21 Sherm, 22 Redy, 23 Faith47, 24 Chour, 25 Chez, 26 Claw & Miss17, 27 Dona, 28 Zori4, 29 Fafi, 30 Yubia, 31 Poise, 32 Venus, 33 Supa B2

Street Art, page 136

1 Aiko, 2 T.W., 3 Aleteia, 4 Psila, 5 Jen Props, 6 Thundercut, 7 Solovei, 8 Koralie, 9 Fairy, 10 Seomra, 11 Nuria, 12 Dani, 13 Lahe, 14 Leeny, 15 Maya Deren, 16 Hope, 17 Den, 18 Hera, 19 Mademoiselle Kat, 20 FUCK YOUR CREW, 21 Rienke Enghardt, 22 Various, 23 Microbo, 24 Nina M., 25 MyMonsters, 26 Mofi, 27 me love, 28 Melina, 29 MyMonsters, 30 Becky Drayson

Graffiti Foldout

1 Sect, 2 Binx151, 3 Duna, 4 Duna, 5 Koube, 6 Duna, 7 Koube, 8 Fern, 9 Mes3, 10 Pesky, 11 Bule, 12 Laia, 13 June, 14 Fern, 15 Laia, 16 Laia, 17 Laia, 18 Meek, 19 Laia, 20 Meek, 21 Pesky, 22 Pesky, 23 Perl, 24 Perl, 25 Wave, 26 Taro-Amie, 27 Miss Chievous, 28 Mes3, 29 Pesky, 30 Flake, 31 Flake, 32 Flake, 33 Flake, 34 Flake, 35 EMS, 36 Utah, 37 Indie, Toofly & Baad4, 38 Dani, 39 Dani, 40 Lady Sound, 41 Dani, 42 Slice, 43 EMS, 44 OGA Crew, 45 Oink, 46 Fairy, 47 Lust (aka Blondie), 48 Oink, 49 Lust, 50 June, 51 Envy, 52 June, 53 Pesky, 54 Envy, 55 Jozki, 56 Jozki, 57 Nish, 58 Nish, 59 Jeyd, 60 OneSevenNine, 61 Cudles, 62 Cudles, 63 Diva NZ, 64 Cudles, 65 Jeyd, 66 Diva NZ, 67 Gloe, 68 Gloe, 69 Weir, 70 Havic-Civah

Street Art Foldout

1 C Damage, 2 C Damage, 3 C Damage, 4 C Damage, 5 C Damage, 6 C Damage, 7 Rina, 8 Rina, 9 Lease, 10 Mia, 11 Astria Superak, 12 Astria Superak, 13 Kika, 14 Kika, 15 Lease, 16 Lease, 17 Kika, 18 Pufferella, 19 Supa, 20 Kika, 21 C Damage, 22 C Damage, 23 C Damage, 24 Kika, 25 Kika, 26 Pufferella, 27 Nikita, 28 Nikita, 29 Trine, 30 Trine, 31 Trine, 32 Katherine Dessert, 33 Katherine Dessert, 34 Peto, 35 Peto, 36 Katherine Dessert, 37 Suez, 38 Ipno, 39 Trine, 40 Peto, 41 Peto, 42 Trine, 43 Peto, 44 Peto, 45 OneSevenNine, 46 Ipno, 47 Ipno, 48 Ipno, 49 Ipno, 50 Ipno, 51 Amanda Lynn, 52 OneSevenNine, 53 Amanda Lynn, 54 Amanda Lynn, 55 Suez, 56 No Name, 57 Amanda Lynn, 58 No Name

About the Artists

Key
g: when an artist started graffiti
b: when an artist was born
f: when a crew was founded
A above; B below/bottom;
C centre; L left; R right; T top

All works are by the artists and
located in the artists' resident
countries, unless indicated.

∞+ (aka Laurie/
The Laboratory of Living Arts)
Ireland/Spain/Belgium
(b: 1974 / g: 1988)
www.the-laboratory.org
138 ∞+ in a skeleton mask; *Boxer,*
Barcelona, 2005
139 Clockwise from TL: *Historia de las
mujeres y estrategias de revolucion
social,* Barcelona, 2004; *Con-sciencia
social,* part of an installation for the
gallery SUBAQUATICA, Madrid, 2004;
La Paz, Barcelona, 2004; *Vigilando
la cultura,* Barcelona, 2005; *Boxer,*
Barcelona, 2005; *Respect,* 2004

ACB Valparaíso, Chile (g: 1996)
www.mundofelizdeacb.com
www.fotolog.com/mundofeliz
www.fotolog.com/andrea_acb
20 All art by ACB

Aiko (aka Faile)
New York, USA (g: 1999)
Crews: 50/50 mix killer www.faile.net
140 *Butterfly Girl,* Zurich, 2004
141 Clockwise from TL: *Lady Skull,*
Barcelona, 2006; *Crest, Dog and
Special Trial Offer from FAILE BAST
and ELIK,* Tokyo, 2004–5; *Dog,* Berlin,
2003; *Girl,* Tokyo, 2004; *The Head,*
Zurich, 2004; *Bunny Boy,* Amsterdam,
2003; *FAILE,* Copenhagen, 2005;
Giant Head, Austin (Texas), 2004;
Smoking, LA, 2005

Akit London, UK (g: 1990–97)
www.akit.co.uk
21 Clockwise from TL: NW10, 1996;
N1, 1994; flyer for *Eternity Rave
Magazine,* 1993; NW5, 1994;
W10, 1994; NW1, 1995; NW5, 1996;
NW5, 1996; N6, 1994

Aleteia Paris, France
(b: 1979 / g: 2003)
Crews: Le mur, The VAO Circus
www.aleteia.fr
www.fotolog.com/aleteia
142 All art by Aleteia

Are2 USA (g: 1993) Crews: BA
22 Are2 & Ugly, Maryland, 2004
23 Clockwise from TL: Maryland, 2004;
Maryland, 2004; Maryland, 2004;
Maryland, 2004; Baltimore, 2004;
Maryland, 2004; Baltimore, 2001;
Maryland, 2004; Rome, 2002

Bitches In Control
Brabant, the Netherlands (f: 2003)
Members: F.lady, Meg & Lowlita
www.fotolog.com/bitchesincontrol
26 Clockwise from TL: F.Lady, Tilburg,
2005; F.Lady, Eindhoven, 2005; Meg,
s Hertogenbosch, 2004; *BIC Fool
Series* sticker design, Lowlita
& F.Lady, the Netherlands, 2003;
Meg, the Netherlands, 2003; Lowlita,
Amsterdam, 2004; *Berliner Bär
und Kleisterfuchs,* Tower & F.Lady,
Berlin, 2003; Meg & F.Lady, Nijmegen,
2004; Meg, Berlin, 2003. Cutout:
BIC Since 2003 poster, Meg & F.Lady,
Berlin, 2003

Blue Gothenburg, Sweden
www.bluesource.se
24–25 Clockwise from TL: *Blueswet,*
Bronx, 1997; *Solbarn,* Dalslands
Museum & Konsthall, Sweden, 2005;
Gettosolbarn, Brooklyn, 1997;
Heavenly Pain, NY, 2001;
Dragonchaser, Gothenburg, 2005;
Dragonpower, Gothenburg, 2005;
Blueblood, Brooklyn, 2000;
GRAFITTA.SE, Gothenburg, 2005

BRING OUT THE GARBAGE
Denmark/Norway
www.bringoutthegarbage.org
143 Clockwise from TL: *WARNING
REGISTRATION ZONE,* Gothenburg,
2003; *WARNING REGISTRATION ZONE,*
Gothenburg, 2003; *WARNING
REGISTRATION ZONE* (sticker), Berlin,
2003; *DYMO,* Copenhagen, 2005;
WARNING REGISTRATION ZONE
(sticker), Germany, 2004; *WARNING
REGISTRATION ZONE* (sticker),
Gothenburg, 2003; *DYMO,*
Copenhagen, 2005; *MIND YOUR OWN
BUSINESS* (poster), Copenhagen,
2005; *Copenhagen – without name*
(stencil), Copenhagen, 2005

Cade (aka Nika Sarabi)
Canada/USA www.cade2.com
144–45 All art by Cade

Cant4 (aka Amanda D)
Toronto, Canada
(g: 1995) Crews: UCM

www.deucetattoo.com
www.them.ca
www.myspace.com/saviorrocks
28 2005
29 TL: *With Water,* Duro3 & Case,
Phoenix, 2004; BR: 2001
All others by Cant4, 2005

Casie Munich, Germany
(g: 1996) Crews: Style Fanatix
www.stylefanatix.de
27 Clockwise from TL: Vienna, 2004;
Munich; Munich, 2003; with Law,
Munich, 2005; Munich, 2004;
with Law, Munich, 2005;
Munich, 2003; Munich, 2005

Che Jen (aka Jiyun)
Brooklyn, New York
Crews: Barnstormers
www.chejiyun.com
146–47 Clockwise from TL: Brooklyn,
2005; London, 2005; NY

Chez Sydney, Australia
(g: 1989) Crews: 21st Century, BH
www.bountyhunterz.net
30 Clockwise from TL: with Slave1,
Sydney, 2003; *Boba Fett,* Wellington
(New Zealand), 2005; Sydney, 2002;
Ninja, Sydney, 2002; *Wave,* Sydney,
2004; *Praying Girl,* 'Bounty Hunterz
Exhibition', Sydney, 2002;
Stealth Girl, 'Festival Exhibition',
Sydney, 2005

Chock (aka Angels)
London, UK
(g: 1998–99) Crews: THC, YRP
www.onallfrequencies.com
31 All art by Chock

Chour France
32–33 All art by Chour

Claw & Miss17 New York, USA
Claw crews: FC, TC5, PMS
Miss17 crews: PMS
www.clawmoney.com
34–37 All art by Claw and Miss17,
NYC, 2000 – present

Coletivo TPM
Rio de Janeiro, Brazil (f: 2004)
Members: Ira, Morgana, Om,
Prima Donna, Z
www.fotolog.com/tpmcrew
38 All art by Coletivo TPM

Constance Brady (aka Cattle)
New York, USA
148 All art by Constance Brady

Dani Halle, Germany
(g: *c.* 1998) Crews: Klub7
www.klub7.de
149 Clockwise from TL: *Creatures,*
Dani/Klub7, Halle (Saale), 2004;
Creature, Dani/Klub7, Halle, 2005;
Creature + Pies, Dani/Klub7, Halle,
2005; *Pies,* Dani/Klub7, Halle, 2005;
Creatures + Cash, Dani/Klub7,
Berlin, 2004

**De Professionella Konstgangstrarna
(DPKG)**
Sweden www.konstgangster.com
39 All art by DPKG

Den Bilbao, Spain
(b: 1978 / g: 1995)
Crews: Extralargos
www.fotolog.com/denparanoia
www.extralargos.net
150 Clockwise from TL: *Lady Day,*
Bilbao, 2004; with Mate, Cade,
Dizebi & Sye (Extralargos crew),
'Write4gold', Torrevieja, 2005; with
Mate, Cade & Soldi, Legutiano, 2005;
'Jam In Line', Pamplona, 2005

Deninja São Paulo, Brazil
(g: 2001) Crews: HDV
www.fotolog.com/deninja
40 Clockwise from TL: Rio Claro, 2004;
Rio Claro, 2005; São Bernardo do
Campo, 2004; Vector Design, 2005;
São Paulo, 2005; Vector Design, 2003

Maya Deren Cambridge, UK
(b: 1984 / g: 2003)
151 All in Cambridge. L: *Flamenco
Dancer,* 2005; C, from T to B: *Madonna
and Child,* 2005; *Venus,* 2004; *Pieta,*
2005; R: *David,* 2004

Diva New York, USA
(b: early 1970s / g: *c.* 1984–85)
Crews: VIC
41 Clockwise from TL: Diva
Blockbuster, Williamsburg Bridge,
Brooklyn, 1997; Brooklyn, 1999;
with K-Star, Queens, 1999; with
Erotica, Sunset Park, Brooklyn, 1998;
Brooklyn, Xmas 1997; Brooklyn, 2000;
Brooklyn, 2000

Dona New York, USA
(b: 1970 / g: 1989)
Crews: BAD, TPA, VIC
42 Clockwise from TL: *BARC Shelter
Dog,* production with Pink, Cycle,
Muck, ACB & Monk, Brooklyn, 2004;
Altoid's 'Wall of Fame', production

with Pink, Smith, Cycle, Dalek, Erni, West, Muck, Yes, Ces, Rebel, Daze, Ezo Skwerm, Kenji, Leia & Bisc, Brooklyn, 2002; *Angel Devil*, with Icon, Queens, 1997; *Pop Goes Graffiti*, with Diva & Jakee, Brooklyn, 2000; *Diva Dona*, Bronx, 2002; *Peak Diva*, with Peak, Canal Street, NYC, 1999

Donna
Rhein-Main District, Germany
(g: 1997) Crews: Zonenkinder
www.fotolog.com/zonenkinder
152 All Zonenkinder productions, Rhein-Main & Berlin, 2004–5

Becky Drayson Cornwall, UK
153 All art by Becky Drayson

Dune Barcelona, Spain
(b: 1986 / g: 2002)
www.fotolog.com/helendune
43 All art by Dune

EGR Toronto, Canada
(g: 1996) www.egrart.com
44 Clockwise from TL: *Mother Nature*, 20"x28"; *Black Panther*, 24"x48"; Toronto; *Dream World*, Toronto; *Angelica*, 8"x10"; *Alien Faerie*, 24"x18"
45 *City of Lost Souls*, 36"x48"

EMA Montpellier, France
(b: 1977 / g: 1996)
Crews: ISK, ICP, PDP
46 Oakland, 2003
47 Clockwise from TL: Trenton, 2005; Queens, 2005; New York, 2005; Brooklyn, 2005; Queens, 2005; Frontignan, 2000

Rienke Enghardt (Hope Box)
The Hague, the Netherlands
www.hopebox.nl
www.vmcaa.nl/hopebox
154 Clockwise from L: *Tree Gallery*, with Gang of Five (Loung, Vinh, Hoa, Dung & Hieu) and Dik & Peertje (Hans & Rienke), Hanoi; *Kite of Life*, with Slobo Spuzevic, Sarajevo/The Hague; *Piece for Peace*, with Ice Cream Specials/NWA (Djordje, Dusan, Angel, Sale, Jovan & Rienke), Belgrade; *Ruin-art*, 'Close Up in Blue Space', Rienke for Tin; *Weather Report*, with Seraphine Pick (Dunedin), Rudina Xhaféri (Pristina), Ilse Edit Pahl (Johannesburg) & Tran Trong Vu (Hanoi)

Erotica67 New York, USA
(b: 1967 / g: 1977)
Crews: Fly I.D.
www.flyidcrew.com
erotica67flyid@aol.com
48 All art by Erotica67 in New York between 1999 and 2002

Ethel London, UK (g: 1994)
49 Clockwise from TL: LA, 2004; London, 2005; San Francisco, 2004; London, 2005; London, 2004; London, 2005; London, 2003

Fafi Paris, France
(b: 1975 / g: 1994)
www.fafi.net
50–53 All art by Fafi

Fairy Bologna, Italy
(b: 1984 / g: 2000) Crews: PG
155 Hand stickers, Bologna, 2005; character, Florence, 2005

Faith47 Cape Town, South Africa
www.faith47.com
info@faith47.com
54 *Abantwana Abahle, Children are Beautiful*, 2005
55 2005; 2005; Örebro (Sweden), 2005; tag; 2004; *One Wish*, with Mak1one, 2005
56–57 *Housing and Security for All*, 2005

Fany Hamburg, Germany
(g: 1998) Crews: AFC www.fany.de
58 Clockwise from TL: Fany (AFC) Hamburg, 2005; Fany (AFC) with Trica(lga), background by Jayn & Fany, Lüneburg, 2005; Fany (AFC), background by Code & Asie, Itzehoe, 2005; Fany (AFC) with Riko, Hamburg, 2005

Femme9 Kansas, USA
(g: 1996)
www.angelfire.com/ok5/femme9
www.whileyouwereon12oz.com/
femme9gallery1.html
59 Clockwise from TL: *Miss Pointing*, Kansas City, 2005; *Miss B Girl Be*, Minneapolis, 2005; *Miss Flower Power*, Kansas City, 2005; *Feme9*, Kentucky, 2005; *Swel*, Kansas City, 2005; *Bread & Miss Roxy*, Kansas City, 2005; *Phem*, St Louis, 2000; *Miss Lady Bug Blue*, Kansas City, 2005

Fever (Lady K) Canada/USA
(g: 1991) Crews: FCS, KD, TDS, TLC, CAC, TLV, WDS, WOTS
www.ladykfever.com
www.graffiti.org/ladyk/index.html
www.feverized.com
60 Clockwise from TL: Graffiti Hall of Fame, Harlem, 2003; 'B-girl Be Summit', St Paul, Minnesota, 2005; Brooklyn, 2003; *Strawberry Shortcake's Candyland*, Brooklyn, 2004; *Strawberry Shortcake's Candyland*, Brooklyn, 2004

Fly/Flai Barcelona, Spain
(g: 2003) Crews: BG, Niñas del Brasil (with Dune, Musa and Elisa from

Freaklüb) and GFM
www.fotolog.com/fly_flai
61 All art by Fly/Flai, Barcelona, 2005

Friendly Vandalism
Zurich, Switzerland
(b: 1969 / g: 2001)
friendly_vandalism@yahoo.com
156 Clockwise from TL: *hier starb sissi*, Zurich, 2001; *milk 2005 (after jeff wall)*, Zurich, 2005; silkscreen on panties, 2004; *tagman no. 5*, Zurich, 2004; 'Art Basel', 2004

FUCK YOUR CREW Germany
(b: 1976 / g: 2002)
Crews: FUCK YOUR CREW, KC
157 Clockwise from TL: Stuttgart, 2004; Berlin, 2004; Stuttgart, 2005; Berlin, 2004; with Miss Riel, Nomad, Gould, London Police, Galo & Brom at 'Gata the Gathering', Berlin, 2004; Berlin, 2004; Stuttgart, 2005; (birds) Berlin, 2003

Girl23 Vancouver, Canada
http://myspace.com/ssgirl23
62 All art by Girl23

Maya Hayuk New York, USA
Crews: Barnstormers
www.mayahayuk.com
158 Clockwise from TL: *roll rampant and free skate ramp*, with Craig Dransfield and ten other skater-painters, Pittsburgh, 2005; *hot tub chicken coop*, with Barnstormers, SECCA museum, Winston-Salem, 2004; *drippy donut*, train yard in Brooklyn, 2003; *love's my favorite color*, with Barnstormers, Cameron, 2004; painted skateboard, with beck(y) hickey bags, Portland, 2005; *roll rampant and free skate ramp*, with Craig Dransfield and ten other skater-painters, Pittsburgh, 2005; *roll rampant and free skate ramp*, with Craig Dransfield and ten other skater-painters, Pittsburgh, 2005
159 *monsters and ghosts in the kingdom of awesome*, Pittsburgh, 2005

Hera Wiesbaden, Germany
Crews: 24, Herakut
160–63 All art by Hera

Hope Montreal, Canada
(b: 1972 / g: c. 1998)
164 All art by Hope

Horsie Pittsburgh, USA
(b: 1964 / g: 2003)
www.fotolog.com/horsie
165 All art by Horsie in Pittsburgh; BR: 2003; bottom row: 2004; rest: 2005

Irena Barcelona, Spain (g: 2002)
166 All art by Irena, Barcelona, 2004–5

Jakee New York, USA (g: 1991)
Crews: 113, TN, ICU
63 Clockwise from TL: Bronx, 1997; Queens, 1997; Bronx, 2002; Brooklyn, 2000; Brooklyn, 2000

Jana Joana Brazil
(b: 1978 / g: 1998)
www.fotolog.com/janajoana
64 All art by Jana Joana, São Paulo, 2005

Jel Los Angeles, USA
(g: 1998) Crews: TKO
www.skateallcities.com
65 Billboard, Denver (Colorado); Virgin Mary, Mexico; all other art, LA

Jen Props New York, USA
(g: 1990) www.jenprops.com
167 Clockwise from TL: Stencil & tag on mailbox, Midtown, Manhattan, 2001; large wave & stencil, on wood, Tokyo, 2003; wave stencil, Brooklyn, 2004; wave painting on wood, Manhattan, 2005; sticker on gumball machine, L.E.S., 2004

Jerk Los Angeles, USA
(g: 1995–96) Crews: GAW
66 All art by Jerk, LA, 2000–4

Karma Stockholm, Sweden
Crews: AK, D/ www.karmaworkshop.com
68 Karma & Blue, Dalsland, 2003
69 Clockwise from TL: Barcelona, 2001; Stockholm, 2000; with Kropp, Stockholm, 2003; Norrköping, 2005; Copenhagen, 2001; detail, Örebro Art Museum, 2005

Keho Brussels, Belgium
(b: 1985 / g: 2001) Crews: EA.CS
www.fotolog.com/durex_keho
67 All art by Keho

Klor France (g: 1992)
Crews: 123, 3HC, CNS, KD
www.123klan.com
70–71 All art by Klor

Koralie Montpellier, France
(b: 1977 / g: 1999)
www.koralie.net
168 All art by Koralie

Lady Bug
Lignano Sabbiadoro, Italy
(g: 1999) www.lady-bug.tk
www.baeldesign.com
169 Clockwise from TL: Genoa, 2002; Alessandria, 2003; Berlin, 2004; Alessandria, 2005; Milan, 2005; Alessandria, 2004

Lady Pink New York, USA
(g: 1979) www.pinksmith.com
72 Clockwise from TL: Jack GOW &
Pink on German train, 1993; Pink
top-to-bottom, NYC subway, 1982;
Pink freight, NYC, 1994; *Welcome to
Heaven* by Pink, NYC subway, 1982
73 Pink 3-D piece, Queens, 1996;
detail of female warrior, Queens,
1994; detail of *Blue Gal*, Brooklyn,
2000; Pink with detail of 9/11
tribute, Queens, 2001; *Brick Woman
Crying*, acrylic on canvas, 36" x 36",
2001, private collection; detail of
green woman, Brooklyn, 1996
74–75 Pink piece at the Aviation
High School Wall, Queens, 1999

Lahe Seville, Spain
(b: 1978 / g: 2001) Crews: SPL
www.ana_langeheldt.com
170–71 All art by Lahe

Leeny
Montreal, Canada (b: 1981)
172 *Self-portrait*, 2004
173 Clockwise from TL: 2005; 2005;
2002; 2005; with Produkt, 2002;
2004; with Produkt, 2004

Louise Antwerp, Belgium
(b: 1978 / g: 2003)
www.eugene-and-louise.be
174–75 Louise creature, Eugene
and Louise, Ghent, 2005

Luna Los Angeles, USA
lunagraf@yahoo.com
76 Clockwise from TL: mural @ La
Esquinita, Echo Park, by Luna, Klee
& Sigma, 2005–6; two photos & slap
tags by Luna, Mexico, 2005; *all about
the light II*, downtown LA, 2005;
Luna & Klee, LA, 2006; *belmont's
last days*, 2005

Lus & Plume Toulouse, France
(g: 1990s) Crews: BAD, Le Club 70
77 All art by Lus & Plume

Mace Germany
Crews: DMA
80 Clockwise from IL: Milan, 2004;
Hamburg, 2001; with Dior, Düsseldorf,
2005; Milan, 2005; Hamburg, 2000;
Germany, 2003

Mad C Dresden, Germany
(b: 1980 / g: 1996)
Crews: Bandits, IAC
www.madc.tv
78–79 Clockwise from TL: Bautzen,
2004; Bautzen, 2002; Dresden, 2003;
(B:) Prague, 2004; (T:) Dresden,
2004; Halle, 2004; Berlin, 2005;
with Mogi, Braunschweig, 2004

Mademoiselle Kat
Toulouse, France
(g: 1992) Crews: BAD
www.mademoisellek.net
176 All art by Mademoiselle Kat,
France, 2003

Makoh Alicante, Spain
(b: 1982 / g: 1996)
Crews: Antiextres, GK, ST, TRS,
Mimi Team
www.fotolog.com/makoh
81 All art by Makoh

Malicia Barcelona, Spain
Crews: 1980, KCP, LH, NM, NOT
www.amoraljamon.tk
maliciawalls@hotmail.com
82–83 All art by Malicia

Andrea May
Salvador, Brazil
(g: 2002) Crews: COLAtivo,
e-lectrolNvasores, Re:Combo
www.fotolog.com/mayart
http://andreamay.multiply.com
177 All art by Andrea May

me love Munich, Germany
(b: 1976 / g: 2000)
Crews: SF, tapetentiere
www.flickr.com/photos/melove
www.fotolog.com/me_love
178 L, TR & BR: Munich, 2004;
T: Munich, 2005; R: First row,
L: Berne, 2005; C: with Bird, Berne,
2005; R: Munich, 2005; Second
row, L: Berne, 2005; C: Berne, 2005;
R: Munich, 2004

Melina New York, USA
(b: 1979 / g: 2001)
www.fotolog.com/iammelina
179 All art by Melina

Mickey Amsterdam, the Netherlands
(g: 1983) www.space-babies.com
84 Clockwise from TL: Study for
canvas, Amsterdam, 2005; Basel,
2005; Amsterdam Bijlmer, 2005;
The Snake Eye, study for canvas,
Amsterdam, 2004
85 *I ♥ NYC*, Queens, 2005;
Amersfoort, 2004; Amsterdam
Bijlmer, 2005; Switzerland, 2005;
part of huge The Split Force crew
wall, The Hague, 2004
86–87 Münster (Germany), 2005

Microbo Milan, Italy (g: 1998)
www.microbo.com
180–81 All art by Microbo

Misako Canberra, Australia
(b: 1987 / g: 2001–2)
182–83 All art by Misako

Miss Lili Shenzhen, China
(b: 1977 / g: 1998)
Crews: CF, I ♥ CHINA
88 With CF Crew, Paris, 2005
89 Clockwise from TL: France, 2005;
Spain, 2004; France, 2000; France,
2005; Robot Hibino Project, France,
1999; Shenzhen, 2005; with Hobsek,
France, 2005

Miss Riel
Reykjavik, Iceland/
Berlin, Germany
(b: 1980 / g: 2001)
Crews: Gata, Big Geezers, Why Kings
198 Clockwise from TL: *Der Affe*,
Reykjavik, 2004; *Yoyogy Stairs*,
Japan, 2005; *Hypnotizer*, Berlin,
2005; *Sad Sweet/Ass Tweed*, Berlin,
2004; Seydhisfjördhur, 2003

Miss Van France www.missvan.com
90–93 All art by Miss Van

Mofi Thessaloniki, Greece
(b: 1980 / g: 2000)
184 Clockwise from TL: Aegean
Islands, 2005; Athens, 2005;
Aegean Islands, 2003; Athens,
2005; Athens, 2005
185 Thessaloniki, 2005

Muck USA (b: 1978 / g: 1994)
94 Clockwise from TL: Brooklyn, 2004;
Brooklyn, 2004; Queens, 2003;
Brooklyn, 2003

Musa (aka Venus/China)
Barcelona, Spain
(b: 1971 / g: 1989) Crews: ROS, WSC
95 All art by Musa

MyMonsters Frankfurt, Germany
(b: 1983 / g: 1997)
www.mymonsters.de
186–87 All art by MyMonsters

Nina São Paulo, Brazil
96–97 All art by Nina

Nina M. Porto Alegre, Brazil
www.fotolog.com/visceras
188–89 All art by Nina M.

Nuria Madrid, Spain
(g: 1999–2000)
www.eltono.com
190 Clockwise from TL: São Paulo,
2005; Ilhéus/Salvador, 2005;
Guimarães (Portugal), 2005; Palma
de Mallorca, 2000; Madrid, 2003
191 Clockwise from TL: Madrid, 2003;
Madrid, 2002; Guimarães, 2005;
Madrid, 2000

Omri Aalst, Belgium (g: 2004)
www.fotolog.com/omri_laila
98 All art by Omri

Panda Manchester, UK (g: 2002)
192 All in Manchester. Clockwise from
TL: 2005; 'Doodlebug', 2005; 2004;
2003; 2005; 2005

Peste Monterrey, Mexico
(b: 1977 / g: 1994)
Crews: KD
www.burnercru.com
99 All art by Peste

Pian Caracas, Venezuela
(b: 1980 / g: 2003)
Crews: La Lucha
www.piancita.com
www.piancita.deviantart.com
193 All art by Pian

Poise Victoria, Australia
(b: 1972 / g: 1988–89)
Crews: TFC, ROT, ladiesluvhiphop
100–1 All art by Poise

Popdesign Rio de Janeiro, Brazil
(b: 1980 / g: 2003)
www.fotolog.com/popdesign_b
www.popdesign.biz
196 All art by Popdesign

Psila Skopje, Macedonia
(b: 1982 / g: 1995)
www.comeclean.com.mk
194–95 All art by Psila

Queen Andrea New York, USA
(b: 1978 / g: 1992)
www.superfreshdesign.com
102 T: Queens, 2004;
B: Queens, 2003
103 T: Queens, 2005;
Bottom row, L: 'Graffiti Hall of Fame',
New York City, 2003; CT: Brooklyn,
2004; CB: 'Graffiti Hall of Fame', NYC,
2004; R: Brooklyn, 2004

RB827 New York, USA
(b: 1982) Crews: FVK
www.fvkillers.com
197 All art by RB827

Ream Hamburg, Germany
(b: 1982 / g: 1996) Crews: AFC
104 All art by Ream

Redy Hong Kong, China
(b: 1983 / g: 2000) Crews: BNS
105 Top row, from L to R: with
Smirk, Taiwan, 2004; with Dofi,
Hong Kong, 2005; Hong Kong, 2003.
Middle rows, clockwise from TL:
with Dofi, Hong Kong, 2002; with
Dofi, Hong Kong, 2004; with BA1,
Hong Kong, 2004; with Dofi,
Barcelona, 2005; with Bushh,
Hong Kong, 2004; Hong Kong,
2005; with Frek, Dofi, BNS, SAG,
FDC, Bane & Kiev, Hong Kong, 2001.

Bottom row: with Tron & Obesk, Hong Kong, 2006

Reminisce (aka 'The Horse Lady') San Francisco, USA
106-7 Art by Reminisce

Ropas New York, USA
(b: 1979 / g: c. 1993)
108-9 Top row: Columbus, Ohio and New York, 1996–2004; Bottom row: New York, 2003–5

Sasu Tokyo, Japan (b: 1974)
www.hitotzuki.com
199 All art by Sasu/Hitotzuki

Seomra Dublin, Ireland
www.theartofasbestos.com/seomra
200 Clockwise from TL: *Little Bo Peep*, Brick Lane, London, 2005; *Little Black Sheep*, Barcelona, 2005; *Little Black Sheep*, Brick Lane, 2005; *Little Black Sheep*, Milan, 2005
201 *Sheep with Water Boy*, Marrakesh, 2005; *Mutton Dresses as Lamb* plates, with Finders Keepers, Milan, 2005

Sherm Los Angeles, USA
(b: 1977 / g: 1994)
Crews: WGS
www.shermgrafik.com
110 All art by Sherm

Shiro Shizuoka, Japan
(g: 1998)
Crews: GCS (Japan), TDS (USA)
www.bj46.com
111 Clockwise from TL: Queens, 2005; canvas, 2004; with Cook, Osaka, 2005; Shizuoka, 2004; Queens, 2005; (CL:) hoody, 2004; (CR:) Shizuoka, 2000

Siloette USA (g: 1998)
Crews: NG, 32D
www.siloette.com
112 Mixed media, 2005
113 Clockwise from TL: Mixed media, 2005; train, 2005; spraypaint, Minneapolis, 2005; spraypaint, New York, 2005; train, 2004

Smirk Switzerland/South Africa
(b: 1977 / g: 1996)
Crews: WOTS
114 Clockwise from TL: with Seemsoe, Ecran & Sky189 (dogs by Smirk & wall commissioned by Sprite), Cape Town, 2002; canvas, Cape Town, 2003; canvas (exhibited in Sydney), Cape Town, 2003; digital image, Basel, 2005; digital image, Basel, 2005; canvas (exhibited in Sydney), Cape Town, 2003; with Seemsoe & Sky189, Dortmund, 2005; Mainz, 2005

Solovei USA
202-3 All art by Solovei

Soma Switzerland (g: 1999)
116–17 All art by Soma

Sonne Chemnitz, Germany
(b: 1979 / g: 1999)
Crews: DSA Girls
www.thenextart.de
115 Clockwise from TL: Dresden; with JMF, Shogun, Yuxa & SU, Döbeln; 'Urban Syndromes Jam', Dresden; Kaiserslautern; Chemnitz

Spice Sydney, Australia
(b: 1972) Crews: BQ, GB, IBS
118 Clockwise from TL: *Underwater*, Mt Druitt Park, 2004; *Straight from the heART*, 2003; *Oh How I Love to Funk Thee*, 2005; *Kangaroo on Van*, 2002; UV paint (glow in the dark) canvases x 3; *Ladies First*, 2004; *Journey 2 the Centre of the Soul*, 2002

Stef Chicago, USA
(g: early 1990s) Crews: ESP, THC, LB
119 All art by Stef

Suez Dresden, Germany
Crews: GRS, MIJA
120 Clockwise from TL: Dresden-Chemnitz line, with Phoenix (character), 2004; train in Dresden main station, with Besd, Hopla & Sezir, 2005; Dresden, 2006; S2 Line, Dresden, with Hopla, 2005

Supa B2 Mestre, Italy
(b: 1980 / g: 1995)
121 Clockwise from TL: Antwerp, 2005; Mogliano, 2004; Alessandria, 2004; Foggia, 2003

Swoon New York, USA
204–7 All art by Swoon

Tash Queensland, Australia
(g: 1990) Crews: 183, BQ
122–23 All art by Tash

T-Girl Sweden
(b: 1984 / g: 2000) Crews: HS
www.t-girl.se
208 Clockwise from TL: 2005; 2005; 2005; with Gangsterboogie, 2005; 2005; with Mir, 2004; with Hola Sombrero Crew , 2005

Thundercut New York, USA
(b: 1974 / g: 2003)
www.thundercut.com
209 Clockwise from TL: *Blue Demon Walker*, 2005; *Nasa Walker*, 2004; *Teen Walker*, 2005; *Shopper Walker*, 2005; *Hip Hop Walker*, 2004; *Rasta Walker*, 2005; *CBGB Girl Walker*, 2004; *Red Devil Walker*, 2005; *CBGB Guy Walker*, 2004

Toofly New York, USA
(b: 1977 / g: early 1990s)
www.tooflydesign.com
124 Toofly & Inks, Brooklyn, 2005
125 Clockwise from TL: Queens, 2005; Patagonia y Necochea Calle, Quito, Ecuador, 2005; Queens, 2005; Brooklyn, 2005; Hall of Fame, 106 Park Ave., New York, 2004; (CL:) Bronx, 2005; (C:) Brooklyn, 2003

Tribe
Los Angeles, USA (g: 1992)
Crews: AWR, MSK, OTR, RTDK, TKO
www.djladytribe.com
126 All art by Tribe

T.W. San Francisco, USA (g: 1994)
210 Top row, clockwise from TL: *Once Upon a Time*, San Francisco, 2004; *Fun*, San Francisco, 2002; *Where was I a minute ago?*, San Francisco, 2004; B: *Action Girls and Boys*, San Francisco, 2001

Various Berlin, Germany (g: 2003)
211 Clockwise from TL: *Shadowfigures Series*, Halle, 2005; *Snowflake*, Berlin, 2005; *Shadowfigure*, Berlin, 2005; postcards, Berlin, 2005; *We Need More Stupidity*, Berlin, 2004; *Shadowfigure*, Berlin, 2005

Venus Lisbon, Portugal (g: 2000)
127 Clockwise from TL: Lisbon, 2005; Lisbon, 2004; Cascais, 2004; canvas; Caldas da Rainha, 2005

Waleska
London, UK/São Paulo, Brazil
Crews: 3rd Decade, Terceiro Mundo Crew, IC, LT, TM, XS www.waleska.co.uk
128 With Zosen, Tom14 & Adam, Barcelona, 2004
129 Top row, clockwise from TL: São Paulo, 2006; London, 2005; Brazil, 2006; with Tinho, Brazil, 2006; Brazil, 2006. Second row: London, 2006; with Adam, Barcelona, 2005; London, 2005. Third row: With Adam, Brazil, 2006; Brazil, 2006
130-31 São Paulo, 2005

Yolie Madrid, Spain
(b: 1974 / g: 1990)
www.graffiti.org/yolie/index.html
132 All art by Yolie & Sace2, Madrid, 1990s

Yubia Bilbao, Spain (g: 2002)
Crews: Kreatitizides, KR+
www.fotolog.com/yubia
133 All art by Yubia, Bilbao, between 2004 & 2005, except bottom row, third image: Barcelona, 2004

YZ Paris, France
(b: 1975 / g: 2000)
www.openyoureyesproject.com
212 *Irruption*, Paris, 2005
213 Clockwise from TL: *Irruption*, Paris, 2005; *We are getting fat*, Brighton, 2004; *Open your eyes*, Berlin, 2004; *Push*, Brighton, 2004
214-15 YZ, EMA, Siner & Meresone, *Open your eyes*, New York, 2005

Zora Lucerne, Switzerland
(b: 1974 / g: 1989)
Crews: AOH, GBF, SUK, WM
www.sukibamboo.com
134 T: with Shark, Hall of Fame, Lucerne, 2000. Second row: *Sukiss Diamond*, Canvas 500x1400 mm, 2005; *Angie & Gepsy*, train, Germany, 1995; *Freaks of the Underground*, 2006; *Danke!*, Hamburg, 2003. Third row: *Sukiss Spades*, canvas 500x1400 mm, 2005; *Sukiss Heart*, canvas, 500 x 1400 mm, 2005; *Sukiss Clubs*, canvas, 500 x 1400 mm, 2005; *Zora Bone-Piece*, with Shark, Mate & Daim, St Moritz, 1996

Zori4 Carolina, Puerto Rico
(b: 1981 / g: 2000)
Crews: BAD, KD, MI, OBW, TDS, Y&I
http://zorifour.deviantart.com
135 Clockwise from TL: 'Kosmopolite Festival', with Lies, France, 2004; scale truck, 2004; *Sunset*, mixed media, canvas; Bayamón, 2005; Carolina, 2005; Carolina, 2005; NY Hall of Fame, Spanish Harlem, 2004; Trujillo Alto, 2005; Guaynabo, 2005

Crews

BA – Burning America, Baltimore Alcoholics

BAD – Boys Are Down

BG (Fly/Flai) – Be Guay, Big Ups

BG (Miss Riel) – Big Geezers

BH – Bounty Hunterz

BNS – Bombing Never Stops

BQ – Bandit Queens

CAC – Crazy Ass Criminal

CNS – Checkin' Nuh Skillz

FUH – Fuck Ur Hood

FVK – Fearless Vampire Killers

GAW – Going Awol, Ghetto Art Work,
       Gods At War

GB – Ghetto Blasters

GBF – Gummi Bärchen Front
       (Jelly Baby Front)

GBR – Graffiteiras Brasil

GCS – Graff Can Sorcery

GFM – Great Fucking Moments

GK – Ghetto Kings

HDV – Hour Do Vandalismo

HS – Hola Sombrero

IBS – International Bomb Squad

IC – Intoxicacao Corrosiva

ISK – Incredible South Kids,
       Iguane Serpent Kameleon

KC – Kaktus Crew

KCP – Karne Con Patatas

KD – Kings Destroy

LH – Love Ham

LT – Latin Terrorists

MIJA – Malen Ist Jungs Angelegenheit

NG – Nitty Gritty

NM – Nobody More

NoT – Not Triumf

OBW – Only 4 Best Writers

PG – Planet Green

PPC – Press Pause Crew

ROT – Reign Of Terror

SF – Sticky Fellaz

SFX – Style FanatiX

SPL – Sprays Platinum

ST – Sur Triboo

SUK – Stick Up Kids

TDS – The Death Squad

TFC – Twenty First Century

TKO – The Knight Owls, TaKing Over,
       Taking Krews Out, The Krowns Ours

TLC – The Ladies Crew

TLV – The Latin Vandals

TM – Terceiro Mundo

VIC – Vandals In Control

WDS – We Destroy Shit

WGS – We Got Style

WK – Why Kings

WOTS (Lady K) – Wizards Of The Style

WOTS (Smirk) – Word On The Street

Bibliography

123Klan, *design&designer 020_123Klan*,
Pyramyd Editions, Paris, 2004

Chalfant, Henry, & James Prigoff, *Spraycan Art*,
Thames & Hudson, London, 1987

Cooper, Martha, & Henry Chalfant, *Subway Art*,
Thames & Hudson, London, 1984

Fafi, *Love and Fafiness*, Marble Books, Tokyo, 2005

Ganz, Nicholas, *Graffiti World: Street Art from Five Continents*,
Thames & Hudson, London, 2004

Macdonald, Nancy, *The Graffiti Subculture: Youth,
Masculinity and Identity in London and New York*,
Palgrave Macmillan, New York, 2001

Microbo, Bo130 & The Don, *IZASTIKUP*,
Drago Arts & Communication, Rome, 2005

Websites

Artcrimes – www.graffiti.org

Catfight Magazine – www.catfightmag.tk

Nicholas Ganz – www.keinom.com
www.graffitiworld.org / www.graffitiwoman.com

Ladys Graff – www.ladysgraff.cjb.net

Lease – www.surfacephotography.com

Trine – www.trine-natskaar.dk

Wooster Collective – www.woostercollective.com

*Written documentation of the female scene is rare.
'A Global Snapshot' referred to a variety of sources,
including existing texts, websites and – most
importantly – the experiences of the artists.*
       Nicholas Ganz

Acknowledgments

I would like to thank all the contributing artists for their fantastic artworks. Without their amazing help, none of this would have been possible. Apologies to all the artists who I haven't been able to include due to lack of space.

Particular thanks go to the people I met on my travels who helped me with the book: Blue, BRING OUT THE GARBAGE, Dallah Cesen, Claw, De Professionella Konstgangstrarna, Diva, Dona, EMA, Rienke Enghardt, EyeOne, Fafi, Faith47, Jen Props, Karma, Lady K-Fever, Lady Pink & Smith, Mickey, Monkey6, Nina, PC Kid, Pesky, RB827, Nika Sarabi, Swoon, Tash, Toofly, Vyal and Waleska.

Very special thanks to my lovely girlfriend Elena Jotow, my mother Corina and my brothers Maurice and René for their huge support and invaluable help. I'd also like to thank Dirk Gwiasda for his technical expertise, Demon for his thoughts, Nancy Macdonald for contributing her unrivalled knowledge, Sam Clark for his great work on the design, Rebecca Pearson, Ginny Liggitt and everyone at Thames & Hudson involved in this book, Jim Prigoff for his fantastic images, Tristan Manco for his photos of Brazil, Michael and Kristen De Feo for a wonderful time in New York, Alison and Adam for their hospitality, Trine Natskaar for a couch in Copenhagen, Gomyo for his work in Japan, Susan Farrell for her unfailing support on graffiti.org, and Mark and Sara from Wooster Collective for their great contribution.

Picture Credits

All pictures were supplied or taken by the artists themselves, unless otherwise indicated.

Alicia – Sepugirl (alisia.malisia@gmail.com) p. 138 (skeleton mask); Ignacio Aronovich pp. 96 & 97 TL, BL, TR, CR; Hans van Bentem p. 154 L; Ralph Borland p. 1; Henry Chalfant p. 72 B; Chock, graffiti foldout nos. 47 & 49; Sam Clark endpaper photo; Martha Cooper p. 15; Cope2 p. 135 BL; Daffy p. 103 B; Nicholas Ganz p. 18 B (third from left), p. 42 CT, p.47 BL, p. 50 TR, graffiti foldout (images 9, 28, 53 & 69), p. 85 T, p. 108 BL, p.110 BL, p.136 CL, p. 141 CBL, street art foldout (images 10, 11, 12 & 19), p. 205 L; Gear p. 55 CR; Gilda van Hecke p. 154 R (second from bottom); Hopla p. 120 TR (& Rina), BR & BL; Jack p. 72 TL; Karma p. 224; Gomyo Kevin graffiti foldout (image 1); Daniel Lacet pp. 188 & 189 R; Tristan Manco p. 97 BR & second row L; Yoann Martineau p. 212, p. 213 TL; Tanya Milosevich p. 210 R (second from top); Nomad p. 198 BC; Sam O'Neil p. 55 TR; Ore p. 184 (except bottom); Peak p. 41 TL & TR; Paula Plim p. 189 L (x4); Jim Prigoff pp. 106–7; Francisco Reyes graffiti foldout (images 5 & 7); Tony Rodriguez p. 103 RC; Sace2 (& Yolie) p. 132; Ilse Schrama p. 154 BR; Jean-Louis Souc p. 2 (YZ); Monique Wijbrands p. 154 TR (X2); Zori4 p. 60 TR

About the Author

Nicholas Ganz (aka Keinom) is a street and fine artist based in Essen, Germany. In 2004 he published the bestseller *Graffiti World*. He works as a freelance artist, author and photographer in various fields, stages exhibitions and gives lectures in the United States and Europe. For more information please log on to www.keinom.com, www.graffitiworld.org or www.graffitiwoman.com.

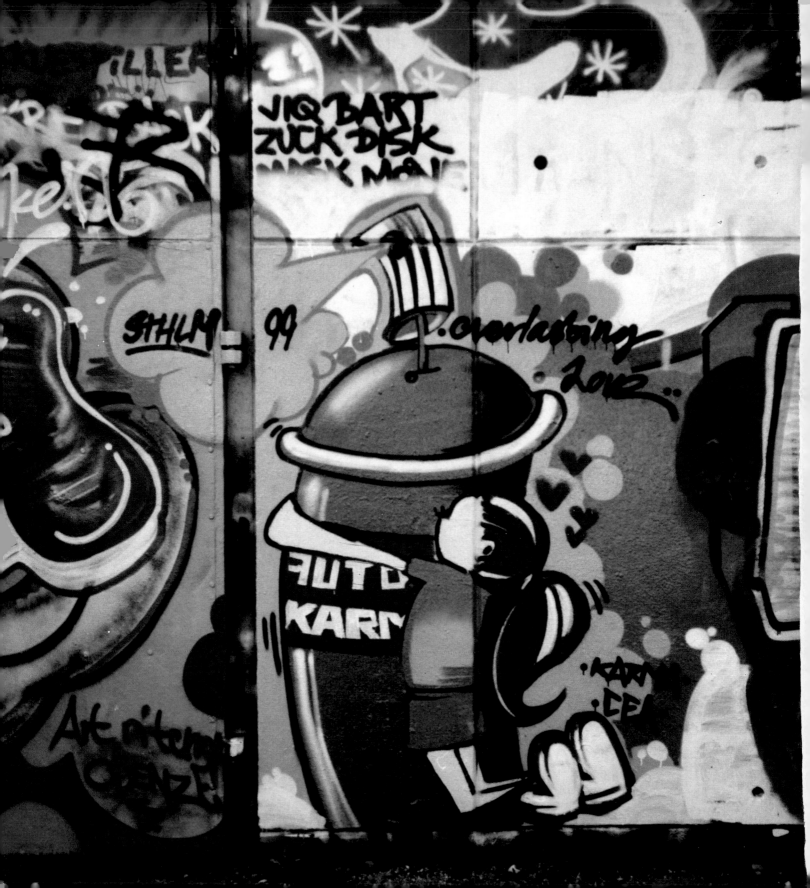

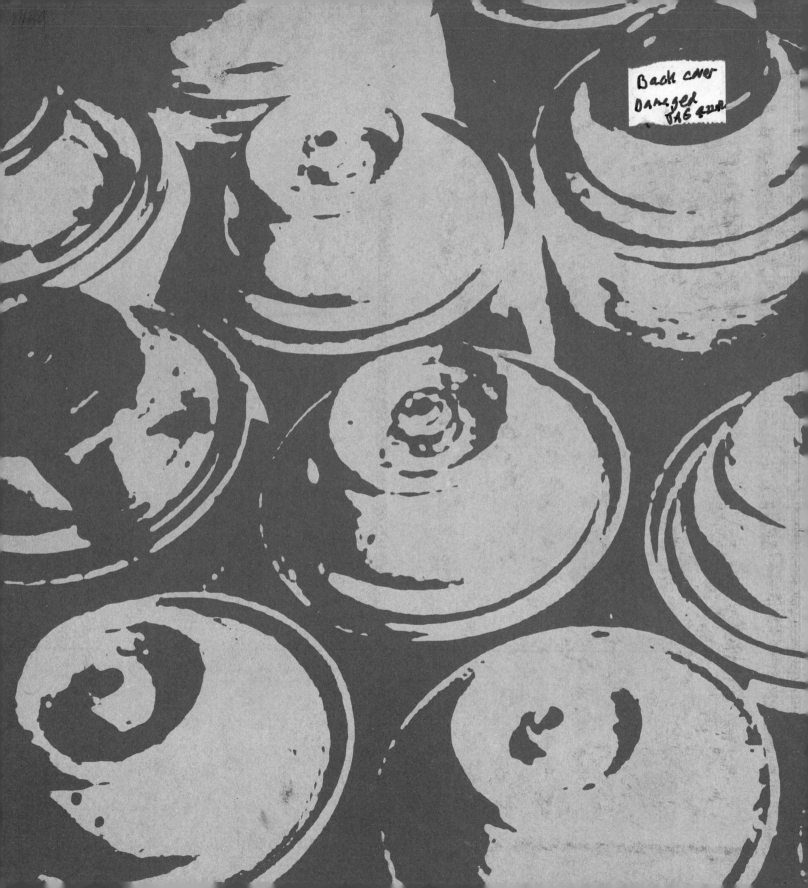